Identity Within Hegemonic Process

Adivasi Ethnicity—Class

Denzil Saldanha

AAKAR

Identity Within Hegemonic Process: Adivasi Ethnicity—Class
Denzil Saldanha

First Published 2019

ISBN 978-93-5002-574-1

Published by
AAKAR BOOKS
28 E Pocket IV, Mayur Vihar Phase I
Delhi 110 091 India
aakarbooks@gmail.com

Laser Typeset at
Sakshi Computers, Delhi

Printed at
Sapra Brothers, Noida

Contents

Acknowledgements

I am grateful to the Indian Council of Social Science Research, Western Regional Centre, Mumbai for financial assistance which enabled me to undertake this study that involved fieldwork and extensive coverage of sources.

My young colleagues and friends at the Tata Institute of Social Sciences, Mumbai and elsewhere deserve my appreciation for helping me to access a range of materials. Some of them provided research assistance and they are too many to name. Ajay Dandekar was kind enough to comment on some of the chapters, to draw my attention to and to provide some materials. In addition, he helped in the translation of some of the documents for which I am extremely grateful. The errors that remain and the interpretations offered are entirely mine. Most importantly, I am grateful to the respondents in the field, especially the adivasis, who shared with me their beliefs and deepest aspirations. My compliments go out to Aakar Books and its editorial team for a task that was efficiently completed.

This work grows out of my earlier publications on the region: *Structure, Consciousness and Social Transformation: The Adivasis in Thane District, Maharashtra*, 2015 which covered the political economy and the process of class formation among the adivasis for close to 200 years to the present and *The Subaltern Subject in Structured Historical Process: Towards an Epistemological Approach*, 2015 which focused on methodological aspects in a comparative perspective with the articles in the volumes of *Subaltern Studies* relating to the peasantry. The present work concentrates on aspects of culture and ethnic identity, as the title suggests. While it may be read independently, it may be seen as a companion volume to the former publications.

I would be grateful for comments, critical and otherwise, at the following email address.

Denzil Saldanha
saldanhadenzil@gmail.com
Mumbai, April 2018

Section 1

Perspectives

CHAPTER 1

Introduction

My last publication, *The Subaltern Subject* (Saldanha 2015 b), had raised the question: How does one epistemologically relate and incorporate culture with the political economy within processes of structured change? The political economy of structured change over the last 200 years from the time of British rule in the then Thane district, Maharashtra, with a focus on political organization and consciousness among the adivasis, especially since 1944 with the entry of the Kisan Sabha, was the primary thrust of *Structure, Consciousness and Social Transformation* (Saldanha 2015 a). The analysis of culture in the material context is a theoretical issue as much as an epistemological one, with political implications. Some tentative answers in the context of a dialogue with relevant articles in the 12 volumes *Subaltern Studies* had been proposed in *The Subaltern Subject* (Saldanha 2015 b). The following publication is an attempt to probe the question more concretely in operational terms around the integrative concept of identity. In more specific terms this publication tries to uncover the relation between the concepts of class and tribal ethnicity using the situation of the adivasis, in particular the Warlis in what is from 2014 Palghar district carved out from Thane district, Maharashtra, as an illustrative case within talukas/administrative blocks of a concentration of adivasis.

The major phases of the **history** of the region may serve as a brief introduction to the geographical space and to the 'objective' social scientific notion of chronology. This history of the political economy of the region which constitutes the basis of class formation and the identity as garib adivasis (poor adivasis), the lok (the people), among the adivasis; in sharp contrast to the 'other', the non-adivasis and their landlord-trader-moneylender nexus, the seth savkars;

underlies the following analysis carried out in the chapters relating to adivasi ethnicity. It is presented here in the introduction so as to avoid repetition and to serve as a constant reference. A detailed version may be found in Saldanha (2015 a, Section 2). The northern talukas of Dahanu and Talasari of the then Thane district, presently Palghar district, lie about 120 kilometres, north of Mumbai city and south of Gujarat state. This region had seen several rulers, all having some impact on the present condition of the Warlis. The district was under Hindu rule till 1300 AD, the subsequent Muslim period till 1660 AD, followed by reigns of partial regional overlap by the Portuguese from 1500 to 1670, the Marathas from 1660 to 1800, followed by the British from 1800 till independence in 1947. There had been a severe decrease in the population of the Warlis in 1901 and 1921. This has been due to famine and plague in the case of the former and a result of a severe epidemic of influenza which covered the country in 1918. The adivasi population formed 28 per cent of the total population numbering 932,733 of the district in 1941. At the time, the Warlis formed 49 per cent of the adivasi population and 14 per cent of the total population of the district. According to Save (1945: 4), based on the Bombay Gazetteer, except for the Mahadeo Kolis who appeared to have come from the Deccan in the 14th century, the other tribes had settled in the district from pre-historic times. The three divisions among the Kolis in the district are the Mahadeo or the Raj Kolis, the Malhar Kolis and the Dhor Kolis, the last being considered as untouchables by the adivasis because of the practice of eating the flesh of carrion. The Son Kolis are considered a distinct cultural group (Save 145: 257). The Warli tribe appears to have had a non-Aryan origin and lived in the Vindhya and Satpura ranges, from which it came southwards via the forests of Dharampur and Bansda. The Bhimbetka rock shelters in Raisen district, Madhya Pradesh represents an archaeological site of the Paleolithic age, perhaps the earliest record of human life on the Indian subcontinent (Santoshi, *Hindustan Times*, Mumbai, April 10, 2017). The images on the rock scape demonstrate a strong resemblance to some of the formal elements of contemporary Warli paintings suggesting that this region of early human civilization might well have been the originating point of the Bhils, and also of the Warlis who appear to have originated from the former. However, this is a matter of further research. According to Enthoven, the Warlis may have some relation to the Bhils (in Save 1945: 5). This view is also supported by Grierson in his *Linguistic Survey of India* (1907), according to Save (1945: 186). The Warlis in the past are supposed to have identified themselves with the Bhils of the forested Dhangs of the present Gujarat state given that this was the single largest forest community of western India with some degree of political dominance even during early British rule (Skaria 1999: 112). The Dongar Bhils are reported by informed observers to be beef eating which sharply distinguishes them from the Warlis who are otherwise. Piles of stones are reported to be presently found in some Warli villages in Dahanu and Jawahar talukas and are referred to as 'Bhilanche dongar', the memorial stones of the Bhils, suggesting traces of a conflict between the Warlis and the Bhils from whom they have likely emerged. The 'scientific' disciplines of spatial geography, temporal history, biological categorization of blood samples and linguistic analysis have been unable to categorize the identity of the Warlis based on origins in any definitive manner. What appears significant is how they defined themselves in the 1940s, in the 1980s and after, based on culture, labour and the manner of attaining livelihood; as garib adivasis (poor adivasis). They see themselves as uplanders, forest dwellers and earliest inhabitants of the region who use brushwood known as waral in order to burn the top soil for agriculture, and hence Warli adivasis; and as Kulambi, cultivators, a term used for themselves even to this day in a number of their rituals over the annual agricultural cycle and the life cycle. The generally amicable relations between the Warlis, a strictly endogamous tribe, and other tribal early inhabitants of the region while experiencing a broad identity based on economic interests, suggest a status hierarchy. Dhodias and Kolis are considered as superior and Dublas and Koknas as equals permitting inter dining. Thakars, Katkaris and Dhor Kolis are treated as inferiors (Save 1945: 258).

Some of the southern Warlis, especially those belonging to the Nihir subdivision, describe themselves as Malhar Kolis in order to seek upward social mobility. It is reported that in 1934 some members of about 50 Warli villages participated in a conference in Dahanu Taluka and passed resolutions related to various adivasi practices, especially relating to marriages. These were largely central and coastal villages and the delegates resolved that they would call themselves Malhar Kunbis instead of Warlis (Save 1945: 95). There is some confusion regarding the distinction between Malhar Kunbis (as mentioned by Save) and Malhar Kolis as a self-identification that is generally used by some Warlis, including the Bholada and Sathvi adivasi Pujaris of the present-day Mahalaxmi Temple Complex. The decision of 1934 would have an impact on the status of the adivasi Pujaris of the Mahalaxmi temple, as we shall see in Chapter 5. The Warli tribe is comprised of several exogamous groups, who are clans or kuls, apart from the generally endogamous division of Davars to the north and Nihir to the south of the district. The general belief is that families within the clan have descended from a common ancestor, which creates a possible blood relationship between the members of the clan and the possibility of breaching the incest taboo if marriage takes place within the clan. The tribe within a village had a system of self-governance through the village panchas who are self-elected persons of influence, and the patel who was considered a leading person in a group of three or four villages. However, with the permeation of the system of panchayati raj of local self-government these institutions of administering justice have been weakened to a considerable extent.

The region came under British rule in 1818. During the first half of the 19th century, the British land and forest policies resulted in converting the majority of the hunting, food gathering and shift cultivating adivasis into settled agriculturists. Throughout the 19th century and especially during the latter half, there was an influx of traders, moneylenders and liquor vendors resulting in the alienation of adivasis' lands and their becoming tenants and bonded labourers; victims of land alienation, indebtedness, forced exactions, torture and sexual oppression. The Kisan Sabha entered the scene in 1944. A militant phase of adivasi struggle till 1948 under the leadership of the Kisan Sabha put an end to most aspects of feudal oppression. The post-independence interplay of party and the non-electoral, non-party based peasant organizations—the latter a phenomenon of the 1970s and after—and the land reforms and development measures of independent India have resulted in a predominantly poor peasant and agricultural labour economy for the adivasis. Malnutrition and disease are increasing and there are sporadic epidemics that afflict the most vulnerable among the adivasis. They are dependent on the state and a class of landlords, capitalist farmers, traders and creditors for employment, inputs into agriculture and for credit for tiding over the lean seasons when there is migration for employment in the informal industrial sector. Alienation of adivasi lands by the state for infrastructural projects and by the private sector for commerce, construction and industry continues. There are increasing restrictions on the use of the forests and a growing commuting for employment in the face of agricultural distress by way of pressures on land and fragmentation of landholdings, poor quality of soil, climate change and ecological factors, rising costs of inputs and uneconomic terms of trade. Seasonal migration and daily commuting, especially among the educated youth, is to the expanding urban centres and industrial sites along the coasts of Maharashtra and Gujarat to the west as well as to the south to the outskirts of the metropolis of Mumbai. Employment in the informal industrial sector is in some ways recreating the feudalism of the past, now in a transformed industrial serfdom.

Over a period of about two centuries the adivasis have been forced into a subordinate position over several modes of production to suit the hegemonic interests of the larger economy. The ethnic identity of the adivasis has been able to survive the trials of the above mentioned historical process, a tribute to their resilience and their capacity to adopt various survival strategies. The circular conception of time in the hunting, food gathering and the pre-settled agricultural society undergoes a perversion of its circularity for the adivasis, in terms of ecology and social context, during the feudal and the post-feudal agricultural era, especially after the British period starting from 1818 (see Chapter 2). Is it that it is only later during a predominantly trading and industrial phase that a linear conception of time emerges? Presently, oppression appears to have lost its 'face' because it cannot be easily individualized to the 'other' and hence identified. It has become increasingly a systemic oppression of the neoliberal and global variety which, while experienced, becomes difficult to perceive and define. At present the adivasis are torn between allegiance to the Communist

Party of India (Marxist), i.e. CPI(M), and its peasant mass organization, the Kisan Sabha popularly known as the Lal Bavta (the red flag) which struggles to maintain an electoral toe hold over the northern talukas of Talasari and Dahanu of Palghar district; the Congress (I); the Bharatiya Janata Party (BJP); the Shiv Sena, and the Nationalist Congress Party (NCP). The present instrumental relations of the adivasis with these parties are primarily one of patronage and clientele. In addition, there are several non-party political organizations that are in contention in the region that coordinate among themselves and take up several economic issues in cooperation or conflict with the government. Some of these organizations have occasional clashes with the electoral political parties. Saldanha (1989) discusses the approaches of some of these organizations with a special focus on education. The significance of these political formations in the contemporary context is that they promote or impede class identity based on adivasi identity. That, very briefly, covers the process of class formation among the adivasis within changes in the political economy of the region over the last two centuries. Generalized, analytic features of the ethnic identity of the adivasis will be discussed in Chapter 3, subsection 5 and empirical aspects in the three Chapters of Section 2.

As this manuscript was going to press there appeared the news (*Times of India*, March 12, 2018) that approximately 34,000 agricultural labourers and farmers were marching to reach Mumbai on March 12 starting from Nashik on March 5, 2018. They were largely from the districts of Nashik, Palghar, Thane and the contiguous districts of Dhule and Nandurbar, as earlier mentioned, and led by the state unit of the All India Kisan Sabha. Ninety per cent of these people were reported to be adivasis. They were joined on the 180 kilometre route by cultivating classes from other districts. The demands were loan wavers, remunerative prices for produce, pension for retired farmers, ration cards and most importantly forest rights and regularization of lands cultivated in forests as part of a strategy for survival. The march was supported by some of the state level opposition parties and by citizen groups and middle class individuals along the route—by way of food, footwear, water, medical assistance—especially in Mumbai. Citizens were especially appreciative of the fact that march was held from the north to the south of the city overnight so as not to disrupt the examinations scheduled the next day. The struggle was called off after a written assurance from the Chief Minister of Maharashtra state. This event, reflective of agricultural distress on a far larger scale throughout the country, may be seen as a significant illustrative example of the articulation of ethnicity with class identity.

Some **demographic characteristics** of the adivasis in the region might be in order so as to provide some indication of the scale of one's analysis. According to Doshi (1990: 8-9), from 1871 the Census attempted to retain adivasi religious ethnicity by creating a category of 'primitive'. In 1901 the adivasis formed 2.92 per cent and by 1911 they had increased by 20 per cent to form 3.28 per cent. After 1911 a category of 'tribal religion' was coined accounting for 3.09 per cent in 1921 and 2.36 per cent in 1931. However, after independence in 1951 the process of adivasi cooption was complete with no such distinct category being retained; rather the adivasi religious identity being hegemonically absorbed into the major non-adivasi religions, namely Islam, Christianity, Buddhism and Hinduism; primarily the last even though no formal ritualistic process of assimilation may have existed. According to the Census of 2011 (TISS 2015, a and b for the following data), the adivasi/scheduled tribe (ST) population of India was 104.5 million, forming 8.63 per cent of the total population. The adivasi population of Maharashtra in 2011 was 10.5 million; 9.35 per cent of the total population of the state. This is the second largest population of adivasis in the country, next only to Madhya Pradesh with 10 per cent of the adivasi population of India. In the then Thane district the adivasi population formed 13.9 per cent of the district total; with large concentrations in Talasari (90), Dahanu (69), Vikramgad (92), Jawahar (92), and Mokhada (92) talukas. The Warli adivasi population was 796,245 in Thane district in 2011, a comparatively low figure. However, together with the contiguous adivasi groups of Bhils, Koknas, Thakars, Katkaris, Koli Malhar, Kolis, and Gamits, in that descending order of population in 2011, they formed close to 55 lakh adivasis. These adivasi groups are to be found in a belt of districts neighbouring Thane and Palghar: Nashik, Dhule, Nandurbar, Jalgaon, and also in South Gujarat. This population constituted the ethnic base of the Kisan Sabha during the high point of the class struggles against feudalism from 1944 to 1948, with a focus on the Warlis in Thane district. The size and geographical spread of the population partly explains why while the Kisan Sabha was able to influence policies regarding land reforms, wages and conditions of labour at the state level in a sporadic manner from the 1940s onwards, it was unable to have any significant national impact emerging from this base.

The percentage of literacy among the adivasis was very low in 1981; it was 14 per cent in Thane district, 11 per cent in Talasari and 10 per cent in Dahanu talukas. The literacy rate of the adivasis in the state of Maharashtra was 65.7 per cent in 2011 as compared to the 82.3 per cent of the total population; the adivasi literacy rate having risen from 55. 2 per cent in 2001. In Thane district the growth rate of literacy was significant, rising from 47 to 59 per cent over the decade. The sharp decline of adivasi males in cultivation in the district from 34 in 1981 to 26 per cent in 2011 suggests a movement of the population form cultivation on owned land to agricultural labour and work in the industrial informal sector in search of livelihood, as a result of loss of land and population pressures. On the other hand the sharp increase in adivasi household phone usage from 5 to 46 per cent over the decade in the district is an indication of greater usage of communication facilities.

The **conceptual framework** starts with the assumption that identity as self-perception within individuals and collectives is multidimensional and multilayered, called forth to consciousness by mobilization within changing historical contexts and circumstances. Some of the major factors influencing identity would be economic concerns of livelihood related to ownership of assets, the agricultural cycle and production process within the particular ecological region, the social relations of production and the 'insider-outsider' conceptualization that has shaped the social relations of production in the region, the relation to various political formations through the electoral process and to the agencies of the state. Since the primary focus of this study would be on the cultural factors that influence ethnic identity, and its relative significance with respect to politico-economic identity such as class and political party affiliation (which has been studied earlier in Saldanha 2015 a); festivals and rituals related to the agricultural cycle and the life cycle and the indigenous agents that play a key role in these practices, oral history of myths and stories, religious practices, aesthetic expressions and the depictions in paintings are some of the data sources that gain special significance. These are presented in Section 2, while Section 1 provides some overarching theoretical perspectives that emerge from an inductive process based on empirical practices as well as a deductive frame of reference. This mode of presentation might help the reader to wade through and facilitate interpretation of Section 2. Further analysis of the conceptual framework underlying our epistemological approach to identity may be found in Chapter 3.

What is the defining character of identity at a given time, what are the social contexts that shape identity at different times and are there more stable, relatively permanent aspects of identity together with more contingent elements, are some important issues. What triggers identity towards collective action in given contexts is another significant question. An answer to these issues constitutes the **central aim** of the project. The more specific **objectives/ questions** with **methods of data collection** of the research are the following. The primary objective is to uncover the present Warli cultural/ethnic identity through an interpretative relation to the adivasi past drawn from secondary sources, observations of contemporary cultural practices in socio-economic and political contexts and documentation of current narratives and incantations, with due consideration to subaltern interpretations through interviews and group discussions. As will be seen, the study is primarily pitched at the level of a relevant social science epistemology in dialogue with adivasi epistemologies relating to cultural practices and the sense of identity that they might provide. Observations and a tentative interpretation of some major studies (Saldanha 2015, Munshi ed. 2013, 2007, 1995, Skaria 1999, Dandekar 1998, Pereira 1990, Hardiman 1987, Dalmia 1982, Parulekar 1975, Save 1945, Enthoven 1920) have suggested that contemporary Warli cultural practices might have implicit significance regarding coming to terms with the tensions, at a temporal level, in relation to the agricultural and the life cycles, between the traditionally held meanings of cultural practices and their relevance in a drastically changed context; at an ecological spatial level, significance in relation to the symbolism of earth and sky, the tensions between the past relations to forests, flora and fauna and the mountains as markers and the present growing alienation from land and seasonal migration in search of employment in the informal sector; and at a social relational level, male-female and insider-outsider relations. These suggestions need to be substantiated and developed into a theory and methodology for comprehending cultural identity based on a sense of community and as seen in a historical context of changes in the political economy.

The foregoing are only some of the tensions within contemporary adivasi cultural identity emerging from a historical process. The objective of this study would be to uncover these socially constitutive processes of identity and thus contribute to the understanding of subaltern Warli identity in particular, and the social scientific concept of subjective identities in general. While the focus of this study would be on adivasi cultural identity, the theoretical research would have wider implications for an understanding of the relation between cultural/ethnic identity and politico-economic class identity. Cultural identity is being seen as one avenue of access to changing socio-economic and political experience. *In very specific terms the objectives of this study might be seen as: Identifying some key cultural practices that might be contributing to present-day adivasi ethnic identity; uncovering their basis, if any, in the agricultural cycle and the struggle for livelihood; thus, analysing the relation between ethnic identity and class as a politico-economic identity; interpreting the essential elements of the belief systems underlying contemporary ritual practices and accompanying incantations and identifying the residual traces, if any, of the ancient Lokayata materialist philosophy, as some scholars have suggested; and finally, drawing out the significance of the foregoing for a theory and practice of adivasi identity within processes of hegemonically structured, social transformation.*

The following is an **introduction to the chapters** of this publication. The first three chapters provide a perspective to the latter three that relate to the cultural practices, belief systems and aesthetic expressions of the adivasis that contribute to their ethnic identity. Though inductively emerging from the last three chapters that are based on field data, the first three chapters are presented at the outset to facilitate the reader who might otherwise get lost in a wealth of ethnographic detail. Indeed, the objective of this study was not primarily to present an ethnographic account of the adivasis nor to undertake an exercise in folklore, but to draw from these cultural practices some conclusions that might have a theoretical relevance and possibly a more generalized application.

Chapter One serves as an introduction to the study. It covers the objectives of the study; the methodology, methods and sources of data; an overview of the political economy of the adivasis, especially in Palghar district, Maharashtra; a brief introduction to the chapters; and finally, some qualifications regarding the study.

Chapter Two provides an interpretation of the adivasi perception of time. The analysis based on field data is carried out at the level of 'objective', historical and socially structured time in relation to the life cycle and the annual agricultural cycles with their associated festivals and rituals that serve as time markers; as well as the 'subjective' experience of the contraction and expansion of time in the context of deprivation. This analysis is relevant since the social scientific notion of chronology might not always correspond with the adivasi understanding of temporality.

Chapter Three which analyses questions of identity at a theoretical level and the relation between ethnic/cultural identity and economic class identity is in effect the crucial concluding chapter. It is presented here for reasons stated above. The chapter covers the ground of epistemological and conceptual issues related to identity, especially the concept of hegemony drawn from Antonio Gramsci, that is crucial to our analysis; the historical origins of the adivasi sense of identity going back from the present to nearly 5,000 years, even before the Indus Valley civilization, based on the writings of D.P. Chattopadhyaya and D.D. Kosambi attempting to trace elements of the commonality of belief systems as suggested by these eminent authors; the question of multiple levels of identity and the manner in which a particular identity is heightened in a given context of political mobilization.

Moving to the chapters related to cultural practices, Chapter Four is a significant chapter that provides a material basis of adivasi cultural practices, covering the highpoints of the life and agricultural cycles together with the accompanying rituals and incantations. A strong relation between the two is analysed around the principles of fertility, both human and agricultural in its natural context and the struggle for livelihood. Data are based on observations, interviews and group discussions over intervals covering close to fifty years right up to the present. This is complemented by several secondary sources.

Chapter Five relates to the peculiar features of the festivals and rituals around the Mahalaxmi temple, at Charoti Naka in Dahanu taluka. The cooption of adivasi practices, their original temple and their animistic priesthood (the bhagats) through a hegemonic process of Brahmanical dominance is uncovered as a result of a historical and contemporary analysis of oral sources.

Chapter Six covers more contemporary aesthetic expressions which, however, have their roots in the past. These are adivasi paintings, songs, dances and stories. An attempt has been made throughout the chapters to uncover the contemporary meanings that these ethnic practices have for the adivasis, their roots in the past and their relation to present community solidarities based on tribal or class identities and their struggles for livelihood.

The References contain a very extensive coverage of materials of a theoretical, historical and empirical character which have been acquired with great difficulty and thanks to research assistance. This should be useful to future research scholars.

There are **some qualifications** to the present study which one needs to place on the table. Interpreting the contemporary ritualistic incantations of the adivasis, attempting to uncover their materialistic basis and deciphering the origins of the belief systems encoded in them over a period dating back to the primitive tribals of pre-Vedic society (as suggested by some scholars such as D.P. Chattopadhyaya and D.D. Kosambi), has been a complex and tenuous analytic process. Wherever there has not been direct evidence for some of our conclusions from a secondary source or from our field observations and interactions, we have been constrained to use a hypothetical language such as may be, perhaps and possibly. The validity of such conclusions emerges from the logic of the total argument. However, one has persisted with putting forward these tentative interpretations with the hope that they could form the hypothesis for further research by others.

The empirical basis and hence the scope of this study is the adivasis, the Warlis in particular, in Palghar district and more specifically in the Dahanu and Talasari talukas of that district. That is where the illustrative cases have been studied in sufficient depth and over an extensive period of time. However, the theoretical generalizations might be found relevant to the situation of adivasis in other parts of the country.

At different places within this publication one might have critically referred to assimilatory, hegemonic, Brahmanic Hindu and casteist practices that, while apparently inclusive in character, are of a subordinating manner of the adivasis. One wishes to clarify and state clearly that this has no reference to Hinduism as a profound and deeply inspiring spiritual and religious practice and surely does not implicate millions of devout believers of that religion for whom one has the deepest respect. One has not analysed in any depth the impact of specific fundamentalist aspects of other beliefs, such as Christianity and a variety of sects within Hinduism such as the Nirankaris, Swami Samarth and Jai Guru, which have influenced the region to a lesser degree. This would have expanded the scope of the study beyond manageable proportions and could be the subject of study in themselves. An additional limitation is that one has not gone into the impact of other symbolical systems of the communication of knowledge such as language, the media and education, in any depth. In this context, one has not analysed the growing influence of the Vishva Hindu Parishad and the schools such as the Vanvasi Kalyan Ashrams and those of other religious denominations.

The focus of this study was on belief systems that had a cultural and religious character resulting in ritualistic and aesthetic practices. The three cases of cultural practices discussed in Section 2 might be considered as illustrative critical examples of the dynamics of dominant hegemonic processes and the impact that they have on ethnic identity. They are certainly not exhaustive of the multifaceted influences on ethnic identity. A significant factor in this exercise of power, however, is the social relations of the political economy and the class struggles and identity that underlie this historical process. A summary might be found earlier in this introductory chapter and an extended version in Saldanha 2015 a.

One's critique is of Brahmanical, casteist practices and beliefs that in a hegemonic manner attempt to assimilate and include subaltern communities within society like the adivasis in a subordinating manner and only has a divisive influence. One is also opposed to the perversion of the nobility of all religious beliefs for political and fundamentalist purposes, thus promoting discrimination and communal hatred and going against the spirit of the Constitution of the country and its pluralist integrity. I have attempted to make a distinction between the positive features of the materialist, Lokayata beliefs of the masses and the negative aspects of an idealistic philosophical position of the dominant Brahmanical castes that resulted in ritualism and casteism. An attempt has also been made to distinguish the latter from the profound experiences and beliefs of an asceticism and spirituality that led to mysticism and to a liberal humanism in some sects at the present time. This discussion may be seen in Chattopadhyaya's analysis of Aurobindo's writings in Chapter 3, subsection 3. One has also been critical of the misuse of religion to reinforce a monopolistic, supposedly nationalist cultural hegemony, thus ending up as a fundamentalist ideology that tends towards fascism. The best of religion in terms of humanistic values is inevitably destroyed in the process. This would only result in a strong majoritarian state, even if it is tyrannical in character; but a weak and wounded nation whose inclusive civilizational process has been distorted from within. As Thapar warns, "A nation needs identities that are broad, inclusive, and that supports its essential requirements of democracy, secularity, equality, rights to the institutions of welfare and to social justice. If we continue to make identities of colonial origin a part of our thinking they will continue to be the quicksand that prevents us from even aspiring to, leave alone reaching, the utopias we had visualized" (2014: 57).

CHAPTER 2

Towards Interpreting the Adivasi Conception of Time

This chapter attempts some reflections and interpretations based on field experiences primarily among the Warli adivasis in Dahanu and Talasari talukas of the then Thane district (presently Palghar district), Maharashtra, especially during 1970-80, updated to the present. It is a revised and updated version of a paper presented at the seminar on "New History", Session 1, Notions of Time, February 20-26, 1983, organized by the Centre for Historical Studies, Jawaharlal Nehru University, New Delhi. Some of these interpretations spring from the problems which I encountered in the field during work towards a doctoral thesis on *A Socio-Psychological Study of the Development of Class Consciousness* (Saldanha: 1984), later published as an edited and updated version (Saldanha: 2015 a). My primary focus was on the socio-historical dynamics of political consciousness among the adivasis and the forms that it takes, especially in the context of the presence of a peasant organization, the Kisan Sabha of the Communist Party of India, Marxist, CPI(M) and within the backdrop of the political economy of the region over a period of 200 years. Epistemological questions of temporality were of a tangential interest at the time. The main problem with respect to temporality arose with reference to the question of chronology and the adivasis' social construction of time. After constructing a history of the region and of the peasant organization from secondary sources, I attempted to reconstruct some of the major events from the recollections of the adivasis. These reflections represent an attempt to interpret what underlines the problems involved in such an exercise. In the process, I hope to present some tentative ideas on the adivasi notion of time. Being an interpretation, the analysis may be seen as a representation whose validity is based on intensive observations, interactions with the adivasis and the internal coherence of the arguments that are presented.

A detailed version of the major phases of the history of the region may serve as an introduction to the geographical space and an 'objective' notion of chronology and may be found in Saldanha (2015 a, Section 2). An abridged version is in Chapter 1, Introduction of this volume.

1. The Problem of Chronology and the Orientation Towards Knowledge

Hardiman in a study on *The Coming of the Devi* in 1922, a phenomenon that covered part of the region for my study, refers to this problem of chronology.

> I did not attempt to obtain certain types of information, such as dates and historical chronology. Most Adivasis whom I interviewed had only a vague idea of how long ago the movement occurred. There was tendency to telescope the time. I could, however, discover the rough age of each informant by determining their age at the time of major events, such as the great famine of 1899-1900 (e.g. 'I was born soon after the Chhapanya famine'), the influenza epidemic of 1918, and the Devi movement itself ('I was a cowherd at the time'—a task carried out by boys aged 6 o 10—or 'the Devi came just before my marriage'—thus, aged 15 to 20) (1987: 222).

I will be drawing attention to what underlines this problem of 'telescoping time' with reference to the past and hence the need to search for socially constructed and subjectively defined cross reference points, coordinates, to formulate before, during and after.

Here are some of my own frustrating attempts at ordering everyday life and at serializing political events:

> When asked when a particular political event such as the Zari meeting took place a more hopeful answer might be 'before the firings at the Talwada meeting'. Or often one might get an answer such as 'When I was that big (with hand outstretched to a height of about three feet) or 'I had just got married and built a house',

or 'The forests were there at that time. They have now been all cut down'. When asked his age the adivasis might answer, 'See me and say', i.e. see my features and bodily structure, what has become of it and decide. The outward appearance, however, often confuses an accurate assessment of the adivasis' age. Sometimes the response might be a more aggressive one as, 'What do I know my age? It's not important. It's all the same. You people count your age and keep. We don't keep an account of our age'.

What appears to be implicit in the above in terms of succession of events and past-present-future (as illustrated below) is the establishing of an interrelation between different temporal rhythms: Individual physical growth—What one does in one's lifetime and one's immediate environment in relation to annual seasons and the agricultural cycle, marked by festivals and ceremonial occasions—And the social historical events that one participates in or that happens to one and changes in the ecology. For example, the elements in defining time among the Trobriand islanders was found to be broadly classified into the astronomical, the meteorological and ecological, and the personal-cultural (Malinowski 1990: 204). As Gurvitch points out, "The total social phenomena both produce and are products of social-time. They give birth to social-time, move and unfold in it...Social-time thus cannot be defined without defining the total social phenomenon...We have defined Social-time as the *convergency and divergency of movements of the total social phenomena, giving birth to time and elapsing in time.* Specifically, the total social phenomenon is an actual total participation of the human in the human involved in an endless movement ebb and flow" (1990: 67, 69). Connerton differentiates the notion of time within market economies of capitalist formations and the conception of the passage of time within more traditional agricultural societies: "The temporality of the market and of the commodities that circulate through it generates an experience of time as quantitative and as flowing in a single direction, an experience in which each moment is different from the other by virtue of coming next, situated in a chronological succession of old and new, earlier and later...When, on the other hand, everyday life is envisaged as a structure of exemplary recurrences, the imaginative persuasiveness of such a perception is wrought through what may be called *a rhetoric of re-enactment*. This rhetoric works by employing at least three distinguishable modes of articulation: we might call them calendrical, verbal and gestural re-enactment" (1989: 64, 65). About social science interactions with informants in agricultural societies, he writes, "When oral historians listen carefully to what their informants have to say, they discover a perception of time that is not linear but cyclical. The life of the interviewee is not a curriculum vitae but a series of cycles. The basic cycle is the day, then the week, the month, the season, the year, the generation" (Connerton, 1989: 20). Aminzade (1992) stresses the importance of four concepts relating to temporal connections that would facilitate our understanding of the choices made by popular actors within the temporal trajectories that govern their lives. He recognizes the difficulties in reconstructing the past despite the use of these concepts. The concepts are: duration, pace or the number of similar events within a given temporal duration, trajectories relating to the patterns and direction underlying change processes, and cycles indicating the rhythms within and between phases. The last two are more qualitative in nature. Discussing events such as wars and revolutions, he underlines the importance of popular perceptions of the length of duration based on the assessment of the costs that would be borne.

Returning to our research among the adivasis of Palghar district, one finds that succession of events is expressed as before /during/ after, within a particular rhythm of activity or by reference points across these articulated rhythms, within a conception of the 'total social phenomenon', as the foregoing discussion by Gurvitch. The days of the week and the months of the year are generally known, but not the date, revealing a weakness with numerical ordering and measurement (time, area, weight, distance and of value) in general. The high points of the month—the Sundays—and the high points of the year, the ritualized festivals (Sankrant, Simga, Diwali and Gav Dev, Khali) and ceremonial occasions serve as the articulated meeting points of the annual lived cycle, the agricultural cycle and the seasonal cycle. These are the days of joyful escape from the rigid pace of the cycle of timed work and employment/unemployment in agriculture and migration, and are used as reference points for expressing before and after. Hence, an adivasi might say: 'I migrated and worked on the outskirts of Mumbai for char Ravivar (four Sundays) after Simga (Holi)'. The adivasis follow the lunar calendar which apart from providing greater and more repetitive periodicity within the annual solar rhythms and the movement over the astrological signs, provides great significance as illumination within a society that generally does not benefit from electrification. Most of the important festivals are held on full moon days.

The following table is an attempt to visualize the articulation of the months of the year with the festivals and ceremonial occasions that are rooted in the life and annual agricultural cycles which, in themselves, are embedded in ecological and seasonal cycles. It is suggested that these dimensions constitute the coordinates for the adivasis for expressing temporal sequence and for the social construction of temporality, with the exception of the social relations with the non-adivasi 'outsider' over a historical period. Reasons for this exception will be discussed.

The Annual Festivals/Ceremonial Occasions and the Agricultural/Seasonal Cycles

Months	Festivals	Ceremonial Occasions	Seasons and Agricultural Cycle
January 14 (Paush)	Sankrant Til is eaten, ceremonial hunting, blood offerings	Divas Pani for the dead.	Winter Threshing, grass processing, migration
February (Magh Shudh 2)	Kul Dev Celebration of Narain (snake god) Vishnu devs, clan deities, stone/ areca nuts mixed with red lead.	Divas Pani for the dead.	Winter Preparation of soil (seed beds), grass processing, migration
March 21 (Phalgun), Vernal Equinox	Simga/ Holi Dholka dances, mango is eaten, ritual stealing, Phalgun Shudh 15, sweet balls of rice flour and jaggery offered	Marriages	Winter-Summer Preparation of soil (seed beds), migration

Contd...

Months	Festivals	Ceremonial Occasions	Seasons and Agricultural Cycle
April (Chaitra)	Mahalaxmi, Ram Navmi, Vagh Dev, begins on Chaitra Shudh 9 and 15 Purnima is Warli main day. Newly married Warlis dance around pole and fire the previous night. Ends on Chaitra Vadya 8.	Marriages	Summer Burning the soil, migration,
May (Vaishak)	A Khatij Various types of grain are immersed in water, for good crops		Summer Burning the soil, migration
June 21 (Jeshta), Summer Solstice, Dakshinayan till December 22			Summer-Rains Ploughing, sowing
July (Ashad)			Rains Transplantation
August (Shravan)	Nagpanchami, snake hill puja by men, Shravan Shudha 5, fasting		Rains Weeding, control of pests
September (Bhadrapad)	Gauri, Pitra Baras (appeasement of ancestral spirits), tarfa dances by Warlis at Mahalaxmi, initiation into bhagat Bhadrapad Vadya 12.		Rains Harvesting

Contd...

Months	Festivals	Ceremonial Occasions	Seasons and Agricultural Cycle
October (Ashvin Shudh 10), Autumnal Equinox	Diwali, Kambdi dance by men, blood offering at durung and Savar Puja, chavali is eaten, Dasara, Ashvin Shudh 10, tarfa dance, Raval begins and ends with Gav Dev (Vagh Baras), Ashwin Vadya 12, Hindu Vasu Baras for cattle		Winter Harvesting
November (Kartik)		Divas Pani for dead	Winter Threshing, grass cutting
December 22 (Margshirsh), Winter Solstice Uttarayan till June 21	Kul Dev (Himmay and Hizara) Ras Khali (Kansari Devi)	Marriages Divas Pani for dead	Winter Threshing, Grass cutting

Equinoxes

March 21 and September 22.

What is the basis of the adivasis' inability to explain their experience of time in terms of the social scientists' conception of historical time in the form of a chronology of events in serial flow? A straightforward answer to this question might be the illiteracy, lack of numeracy and the constricted spatial and socio-economic mobility among the adivasis. The non-literate adivasis, especially those of an older generation, express numbers by counting on the fingers and exceeding ten by multiples of ten. Most have a clear conception of the village with its padas (hamlets) and the taluka with its villages, and a sense of direction and distance in experiential terms. Most know the name of the district and have a conception of it in vague terms, i.e. the immediate extension of the taluka of location into the surrounding talukas. The majority would know the name of the state, having participated in or heard of the Maharashtra-Gujarat border struggle under the Kisan Sabha and only some of them would have a conception of the districts that comprise the state. About two-thirds would know the name of the country, but with only a few having a nebulous understanding of what it comprises. The question arises, what does India mean to the adivasis of a particular taluka in Palghar district? What is the qualitative and quantitative content of the term India for one who has rarely read the newspapers, rarely heard the radio and only for its music, never seen a map, travelled as far as Talasari, Sanjan, Dahanu, Mahalaxmi and perhaps Mumbai for a morcha (demonstration march), whose external human contact is largely with the landlord, the moneylender, shopkeeper, the political worker and the government official, who has heard spoken of 'Dilli' where the 'Kayda' (law) is made and from where it is brought to the village; who has been to or heard of Mumbai where the elected representatives can raise their voices in the meetings? What significance does the subjective meaning of India have for the adivasis' conception of ethnic and class identity in socially extensive terms and an understanding of the strategic alliances within the 'people' in their conflict with the conceived 'class enemy' and the conceived state? These were significant questions that arose during one's study in the 1980s (Saldanha 1984 and 2015 a). Today, the adivasis have to some degree grown out of individual lives, subjective experience of space, time and value and have been introduced to an external, wider and more 'objective' conception. This has been primarily due to state intervention with the introduction of symbolic systems of measurement of area, weight, length, private property, money and the market; and improved means of communication and education. The advancement of commerce, private property and a monetized economy, while implying growing exploitation, have promoted measurement of value and exchange in monetary terms. Growing decentralized administration has meant centres of authority at different levels, in different places for varying purposes with facilities that specify time and monetary value.

For the adivasis, the conceptions of space (a sense of extensiveness related to social and physical mobility, time to travel over distance) and time (the duration necessary for undertaking an activity within a given social and ecological space) undoubtedly coalesce and are implicit in the conceptualization of temporality and are based in activity, especially the quest for livelihood in agriculture. For example, describing the experience of time of the Kabyle, Bourdieu writes, "Inwardly felt, as the very movement of life rather than as a constraining limit, time cannot be disassociated from the experience of activity and of the space in which that activity takes place. Duration and space are described by reference to the performance of a concrete task; e.g. the unit of duration is the time one needs to do a job, to work a piece of land with a pair of oxen. Equally, space is evaluated in terms of duration, or better, by reference to the activity occupying a definite lapse of time, for example, a day at the plough or a day's walk. The common denominator and foundation of the equivalence is nothing other than the experience of activity" (1990: 224).

The adivasi conception of time is closely related to an understanding of spatial features characterized by ecology and social relations of production in an historical context. This has been adequately elaborated by Chattopadhyaya (1978 a/1959) and Gadgil and Guha (1992) in Chapter 3. Time and space get condensed into the memory of past activities within social contexts. Presently recollections of the past are codified in verbal incantations and ritualized (repetition at particular times) through habitual practices. Incantations during rituals that mark the high points of the life and agricultural cycles may be seen as recollections of a happier past and future wish fulfilment. There are specified places for rituals, for example for the Gav Dev (the tiger, the village deity). These spaces are populated by adivasi participants and the bhagat who faces a specific geographic direction; east in the direction of the rising sun. Both time and space are embodied through dances on festival occasions and playfulness sanctified and assisted by alcohol.

While Bogoras presents an insightful understanding of the tribal cosmology of space, this interpretation lacks an adequate explanation of its material basis, as for example: "At the same time the Upper World somehow coincides with the region of sunrise and the East, of zenith or midday, and also with all regions connected with light and the sun, and with the direction up-stream and to the right of the person speaking. The Nether World coincides with the Region of Sunset and the West, of nadir and midnight, i.e. with all the regions connected with night and darkness (and also with the moon), with the direction down-river and to the left of the person speaking" (Bogoras 1925: 213). Such an interpretation of East and West, North and South or one's location during ritual practices, especially at the time of the Gav Dev festival may be found among the adivasis in Palghar district as discussed in Chapter 4. The conception of a Superior Deity, though not one seen as religiously enshrined in places of worship such as temples, may be found among these adivasis; as also the articulation of life and death as well as of beneficial and malignant spirits that influence these processes. Bogoras provides a plausible interpretation of this popular understanding that draws on tribal and non-tribal communities, ranging from pre-animistic to animistic practices and moving on to religious formulations: "What is the primary source of these peculiar conceptions? For what reason is the Superior Deity Almighty and Benevolent, represented as retired, and whence have originated the posterior shapes, evil and malevolent? The conception of the Superior Deity must have sprung from some psychical source even more ancient and primitive than animism. This source is evidently nothing else than the impersonal *mana*. In the very first stage of the religious sentiment in the blending of the self with the universe, the microcosm with macrocosm, with full disavowal of death, the sentiment of *mana* must have been rather bright, buoyant, leading to the optimistic way of thinking and feeling. The clearing of the whole in two parts, the detaching of the self from the universe, leads to the sense of the danger, of the human loneliness in the wide world and ultimately to the perception of death. So the individual spirits which are born from this process are evil and death-bringing. They arise on the periphery of the consciousness of the universe and arrange themselves as in a circle around mankind. The periphery of the universe is opposite and hostile to the self" (Bogoras 1925: 265).

A more basic issue regarding the non-correspondence between the adivasis' conception of time and that of social science would be to understand the real, existential dynamics of the adivasis' conceptualization and communication of temporality, closely related to the lack of symbolic systems implicit in literacy and numeracy which may be considered of lesser significance. I would suggest that a major explanation for the frustrations involved in drawing information with a temporal dimension from the adivasis is the non-correspondence between science as a hegemonic process and the spontaneous viewpoints of subaltern groups with respect to orientations towards space, time and knowledge. The time frames just do not fit. The scientific desire to understand processes, both natural and social historical, in terms of a succession of events (before, during and after) and temporal properties (past, present and future) contains implicit notions of casualty, determination and intention/motivation, of directing the course of events through controls and measurements. This might take more aggressive forms or more empathetic ones. Science is explanation, is comprehension (grasping). Seeking an 'objective' basis for ordering reality, the scientist has to look for standards outside immediate contexts—oneself, spontaneous individual and social experiences, the quality of which might expand or contract the experience of time. This external basis, outside subjective experience, may be found in an historical event that is culturally specific and serves as a reference point (birth of Christ), and the relatively stable and regular motions of planetary bodies and instruments for measurement such as watches and clocks. The history of clock time and the development of symbolic systems of representing succession and, in particular, measurement in quantitative terms, might then be seen in the context of the development of science and technology and of transportation with the need for synchronization of activities. That this process is auto-reflexive, that one is controlled in more novel ways in the very act of exercising control, is another matter. Ordering demands its own reordering. Temporality takes on a self-confident linear dimension of past and present in which one can plan the future. The differences between the scientific notion of time which implies measurement of sequence and duration through standardized techniques and the adivasi existential experience of time as activities within socio-ecological contexts driven by motivation and subjective experience may be understood in relation to the distinctions between the concepts of chronos and kairos, respectively (Jaques 1990: 33).

I do not wish to deny the operation of the hegemony of science in my own interpretative dialogue with the common sense of the adivasis in this and my earlier related publications, despite my efforts. One's limited claim is that it is possible for social science to break out of dominant hegemonic positions and empathize, identify with and articulate contesting, alternative subordinate hegemonic world views in an honest and embedded manner; so that the ensuing interpretations and representations are still as close as possible to the subaltern voice. This has led to the confrontation with realities and the elaboration of concepts such as the experience of community within given ecological contexts and the sense of multiple-layered identities based on ethinicity and the struggle for survival which were generally not part of one's Marxian predelective repertoire.

For the Warlis, what would be our notions of the linear dimension of time tends to collapse into an insecure, limited present over which they have little or no control. Over the course of close to two centuries, the Warlis as a tribe have experienced abrupt changes in their lives: from hunters, fruit gatherers and shift cultivators; to forcibly settled agriculturists; only to lose their lands to the encroaching non-adivasis and to become tenants and bonded labourers. The post-independence land reforms and development schemes, partly in response to their organized struggles, have only served to make them poor peasants and agricultural labourers in constant search for employment over the annual cycle. While changes have taken place, they have generally not experienced themselves as conscious, collective subjects of that process. Except for a brief militant phase of the peasant movement from 1944 to 1948, history has generally happened to them rather than them making history.

The cunning rationality of the past in one's accommodative relation to nature is dying out. In the distant past of a predominantly hunting, foraging and shift cultivating existence what could not be controlled was deified and placated. Vagaya (the tiger) became a major adivasi deity, ironically the protector of cattle. Today this quiet rationality may be seen in their relations with their human oppressors. Some indication of the breakdown of what might have been a more positive attitude to knowledge in harmony with seasonal and ecological cycles might be found in the relation between the bhagat (the medicine man) and bhutali (the witch). The bhagat who acts as a mediator between nature, humans and the spirit world, presides at ceremonial occasions related to the life and agricultural/seasonal cycles and serves as a healer with medicinal plants, finds himself increasingly deprived of traditional sources of medicine with growing deforestation. Activists in non-governmental organizations in the region have established a clear relation between deforestation, increasing incidence of disease and the identification of the bhutali—the woman bearer of an evil spirit, generally a destitute person—as the source of disease with some incidents of their being stoned to death. The attitude towards the schooling system, especially of the older generation, is one of awe at the ritualization of symbols and knowledge content that is considered alien to their culture and their immediate needs. At best it is seen with an instrumental orientation; as a passport to lower middle class status, a gamble that is open to only a few. The attitude towards knowledge is one of passive receptivity. Understanding is generally expressed as 'entry into one's ear' (magya kanant ale), a receptive act where one becomes the object of knowledge of events and not as 'comprehension ' where the subject encompasses events through enlarging the sphere of critical awareness and thus one's grasp over time. The scientific act of relatively controlling time in spatial terms, a cognitive and sensory process, may be got through the telescope or the microscope. For the adivasi it is mainly through transcending a constricted awareness and existence in the present, by stilling that consciousness and escaping into a 'timelessness' on special occasions, as will be described below.

2. The Experience of Limitedness and of Reification: The Contraction (Time for Survival) and Expansion (Time for Escape) of Temporality

I suggest that there are two basic subjective experiences underlying the present adivasi notion of temporality. The painful realization of the limitedness of the life cycle which inevitably ends in death is brought out in the following extract from different incantations at the time of the death rituals found in Save (1944: 137):

> The soul has no death; only the body dies (Jivala maran nahi, kay komate). This body (chest) is the home of life (soul). As a fruit is plucked from the tree, so is life plucked from the body. This soul gives up its outer form like a snake giving up its outer skin. Death is inevitable. God giveth and He taketh (Paramesar deta na toch neta) A man should neither fear nor hate death. This circle of life and death is externally going on. Body is like a lac-dye melting away by fire. It is like a full moon setting all of a sudden and like a plantain stalk breaking in the middle. An earthen pot can last at least for few days, but none can predict how long the body can live.

Save observes that "in one song the nature gods like Sun, Moon, Clouds, Rain and Lightning are described as exempted from the death list, as they have to keep the cycle of the worldly existence ever moving. None of the (other) tribal deities, like Narandev, Hirva or Waghaya have been associated with death" (1944: 138). The notion of the limitedness of human existence is accompanied with the idea of the timelessness of natural phenomena.

The other factor which is important for the understanding of the adivasi notion of temporality is the reality and experience of reification. Over the last two centuries the adivasis have increasingly experienced the commoditization of their activities and labour, the atomization of their communitarian bonds and the objectification of their very existence. G. Parulekar (1975: IX and 92) provides a vivid description of the daily and annual lived cycle of the bonded labourers in early 1940.

> In those days the landowners of these villages had their khatlas. The labourers of this khatlas went to work in the morning at the sound of the bell, and toiled till noon. Then an Adivasi was given paddy sufficient for one person. He took this away and pounded it in a wooden mortar with a wooden pestle to remove the husks. He then cooked the rice he thus cleaned, and ate it with the lump of salt. He forced this meal down the throat with water. He went back to work again at the given time, and toiled till dusk when his working day came to an end. His only wages were a miserly portion of rice. He followed the same routine on all days with no special concession for festivals or holidays both being unknown words for him. He could not even afford to be ill. Every morning

> he had to return to his yoke like some dumb animal, and work himself to the bone on the strength of a handful of rice. At nightfall he had just enough energy left to collapse into sleep. In the morning once again, he was back at the grindstone. It was a life without joy, without variety, without freedom, without zest, a blinkered life which neither saw nor knew of anything beyond the village and the landlord. This was the life that Adivasis led day after day, and year after year...To see them going about their work with bent head one almost suspected that they were dumb, blind and deaf.

The 'moronic', obsessive—compulsive manner in which the adivasi is described as having gone through the round of duties by stilling senses and emotions may be interpreted as a defensive reaction; a rational ritualization of actions aimed at preserving one's human dignity in the face of compulsions.

Capitalist penetration in agriculture, the spread of the market economy, land reforms and some development schemes, especially during the post-independence period, and the militant phase of the Warli struggle from 1944-48 have presently given the adivasis some degree of freedom from feudal exploitation. While a poor peasant-agricultural wage labour economy has grown, newer forms of dependence have emerged. The adivasis find themselves overwhelmed with symbolic systems of measuring area, weight, length, the value of labour and produce. Private property in and alienation of land and restrictions on the use of the forests have confined their existence. The system of local self-government has introduced centres of authority at graded levels, in different places for varying purposes and facilities that specify time and monetary value. Limited class differentiation has emerged among the adivasi peasantry, so that a middle peasant with a fragile security from his small holding could define an agricultural labourer to me as "one who is so overcome by his daily, annual search for employment and wages that he does not have the time to take off and go to dance at a wedding." Today there is a limited scope for 'laziness' on the job and for 'shirking' work; that is, when one does get employment. Upadhyaya (1980: A-145) justifiably interprets this as a way of conserving one's labour power in a situation of undernourishment and exploitation through the wage relation.

It is within the foregoing context of the experience of limitedness and of reification that one might interpret the adivasi notion of the collapse of the linear dimension of time into a focus on the immediate present; an endless, repetitive, cycle of days with relative invariance over the years. Time tends to contract as the ongoing Time for Survival or to expand during festivals and ceremonial occasions as the Time for Escape into timelessness. Time for survival is the shrinking of the notion of time to the level of individual experience whose primary driving force is physical survival despite the alienation of labour in a hostile social and natural environment, over the daily and annual lived cycle. This is timed existence. Time for escape is the expansion of a normally constricted awareness during the few high points of the annual cycle, at the time of festivals and ceremonial occasions. Escape into timelessness on these occasions becomes the only human way of seeking explanations, experiencing freedom and exercising control.

I would suggest that this sense of timelessness among the adivasis, this experience of 'freely floating' with time is exercised through some of the following ways:

Drink: Alcoholism among the adivasis is a very general phenomenon and reinforces impoverishment. But one might take a more understanding view of their addiction to drink. It is one way of surviving the daily work cycle and is used during most ceremonial occasions over the annual cycle. A drinking session is the time when the adivasis can laugh and make small talk (goshti karne) in the company of one's fellows. It is the time when they can raise their voice without any hindrance and curse their lot or swear at the landed, provided that one is in the privacy of the family or in the secluded company of those who share the same experience in a bhonga (country drinking place) on a hillock.

Dance is the time when the adivasis' entire being vibrates to the overpowering, rhythmic sound of the tarpha (a horn musical instrument made out of a gourd) and the drum and is lost in the steps of a collective movement. I have sometimes played back the taped sound of the tarpha and witnessed the transformation that would come over a listless, shrunken, squatting man. He would become restless and a smile would gradually light up his face. He would slowly get onto his feet and suddenly erupt into a cry, with stamping feet and flaying hands—a harmonious blending of powerful self-expression and being lost to the control of a timeless rhythm. No wonder then the tarpha and some other musical instruments are considered sacred, played only during the particular phases of the seasonal and agricultural cycle and are used to represent the divine.

Dreams and entering into trances are the way of transcending 'rationalized', discursive discourse and entering into the limitlessness of fantasy and myth. The recollections of a collective, relatively emancipated past as 'kings of the jungle' (jungle che rage, as they sometimes call themselves) are elaborated upon on these occasions by the bhagat. Younger adivasis are initiated into the traditions of the people at the raval (a learning and induction ceremony of the young by an established bhagat, away from the community settlement). Incantations are recited at festivals, ceremonial occasions and at times of distress (see Chapter 4). The bhagat is both a medium from everyday life into timelessness, a healer and a provider of meaning; by mediating between and explaining the articulations of different temporal rhythms with respect to the immediate. Based on records of some of these incantations one might tentatively infer that their content have little relation to the exploitative social relations and the encroachments on the lives of the adivasis during the last two centuries, but rather are a way of coping with this experience through a process of reaction formation, sublimation, and projection onto a distant past of more harmonious times. It is thus that the present and the more violent history of post-colonial and post-independence rule is transcended and the identity of a people through communion in shared rituals during ceremonial occasions is preserved. As a Warli painter once told me when I drew his attention to the idealized situations that he was creating almost as a wish fulfilment, of extensive and abundant fields ripe with harvest, unrelated to the harsh realities of everyday life, "I paint in order to get rid of sorrow". This is unlike the more popular songs among the adivasis which are of more recent origin and reveal a greater non-tribal influence.

The hunt and food gathering once served to exercise control in harmony with the natural environment. It was the blending of the time for survival and the time for joyful escape. Today, with the denuded forests and near extinct animal life, the occasional hunt (for a squirrel or a rabbit) has only symbolic significance. One might interpret the regular use of alcohol and animal sacrifice (the cutting of chickens, goats and the letting of blood) on ceremonial occasions as harking back to the past and a carryover from the practices of a pre-settled agricultural society. The forays into the forest for gathering roots (kand mul) and forest produce are a necessary supplement to below subsistence agriculture, especially in times of scarcity.

It is in the foregoing context that one might see the special significance of festivals and ceremonial occasions as high points and reference points in the annual cycle. They are the ritualization of the meeting points of the temporal rhythms related to the *Time for Survival*:

The annual work cycle as subjectively experienced in consciousness articulated with the relatively externalized, object referent of the agricultural cycle: Preparation of the top soil (rab), sowing and tending the seeds beds, ploughing, transplantation, control of pests and weeding, harvesting, threshing and storing of food grains, migration for grass cutting and processing and for other forms of casual, manual labour in the informal agricultural and industrial sectors; and the seasonal cycle (summer, rains, winter) related to the lunar calendar.

The life cycle (birth, puberty, marriage, the new house, child bearing, illness and death) linked to the biological time of human growth.

The generational cycle reaching out to a wider time frame of the natural environment for reference points which might be termed as ecological or nature's time—major droughts, famines, epidemics, changes in forest cover and quality of soil. In more recent times, the ravages of climate change as well as dams and other major infrastructural projects that give rise to significant ecological changes serve the purpose of time markers. In this context, one might see the significance of ancestor worship as establishing clan lineage and pacifying the unfulfilled wishes of the dead.

The consciously experienced social historical time (which some historians might call 'the long duration') that is articulated with the widest and the near eternal frontiers of cosmological time which is the subject matter of several myths and fantasies reportedly recovered by bhagats and davleris (married women who preside at marriages) through dreams and spirit possession and expressed through chants and stories of origin. It is significant that the adivasi-non-adivasis' contact and the changing, repressive character of the social relations of production rarely find a mention in these incantations.

One might infer that the adivasi is able to cope with and transcend the foregoing articulated cycles of the *Time for Survival* by seeking release through the timeless rhythms of the *Time for Escape* (drink, music and dance, dreams and entering into trances, the incantations of the bhagat and the davleris, the ceremonial hunt and animal sacrifice). The very repetitiveness of the cycles of the time for survival does provide some continuity and stability to existence. The high points in the temporal cycles related to survival are celebrated through the different expressions of the experiences of timelessness. Festivals and ceremonial occasions are bright landmarks in the dreary lives of the adivasis and serve as reference points in their recreation of chronology. The subjective experience of time tends to shrink to the level of individual experience whose primary driving force is physical survival through the alienation of labour in a hostile natural and social environment; or time tends to expand to the limitless reaches of fantasy and myth whose motivation is escape from the drudgery of survival, i.e. seeking explanation through fantasy. Escape becomes the only human way of experiencing freedom and exercising control. Just as identities are multilayered and coexistent within individuals as well as within collectives, at various stages of predominance and salience to context in a manner of figure and ground in Gestaltic terminology; the experience of varying rhythms of time could be interpreted as acting in a similar manner as variably covalent with respect to specific identities within their diversity that are distinctively called forth to consciousness depending on context and mobilization.

A Schematic Attempt at Conceptualizing the Temporal Rhythms of the Adivasis

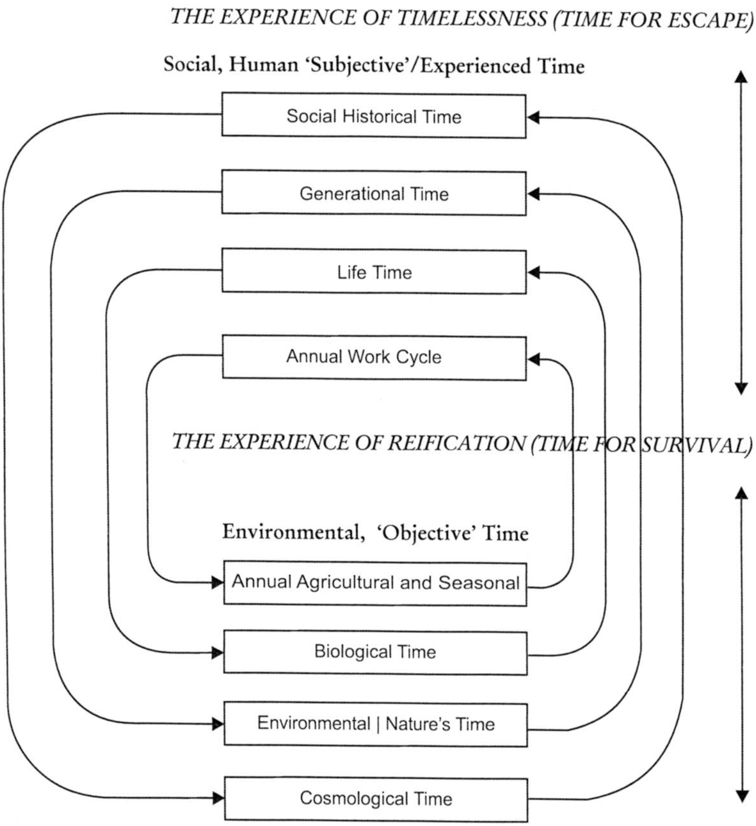

3. Past, Present and Future and the Significance of the Present

It is in this context of the experience of limitedness (insecurity of life) and of reification that one needs to understand the adivasis' absorption with and by a threatening present. The sequential ordering of time where one is relatively in control of events breaks down in the face of a chaotically structured time for survival. The experience of timelessness in the present is the transcending of a reified, relatively changeless repetitive present that is structured by a system of disarticulated temporal rhythms and that is experienced as an inability to exercise choice towards a future alternative. This transcending takes place through different forms, described above, into a distant past that was in relative harmony with the system of articulated temporal rhythms in hunting, food gathering and in shift cultivation of communally held lands largely within forests. My research on the Kisan Sabha in the region suggests that the transcending of the present also takes place through the enthusiastic recall of a more immediate past—the militant phase of the movement from 1944 to 1948—which was experienced by the adivasis as an exercise of collective choice towards the creation of an alternative. The past is present in everyday life, not as a chronologically ordered past but as a phenomenon, logically/ existentially experienced transcendence of the present, through various expressions on festivals and ceremonial occasions and through the narratives of the elderly which revive the memory of the past. The focus on the present, with the lack of planning and saving habits attributed to the adivasis, may also be seen in the context of a bleak future with no definite signs of an alternative. The future is often seen as more of the past. As an adivasi, in a moment of despondency, told me:

> It is as if it is night and one has to drive a cart. The people will just drive. One has to drive, so let's drive. Where lies the path, where lies the ditch, that's not seen. Some even grow old and die, but don't understand (Saldanha 2015 a).

Flinders (2002) offers a very sensitive formulation of the values and belief systems that marked the temporal process of transition from a mode of survival based on hunting and foraging to one engaged with settled agriculture that took place in a world historical perspective about ten thousand years ago beginning in the river valleys of West Asia. She refers to the former as the 'culture of belonging' as different to the latter 'culture of enterprise' that would be gradually enhanced during the settled agricultural phase and later. "The extent of changes involved is almost impossible to take in: For a couple of million years, the vast majority of human beings had been nomadic, tribal, egalitarian, subsistence-level folk with a very modest inventory of tools; after a remarkably brief period of transition—just a few thousand years—they developed settled, politically centralized, socially stratified, economically complex, and technologically innovative societies" (2002: 62). For the adivasis of Palghar district this transition could not have been from most accounts much earlier than 700 years ago under different rulers and their land legislations and accompanying social relations of production that gradually forced adivasis into settlements: Hindu rule till 1300 AD, a subsequent Muslim period till 1660 AD, followed by reigns of partial regional overlap by the Portuguese from 1500 to 1670, the Marathas from 1660 to 1800, followed by the British from 1800 till independence in 1947; with the most significant changes taking place post-1818 under British rule. The relatively late transition of the adivasis in the region might account for their dual consciousness with the persistence of the 'culture of belonging'. The two contrasting cultures referred to above by Flinders (2002: 71), and as illustrated according to one's triangulated and interrelated conception of context, process and consciousness, may be visualized as follows:

Cultures of Belonging Contrasted with Cultures of Enterprise

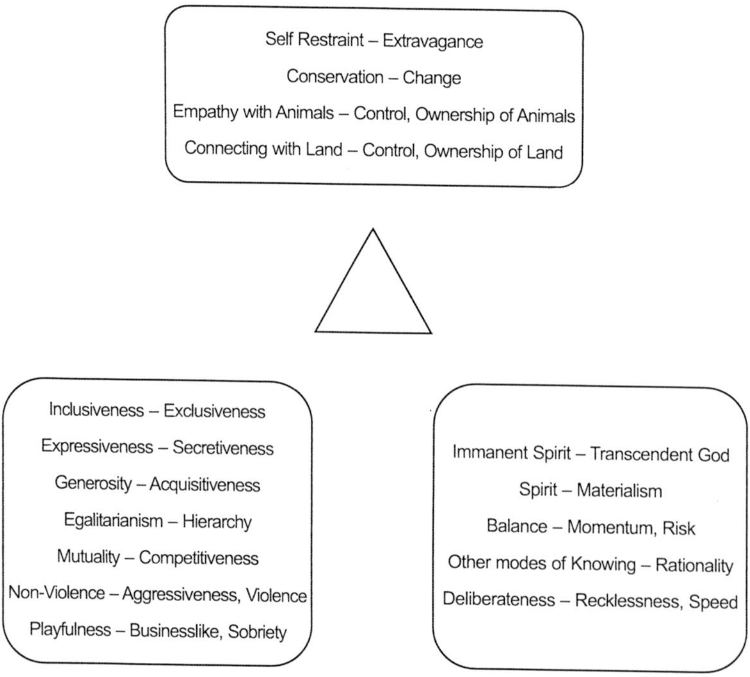

Early human tribal communities during their hunting and foraging stage were in tune with nature, with one another and with the spirit. The modality of exclusion during the agricultural and industrial phase, rather than the inclusiveness of old, and the relegation of the 'values of belonging' to women under the new patriarchal order, prevented the harmonization of the two perspectives over the period of transition and later (Flinders 2002: 87-89).

One's preoccupation during this exercise has been similar to that of J.R. Hall when he suggests the need for a 'comparative phenomenology of time' in order to resolve the tension between social action within structured contexts and the flow of historical processes: "But the more basic concern is to sketch an approach to historiography which recognizes that because subjective and social temporal orientations themselves differ among individuals and groups and over chronological time, knowledge of historically given temporal orientations can tremendously enrich understandings of social order and social change...Measured objective time exists simply as a social convention, clearly more or less important in different ways for various participants and arenas of social life, as well as for historians" (J.R. Hall 1980: 114, 118). One might conclude with the following suggestion. There cannot be a conceptual approach to time that stands conceptually outside of time. The chronology of social scientific discourse needs to open itself to a critique from the chronology of socially and symbolically structured lived experiences, especially of subaltern groups. A history that incorporates the temporalities of these groups would be all the richer for it and would help to give them a voice. How this is to be done is a matter for ongoing dialogue with the subaltern and within the social scientific community. What I have offered is one interpreted representation.

CHAPTER 3

Identity: Adivasi Ethnicity—Class

1. The Issues

An important theoretical question, with significant implications for practice, is how to weave popular culture, consciousness and ethnic identity into dialectical and historical materialism; and to do so by giving it a distinctive and relevant space for solidarity and political action. It is important to do so without setting out on a tangential flight of subjectivist and linguistic fantasy and in a manner that remains grounded in a social structured context and historical practice. The nature of ethnic identity and class identity would then become key concepts, both independently and in their mutual relation, for our understanding of historical transformatory processes. At a more general level, it would be the relation between collective consciousness, culture and symbolic systems understood in a broad sense in the realm of human subjectivity on the one hand, and livelihood within the political economy as constitutive of identity and that might serve as collective driving forces for change in given contexts. Identity is imbibed through the struggle for livelihood, through socialization, community interaction, political organizational affiliation and mutual perception of the 'other', within experienced political and socio-economic structures and the perceived character of past historical processes and future alternatives (Saldanha 2015 a and b). With the considerable weakening of political organizations based on issues related to the economy and the growing number of formations that appeal to ethnicity, identity tends to take on an ethnic colour in appearance and manifestation; if not always in essential substance. However, even in these overt ethnic manifestations through slogans, banners and ideological articulations, the ecological and economic basis of identity and the struggle for livelihood remains underlying and implicit. The issue then is the nature of the relation between ethnic and class identity, their sources and formative influences and their relative salience in collective transformative processes.

Just as paintings are a form of communicative expression of Warli ritualistic, ethnic identity in the sphere of functionality and aesthetics and as facilitated in the past by the Bhagats, Davlaris and Savasinis, and today by commercial art houses; political actions may be seen as a form of communicative expression of the same ethnic identity in the arena of politics facilitated historically in the past by the heads of clans, Karbharis and Patils and presently by political leaders, ideology and electoral party organization. The dichotomy between ethnic identity as traditional and class identity as modern is unsustainable in societies that are transiting from hunting, food gathering, pastoral and agricultural economies to industry and the service professions which very often is in the form of industrial serfdom in the informal sector for the vast majority. The challenge is to establish the relation between these identities in the synchronic present and within a process of diachronic transformation. The nature of the relation between ethnicity and class can best be understood by contextualizing them in processes of socio-economic transition.

An issue that has assumed importance in the contemporary context of the rise of fundamentalist forces and historical attempts at inclusion of the subaltern, though in a subordinating manner so as to affirm hegemony in a majoritarian sense, is whether todays adivasis were all along and are in reality Hindus or whether Brahmanical Hinduism as practised in the present is to a great extent a Brahmanized animism emerging historically from mutual contact with the former 'tribal' identity and practice of the early humans of pre-Vedic times or relatively independently from the pre-Vedic, primitive tribal economies which were a shared ancestry. The human condition is such that the self must create the other, either to integrate with it or to politically and economically dominate it. One is conscious of one's identity in the process of discovering one's being through becoming, in relation to the other. In this context, the character of the mutual relation between adivasis and non-adivasis within the dominance of contemporary state hegemony assumes significance.

The themes covered, especially in the empirical chapters of cultural practices in Section 2:

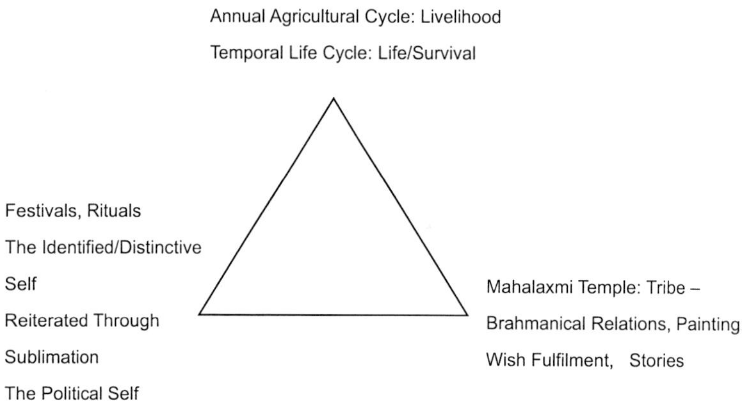

2. Identity: Ethnic/Cultural, Class/Livelihood; Some Epistemological Considerations

The conceptual analysis that follows may be found in greater detail in Saldanha, *Structure, Consciousness and Social Transformation* (2015 a), which covers a 200-year history of the political economy of the then Thane district, Maharashtra, with a special emphasis on adivasi political consciousness. This was followed with an exploration of the epistemological approach to the consciousness of the *Subaltern Subject* (2015 b), together with a comparative critical appreciation of the work in the volumes on *Subaltern Studies* relating to the peasantry. The present study hopes to analyse the theoretical and historical relation between class identity, covered in a major way as regards the adivasis in the region in the two former studies, and ethnic/cultural identity which is the primary focus of this study.

Survival as a biological organism, and hence economic survival as related to livelihood, is the basis or bottom line of existential experience. This experience expresses itself in a community of subjectivity in action and shared cultural symbolism understood in a broad sense (language, regional affiliation, religion, ritual practices, caste, tribe, gender, nationality) and/or a community of shared economic interests or class. Both senses of community as 'collective self' are experienced in relation to the 'other' in given historical contexts. The latter sense of identity as class requires organization, ideology and collective action to facilitate articulation. In general, the existential experience of the struggle for economic survival more spontaneously takes the form of the former cultural identity given that it is more primordial/'traditional' (corresponding to an earlier historical period) in nature. The foregoing could be briefly illustrated as follows:

A Conceptual Framework for Social Systems in Transformation

THE ECOLOGICAL AND SOCIO-ECONOMIC, SPACE, CONTEXT

Structure (Class, Caste, Tribe, Gender, Religion)

Livelihood

Question of Where? With Whom?

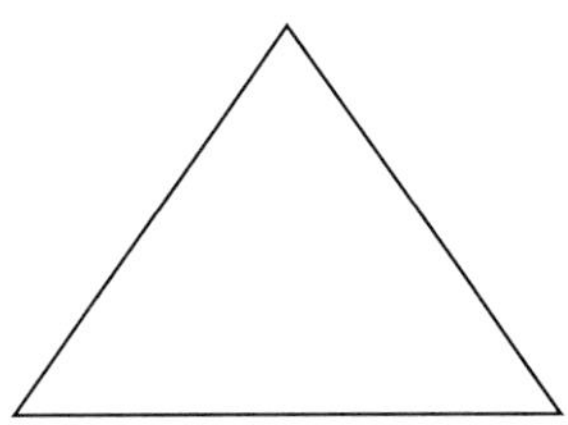

THE SOCIO-POLITICAL PROCESS, TIME

Agency (Actors)

Power (Mobilization, Organization, Strategy, Action)

Questions of How? When? Who? With Whom?

THE SOCIO-CULTURAL CONSCIOUSNESS, ENERGY

Ideology, Motivation, Values, Culture, Symbolic Communication

Questions of Why? For Whom?

One will be elaborating the aspect of the socio-cultural in this study. The following terms might be useful for illustrating the unity of the three dimensions depicted above which in effect constitute a unitary whole: confluence, convergence, concatenation, articulation. It has been noticed from one's research experience that the epistemological tensions and unresolved issues in considering any of the above mentioned two dimensions tend to be solved by taking recourse to the third dimension within social situations through a process of triangulation. One's understanding of dialectics is closely associated with a dynamic analytic process of triangulation which corresponds with the dynamics of the articulation of actual social forces. The synthetic outcome of a process of tension between any two social forces may be seen as a consideration of the third element, as illustrated above. This synthesis is embedded in the dynamics of the relation between the other two. The synthesis does not transcend the dialectics, but evolves as a working out of tensions within the dual dialectical process.

The foregoing illustration might be elaborated as follows. One will be elaborating the dimension of subaltern identity and agency working under the constraints of dominant hegemony in this study.

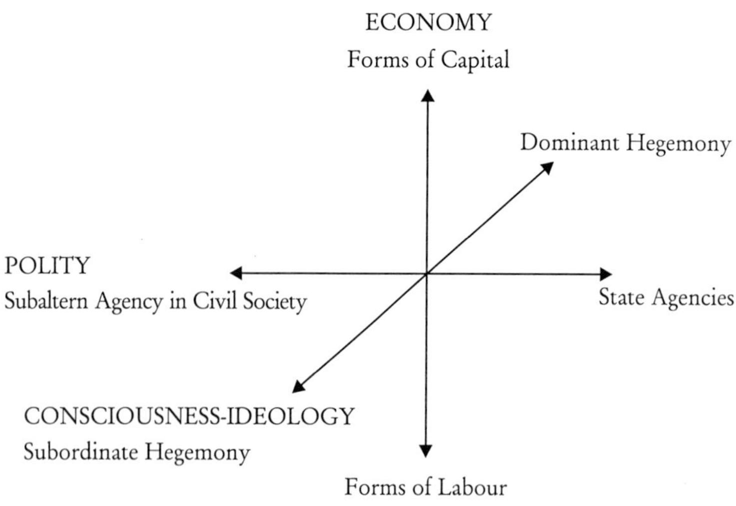

Discussing related concepts of cultural and religious incorporation, K.S. Singh rejects the conception of the tribal as the 'noble savage', an understanding held by the colonialists which only served to justify their rule and make sense of the other; as well as considering them as 'backward Hindus', a notion held by Ghurye (1943/1963) which led to the understanding of 'the Hindu mode of absorption' into caste society as elaborated by Bose (1949/1975). He settles for the concept of 'Sanskritization' as proposed by Srinivas (1952) of positional upward mobility through imitation, and adds a concept of 'tribalization' to bring out the polarity in the tension. Singh emphasizes that the tribal-non-tribal interaction was more secular in character as a result of changing systems of production, market forces and the reach of the state (Singh 1985: 1-2, 87ff).

Since hegemony constitutes a key concept as regards the tribal-non-tribal cultural interface in the analytical framework of this publication, it would be relevant to dwell for some time on its interpretative significance. It is one's understanding that the concept of hegemonies in contention is far more relevant in comprehending Indian realities, as different from the concepts in the previous paragraph, since it preserves the secular thrust of the process while underscoring the tensions within the sphere of culture, taking into consideration issues of power and dominance as exercised over belief systems and the economy. The concept is drawn from Gramsci and in particular from his *Prison Notebooks* (1971). He views hegemony as primarily a cultural process of symbolic systems and institutional practices. Though primarily a matter of belief systems, hegemony requires a material basis, "for though hegemony is ethical-political, it must also be economic, must necessarily be based on the decisive function exercised by the leading group in the decisive nucleus of economic activity" (1971: 161). Dominant hegemony presents itself as representing universal interests, including those of the subordinate, so as to more effectively dominate the subaltern with their consent while appearing to incorporate them. "The development and expansion of the particular group (the dominant) are conceived of, and presented, as being the motor force of a universal expansion, of a development of all the 'national' energies. In other words, the dominant group is coordinated concretely with the general interests of the subordinate groups, and the life of the State is conceived as a continuous process of formation and superseding of unstable equilibria (on the juridical plane) between the interests of the fundamental group and those of the subordinate groups—equilibria in which the interests of the dominant group prevail, but only up to a certain point, i.e. stopping short of narrowly corporate economic interest (1971: 182). According to Przeworski, the political conflicts arising from capitalist surplus extraction tend to be confined within the capitalist system as a whole. "Social relations constitute structures of choices within which people perceive, evaluate, and act. They consent when they choose particular courses of action and when they follow these choices in their practice...Hegemony consists of exploitation with consent" (1985: 146, 148). While this process serves to reproduce the social relations, the consent to capitalism of the subordinate is 'permanently conditional'.

There are a constellation of Gramscian concepts that revolve around the conception of hegemony: the *common sense* consciousness of the masses of a *subaltern class*, the *contradictory* nature of this consciousness, the subordinate world view that stands as an *alternative hegemony in contention* with the dominant one that seeks the *consent* of the subaltern, the role of *organic intellectuals* of the subaltern to articulate subaltern potential hegemony and transform it into an ideology for action. One has elaborated and operationalized these concepts in our earlier publications: on epistemological and methodological questions (1988 and 2015 b), literacy interventions by people's organizations in relation to adivasi common sense (1989), popular cultural processes within literacy campaigns (1993), in relation to literacy campaigns and education in general (2010 and 2008 a and b), and especially in one's analysis of social transformations and adivasi consciousness during the historical period of 1818 to the present in one district (2015 a). In the context of the present study it would be relevant to draw attention primarily to the *contradictory* nature of common sense and the consistent attempts by dominant hegemony to seek the *consent* of the subordinate, only to dominate more effectively and with the least recourse to violence. Describing the contradictions within common sense, Gramsci writes, "When one's conception of the world is not critical and coherent but disjointed and episodic, one belongs simultaneously to a multiplicity of mass human groups. The personality is strangely composite: it contains

Stone Age elements and principles of a more advanced science... The starting point of critical elaboration is the consciousness of what one really is, and is, 'knowing thyself' as a product of the historical process to date which has deposited in you an infinity of traces, without leaving an inventory" (1971: 324). Common sense is, writes Gramsci, "the conception of the world that is uncritically absorbed by the various social and cultural environments in which the moral individuality of the average man is developed. Common sense is not a single unique conception, identical in time and space. It is the 'folklore' of philosophy, and, like folklore, it takes countless different forms. Its most fundamental characteristic is that it is a conception which, even in the brain of one individual, is fragmentary, incoherent and inconsequential, in conformity with the social and cultural position of those masses whose philosophy it is...(but) at those times in history when a homogeneous social group is brought into being, there comes into being also, in opposition to commonsense, a homogeneous—in other words a coherent and systematic—philosophy" (1971: 419, bracket added). One might read the foregoing texts in the context of our discussion of the traces of the materialistic philosophy of Lokayata among present-day adivasis, multiple levels of identity that are called forth to consciousness according to context, and the relatively coherent articulation of identity within political mobilization (in Sections 3, 4, and 5 of this Chapter); and the incoherent character of the materialistic basis of belief systems related to the life and agricultural cycles within the struggle for livelihood (in Chapter 4, in particular). As regards dominant hegemony seeking the consent of the subaltern, the following passages from Gramsci are especially insightful. The hegemonic permeation of the state and the ruling classes is seen to be through institutionalized practices, especially related to culture and religion, since they are the bearers of belief systems that ensure subordination through consent. The state in its function of seeking consent is "the entire complex of practical and theoretical activities with which the ruling class not only justifies and maintains its dominance, but manages to win the active consent of those over whom it rules..." (1971: 244). Gramsci uses the term 'intellectual and moral leadership' while discussing the ethical function of the state "...every state is ethical in as much as one of its most important functions is to raise the great mass of the population to a particular cultural and moral level, a level (or type) which corresponds to the needs of the productive forces for development" (1971: 258). Discussing the ambivalent and dual conceptions within subaltern consciousness, he writes, "It signifies that the social group in question may indeed have its own conception of the world, even if only embryonic; a conception which manifests itself in action, but occasionally and in flashes—when, that is, the group is acting as an organic totality. But this same group has, for reasons of submission and intellectual subordination, adopted a conception which is not its own but is borrowed from another group; and it affirms this conception verbally and believes itself to be following it, because this is the conception that it follows in 'normal times'—that is when its conduct is not independent and autonomous, but is submissive and subordinate" (1971: 327). The foregoing analytical statements might be read in the context of our discussions in the empirical chapters on cultural practices in Section 2 of this publication, especially on the Temple Complex of Mahalaxmi (Chapter 5) and the paintings and other aesthetic expressions of the adivasis (Chapter 6).

In another context of contemporary advanced capitalism, Castells in his *The Rise of the Network Society* provides relevant epistemological insights; the abstract principles of his analytical framework in their elementary forms being perhaps equally applicable to adivasi societies. He writes, "...all major social changes are ultimately characterised by a transformation of space and time in the human experience...all realities are communicated through symbols and a human interactive communication regardless of the medium, all symbols are somewhat displaced in relation to their assigned semantic meaning. In a sense, all reality is virtually perceived...The *space of flows* and *timeless time* are the material foundations of a new culture that transcends and includes the diversity of historically transmitted systems of representation: the culture of real virtuality where make-believe is belief in the making" (Castells, Vol. 1, 2010: xxxi, 404, 406). The relation between social space, historical time and experienced meaning have also been independently elaborated in one's study of *The Subaltern Subject* (2015 b) and a clearer and earlier articulation with respect to advanced capitalism may be found in Castells (2010: 441 ff) and Harvey (1990).

Discussing the social construction of identity, Castells affirms that "identities are stronger sources of meaning than roles, because of the process of self-construction and individuation that they involve. In simple terms identities organize the meaning while roles organize the functions. I define *meaning* as the symbolic identification by a social actor of the purpose of her/his actions... It is easy to agree on the fact that, from a sociological perspective, all identities are constructed. The real issue is how, from what, by whom, and for what. The construction of identities uses building materials from history, from geography, from biology, from productive and reproductive institutions, from collective memory and from the personal fantasies, from power apparatuses and religious revelations. But individuals, social groups, and societies process all these materials, and rearrange their meaning, according to social determinations and cultural projects that are rooted in their social structure, and in their space/time framework" (Castells, Vol. 2, 1997). Drawing attention to the limitations of movements based on ethnic identity, he writes that "Ethnicity, while being an essential ingredient of both oppression and liberation, seems to be usually framed in support of other communal identities (religious, national, territorial), rather than inducing either resistance or new projects by itself." (ibid.: 257). However, this does not undermine the salience of the cultural factor, for according to him, "A new society emerges when and if a structural transformation can be observed in the relationships of production, in the relationships of power, and in the relationships of experience. These transformations lead to an equally substantial modification of social forms of space and time, and to the emergence of a new culture" (Castells, Vol. 3, 1998: 361).

The following are some propositions underlying one's conception of adivasi identity, based on our field studies in Palghar district (Saldanha: 2015 a and b):

The definition of the collective self is necessarily in relation to the 'other', especially in the context of iniquitous adivasi-non-adivasi interactions extending over more than two hundred years.

On this axis of insider self and outsider other, the parameters and contexts that define the collective self-identity of the adivasis are poverty, enforced dependence on the other, and ethnicity; an expressed self-identity as 'garib adivasis' (poor adivasis), generally in that order of salience which may vary according to context over time.

These parameters of self-recognition are closely related to politics, especially in the present era of post-independence electoral democracy; i.e. party organizational affiliation based on an instrumental, opportunistic access to economic opportunity in a relation of patronage and clientele (rajkaran, as popularly understood), and an ambivalent relation to the executive and judicial officialdom (sarkar) based on their sense of the monopolistic, dominant exercise of hegemonic power by the other.

A perception of the past as a dynamic cause of the present and the possibilities of future alternatives decide whether the present collective self is seen in anomic or optimistic terms.

While the sense of identity of class reinforced by ethnicity remains strong, the solidarity in action is presently to some extent fractured and individualized.

The foregoing might be expressed diagrammatically as:

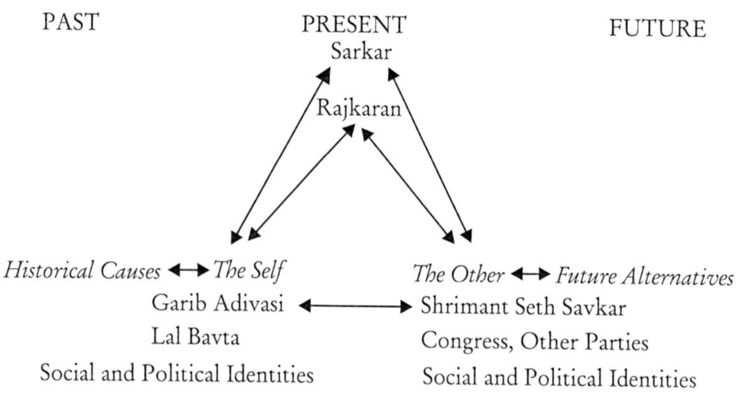

It is highly problematic to identify and classify a distinctive collective, a specific social formation, as ethnic or class at the outset. This is because as relatively static, synchronic, objectively structured phenomena, each identity in a multilayered identity context is socially constituted by an element of culture, the internalization of a dominant hegemony of an imposed identity, as well by a position in the economy and the quality of seeking livelihood. From a purely biological perspective this basis for classification might be tentatively true for gender and race, with several qualifications, and from a geographic point of view for language and regional affiliation in a given context. But the social scientific approach to collective identity is much more than factual considerations of biology and geography, and includes overlapping aspects of culture, economy and political action. Hence, the predominance of identity needs to be identified on the basis of effective, self-conscious mobilizations imbued by an ideology towards set purposes, the nature of the organization and the actual impact within the political economy. Identity may thus be more realistically identified within a diachronic process of flux and political action for social transformation. The concept of identity is an in-between concept; it mediates between self-consciousness, culture and power within given socio-economic contexts. When self-consciousness based on ethnicity or economic interests takes on ideological and organizational characteristics of collective solidarity, we have the beginnings of identity as a political force for change in the political economy. A combination of synchronic structural analysis and of a diachronic social historical approach might be useful to uncover the fluctuating predominant identities in given contexts (Thompson 1977: 260). Thompson understands the nature of class in the following manner: "Class, in the Marxist tradition, is (or ought to be) a *historical category*, describing *people in relationship over time*, and the ways that they become conscious of their relationships, separate, unite, enter into struggle, form institutions and transmit values in class ways. Hence class is an 'economic' and it is also a 'cultural' formation: it is impossible to give any theoretical priority to one aspect over the other. And it follows that 'in the last instance' determination may equally well work its way out through cultural as through economic forms. What changes, as the mode of production and productive relations change, is the *experience* of living men and women. And this experience is sorted out in class ways, in social life and in consciousness, in the assent, the resistance, and the choices of men and women" (Thompson 1977: 264-265, italics in original).

The following is an attempt to identify some of the distinctive features of one's epistemological approach to subaltern consciousness of collective identity, as attempted in one's studies of the adivasis in Palghar district (especially Saldanha 2015 b). One might suggest that consciousness has some internal, covert features that are necessarily related to external, overt contexts, given that collective consciousness is socially constituted. These features in their essentials might be visualized as follows:

Internalities (Covert)

Collective consciousness exists, is real, meaningful and worth analysis,

It is relevant, contextually derived and with context reference,

It is multilayered, relational, in process and in flux; contextuality is assumed or is given by the 'other',

Is specific, articulated with respect to definitive cognitive areas (cognitions); yet holistic with an internally consistent and comprehensive argument (conceptions),

It has elements of past, present and/or future and suggests a movement from the individual to collective consciousness.

Externalities (Overt)

It evolves within the social relations of the political economy (contextual structures) and within historical, organized/ unorganized, transformatory processes,

It suggests a movement from the economic to the political and from the individual to the collective.

The holistic epistemological approach of social science is only an effort that seeks interpretive adequacy with the holistic epistemology of subaltern consciousness, within social scientifically analysed systems that are viewed as structured wholes. Subaltern consciousness is an inter-subjective process within structured contexts and historical processes, drawing from and contributing to the latter. So also is the social scientific process of interpreting the subaltern consciousness, an inter-subjective process between science and common sense.

Some of the propositions underlying the proposed holistic epistemological approach suggest the following analytical dynamics:

A movement from the individual to the collective; to bridge the subject-object distinction and to arrive at the adequate subject/ agency for historical change; as well as the movement from collective practice to consciousness in given structured contexts,

The significance of the concept of identity so as to relate class to other ethnic/cultural processes and to establish the relation/ distinction between the self and the other,

The relation of these identities to the state and to political processes in order to view the relation between the eco-cultural in the present to the political, and to the perception of past causes and of future alternatives to the present within the contention between dominant and subordinate hegemonies.

Interrelated holism is understood not only as a multiplicity of parts or thematic aspects as related parts of a whole, but also as a relation between different levels of complexity, abstraction and inclusiveness of parts. This may be represented as follows, as discussed in Saldanha (2015 b):

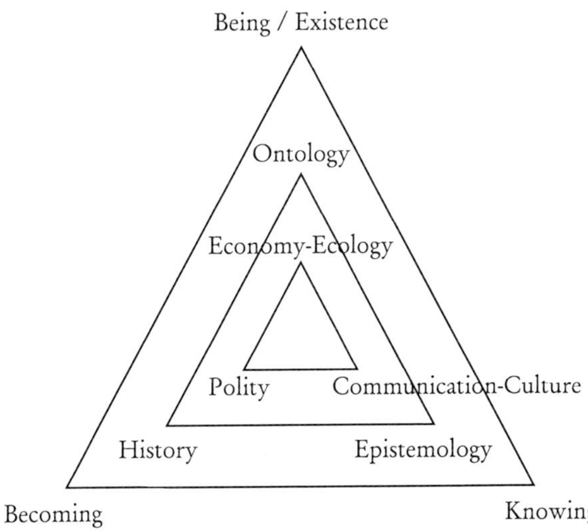

Identities tend to get polarized at the time of intense social transformation. It is at such times that the relation between

ethnic/cultural identity and class/economic identity tends to become transparent, the one reinforcing the other. As Malesevic points out while referring to his earlier publications, "...rather than being a synonym for cultural diversity, ethnicity is a politicized social action. It is a social relation through which some cultural markers become socially and politically meaningful in the process of intensive group interaction...In other words ethnicity and nationhood are not mutually exclusive categories but are diverse and often compatible understandings of social reality" (Malesevic 2010: 71, 72). The cultural expressions that apparently ethnic movements take on can be quite diverse depending on the context and nature of mobilization. "As culture itself is inherently ambiguous the process of its politicization can only be even more multifaceted resulting in extremely diverse forms of social action and corresponding ethnic configurations" (Malesevic 2010: 77). Malesevic undertakes a holistic analysis of the role of ethnic identity in processes of social transformation in a manner that is similar to what has been elaborated by us (Saldanha 2015 b). Identity is analysed within a system of social relations and processes that embrace ecological and economic contexts and political action, while preserving the relative autonomy of the social interpretive processes within the consciousness of subaltern groups. He writes, "interpretations and discourses are important in making individual and collective experience meaningful, but much of this experience has a strong material underpinning: the changing geo-political conditions, visible economic inequalities, institutionalized or informal mechanisms of collective discrimination, the actions of social movements, state agencies or mass media associated with collective humiliation, fear or threat and so on" (Malesevic 2010: 78).

In this context, one might also draw attention to the critical epistemological approach used by Hall to the question of identity and its post-structuralist deviations. According to him, "...events, relations, structures do have conditions of existence out of the sphere of the discursive, but that it is only within the discursive, and subject to its specific conditions, limits and modalities, do they have or can they be constructed within meaning. Thus, while not wanting to expand the territorial claims of the discursive infinitely, how things are represented and the 'machineries' and regimes of representation in a culture do play a *constitutive*, not merely a reflexive, after-the-event role. This gives questions of culture and ideology, and the scenarios of representation—subjectivity, identity, politics—a formative, not merely an expressive, place in the constitution of social and political life...The term ethnicity acknowledges the place of history, language and culture in the construction of subjectivity and identity, as well as the fact that all discourse is placed, positioned, situated, and all knowledge is contextual" (Hall 1996 b: 224, 226). In an earlier article, while elaborating his critical appreciation of discourse theory, he underlines his differences with that body of knowledge: "If you look at discourse theory, for example—at post-structuralism or at Foucault—you will see there, not only the shift from practice to discourse, but also how the emphasis on difference—on the plurality of discourses, on the perpetual slippage of meaning, on the endless sliding of the signifier—is now pushed *beyond* the point where it is capable of theorizing the necessary unevenness of a complex unity, or even the 'unity in difference' of a complex structure" (Hall 1985: 92).

Bonacich distinguishes 'communalistic' forms of social affiliation such as race, nationality and tribe, which she considers as a common phenomenon under the head of ethnicity, from affiliations based on economic and political solidarity such as class. "Thus, ethnocentrism, racism, nationalism, and tribalism are similar kinds of sentiments, dividing people along lines of shared ancestry rather than other possible lines of affiliation and conflict, such as common economic and political interest" (1980: 9). She holds the position that a class approach to issues of social transformation might be closer to reality and uncover a 'deeper' meaning than the apparently 'primordial' ethnic manifestations. "The field of ethnic and race relations has recently tended to be dominated by an assumption that race and ethnicity are 'primordial' bases of affiliation, rooted in 'human nature'. This assumption is being increasingly challenged by authors who contend that, while race and ethnicity may appear to be primordial attachments, in fact they reflect a deeper reality, namely, class relations and dynamics. I believe that class approaches are the most fruitful way to study ethnicity and race. Not only are they more in accord with a 'deeper' level of reality that enables us to understand phenomena at the surface of society, but they also provide us with the tools for changing that reality" (1980: 9). Ethnic phenomena are not a given reality, but need to be socially mobilized and require explanation of under what social conditions they would come to the fore.

3. Adivasi Ethnic Identity: Historical Origins

Before we immerse ourselves within some analytical details relating to the relation between class and ethnic identities among the adivasis of Thane district, Maharashtra, that was later carved out as Palghar district to the north to include the predominantly adivasi areas, it would be relevant to briefly traverse the historical process of identity formation among the tribals in the Indian subcontinent, based on secondary sources. ***As mentioned, the concept of 'tribal' was not relevant at the time and was a latter day ascription for administrative purposes. However, one is using the term tribe for purposes of presentation to distinguish what might be more appropriately called ancient/early humans from the remains of these peoples later called tribals and now termed as adivasis in the contemporary context.*** This forms the backdrop to the adivasis in the specific region of our concern. One of the most insightful accounts of the origins of present-day adivasi cultural practices, with all the complex changes that these practices have undergone over time in the context of different modes of seeking livelihood within changing social relations, is that of Chattopadhyaya (especially 1978 a, first published in 1959). We have used this text as a primary source for referential interpretation of the adivasi cultural practices, especially the relation between the rituals of the annual agricultural cycle and the life cycle, in Palghar district. He holds the position that traces of the oppositional materialistic world view held by early tribal society, dating back to before the Indus Valley Civilization, may be found in the ritual practices and the incantations of contemporary adivasis. This publication is a tentative attempt to establish this cultural relation with the adivasi past and in so doing it is important to arrive at a broad trend and to uncover the semblance of a pattern that links the tribal past with the adivasi present. In addition, this would facilitate a deeper and context-based interpretation of these rituals, their historical wellsprings and their felt meanings in the present. Undoubtedly, this exercise would be fraught with variations across and within adivasi communities, over time and context, given the continuing mutual impact of changing social relations and ecological contexts. Chattopadhyaya engages with a thoroughly research-based interpretation of ancient scriptures together with a critical dialogue with alternative perspectives of contemporary scholars. We will not go into these detailed analyses but focus on his central propositions with due references, that are relevant for our study.

Chattopadhyaya (1978 a) establishes the fundamental, ancient subaltern, materialistic belief in the close relation between the human body and earth/nature, the parallelism between human reproduction and the productivity of nature and the similarities between the birth of human beings and the origin of the universe, given that the 'human body is the microcosm of the universe'. He writes this in the context of his analysis of Tantrism which drew on the primitive tribal worldview and was a later philosophical development related to social practice. ***Understandably, no such concept of tribe existed at the time to designate early humans. However, in this chapter and throughout this publication, we are generally using the term tribe for these early social formations to distinguish from their carryovers into contemporary 'adivasi' society.*** Primitive Tantrism needs to be distinguished from the deviations in interpretation and the perversions in practice that might have taken place at a later date. "Agricultural ritual, in which it has its ultimate source, rests on the assumption that the productivity of nature—of mother earth—can be enhanced or induced by the imitation of human reproduction and conversely, human fertility is similarly related to natural fertility. In the primitive stage these principles were not, of course, consciously formulated. But if we look back and are at all justified in theoretically formulating the fundamentals of this primitive view, we may look at it as an instinctive groping at a theory according to which the human body and the earth are assumed to have the same nature, the two being taken as interacting and as inter-dependent. The corollaries are two fold. First, it should be possible to understand the mystery of nature if we can understand the mystery of the human body—the *deha* or the material human body is the microcosm of the universe. Secondly, the birth of the universe is the result of the same or a similar process as the birth of the human beings. The *deha-vada* and the cosmogony of Tantrism are but elaborations of these two corollaries....This is not materialism in the mature sense; nevertheless, in the sense of an instinctive acceptance of the primacy of the material human body and the material earth on which it lives, it can be characterised as some form of primitive proto-materialism" (1978 a, Introduction: xxi). Original Tantrism is seen as having the potential of developing into a science, especially contributing to physiology and alchemy, thanks to its material basis in human manual labour in agriculture. Evidence based on practice and inference and understanding the true nature of everything in nature, animate as well as inanimate, as constituted of matter were seen to be the criteria of truth by Vatsyana (c. fourth/fifth century AD) in his Nyaya-Vaisesikas (Chattopadhyaya 1989: 14-15, 107-108). Primitive tribal thought has been referred to interchangeably by Chattopadhyaya as Lokayata given its early origins and basis in popular culture; Carvaka, a pejorative term used by idealist thought from the eighth century AD; Brahaspatya with reference to some of its earliest formulators; and the 'Asura' view as opposed to the dominant Vedic Brahmanical 'Deva' formulations. "There is no doubt that the Lokayatikas denied the authority of *sruti* and *smriti*, ridiculed the Brahmanical rituals and mocked at the idea of the other-world or heaven....In all probability, it was a body of beliefs and practices, deeply rooted in the lives of the masses and at the same time hostile to the Brahmanical doctrines" (1978 a: 36). A similar tension may be seen in the world view underlying the ancient medical practices of the physicians that held promises of a scientific materialism and the idealism of Vedic beliefs that was becoming hegemonically dominant. In his brilliant interpretation of ancient medical texts relating to ayurveda, Chattopadhyaya (1977) draws attention to the former belief system, "The move towards an uninhibited understanding of world and man—viewing both as made of the same fundamental stuff, which they called *bhuta* or matter and which they are inclined to understand as existing in five root forms—the *panca-bhuta*. They argue that this matter gets transformed into the infinite variety of inanimate and animate things of the universe because of laws inherent in nature or *svabhava*—the laws because of which for example fire is hot and water cold. Therapeutic power is conceived by them mainly in terms of the knowledge of these laws: the clearer the physician's insight into these the better is his prospect of regulating the interaction between body-matter and environmental matter, which determines disease and health" (1977: 8). However, in their attempts to understand 'nature as a whole' with an intellectual discipline termed as '*yukti*', the texts as they come to us today suffer from several contradictions, an admixture of science and superstition, because "These are of the nature of ransoms offered to the counter-ideology—the stamp of religion given on science with the hope of making it acceptable to orthodoxy" (1977: 18). As one of the many examples provided, Chattopadhyaya quotes the Susruta-samhita to the effect that, "Ayurveda with its eight sections is revealed by (god) Brahma as a discipline subsidiary to the Veda. Hence, the doctor aware of his role, must act in subservience to the priest (because the latter is the custodian of the Veda)" (1977: 36, brackets in original). A similar contradictory consciousness might be found expressed by the bhagats of Palghar district; a consciousness overlaid by a history of exploitation and under the weight of a dominant hegemony (Chapters 4 and 5).

Chattopadhyaya underlines a clash of cultures implicit in the Brahmanical rituals and the ritualistic practices based in the agriculture of the common people: "If all these be true, then, in spite of its rejection of the authority of *sruti* and *smriti* and in spite of its denial of God, the other-world and the efficacy of the Brahmanical rituals, the Lokayata could have hardly been the philosophy of scepticism and materialism in our usual sense, that is in the sense of being propounded by some individual philosophers. Rather, the clash between Brahmanism and the Lokayata assumes for us the appearance of a clash of two distinct cultures, the latter being deeply rooted in the lives of the masses" (1978 a: 40). Even the ancient, early Rig Vedic texts contained some elements of a 'primitive pro-materialism' as seen from the veneration of food as a deity, thanks to the independent existential tribal origins of this tradition. Chattopadhyaya (1976 b: 108) quotes from the Rig Veda i.187 to make his point:

> Savoury food, honeyed food, we welcome thee; be our protector. Come to us, beneficial food, we welcome thee; be our protector.... Your flavours, oh food, are diffused through regions, as the winds are spreading through the sky. These men, oh food, who are your distributors, oh most sweet food, they who are the eaters of thee and thy juices, increase like you with elongated necks. The minds of the mighty deities, oh food, are fixed upon thee....Oh food, the wealth which is associated with the mountains went to thee. Oh sweet one, listen to us and be accessible to our eating. And since we enjoy the abundance of the waters and plants, therefore oh body may you grow fat. And since we enjoy the drink soma, thy mixture with boiled milk and boiled barley, therefore oh body may you grow fat...

Illuminating similarities might be seen with the ritualistic incantations at the time of the harvest festivals of Gav Dev of the village community and Khali, the household threshing ritual, where the present-day adivasis in Palghar district gather together in appreciation of the new crops with drink and a shared meal; as may be seen in Chapter 4. We find that food/grain is now humanized and placated as the female deity Kansari, as also the forces of nature and various natural elements; together with a sharp tone of desperation in contrast with the relatively joyous and celebratory vibrations of the Rig Veda. The songs of the Rig Veda were considered as 'making verses by the mouth' in a manner similar to the appreciation of the manual craft of carpentry and chariot making (1976 b: 139 ff).

The origins of the idealistic Brahmanical outlook is seen by Chattopadhyaya within the emerging separation of mental and manual labour and the downgrading of and the disparaging view that was taken towards the latter, which was also the beginnings of the destruction of the contrasting Lokayata perspective (1978 a: 230). The idealistic view reinforced and legitimized the emerging division of labour within society, primarily between the mental and the manual, a stratified social division that was forming as a result of the hegemonic force of military might, economic dominance, political power, and a monopolization of what was considered to be knowledge. The contrasting idealist view is seen by Chattopadhyaya to have originated in the Upanishads approximately in the sixth century BC where the ultimate reality, Brahman, was identified with the soul, Atman, in the sense of pure spirit or consciousness; later to be elaborated by the Buddhist philosopher Nagarjuna as the theory of Sunyavada in the first or second century AD and even later by Samkara in the eight century AD in his theory of Advaita Vedanta and by the law makers in the Dharmasastras as a structuring of society in terms of Varnashramas, the caste system (1989: 3-5, 18). The epics of Mahabharata and Ramayana are seen to be used as instruments by the higher castes and the lawmakers who were architects of the dominant hegemony to reinforce the status quo of the caste structure through the propagation of values implicit in the belief of karma among the masses (1989: 121). To return to the materialist tradition, we find that Tantra, Samkhya and Yoga are interpreted by Chattopadhyaya as overlapping articulations in a relatively parallel materialist philosophical stream of the early Lokayata perspective, in that rough chronological sequence given the uneven development within the country dating back to the Indus Valley Civilization. "Tantrism was the original complex out of which emerged the Samkhya and the Yoga of the later times. But just as, because of the uneven development, people in the primitive tribal conditions have continued to live in India side by side the civilized and sophisticated societies, so, in the field of ideology, by the side of the later sophisticated Samkhya and Yoga there survived also the Tantric beliefs and practices, still representing the primordial complex out of which Samkhya and Yoga eventually developed" (1978 a: 63; see also 1976 b: 286).

Chattopadhyaya goes on to uncover the relation between gender relations, changes in the modes of acquiring livelihood over the period of ancient history, the consequent relative preponderance of the sexes in the performance of ritualistic cultural practices, and the contagious mutual influence believed to be between human reproduction and agricultural productivity among the early tribals. This is of special significance in our interpretation of present-day ritualistic practices among the adivasis in Palghar district. "We are going to argue that because agriculture is the discovery of women and which remains their exclusive preoccupation in its early stages, it created conditions for the economic—and, therefore, also of social-supremacy of the female. It is here that we find a material basis of the ideological emphasis of *prakriti* (*prakriti pradhanya*) of the Lokayata trend in Indian philosophy. By contrast, the Vedic ideology was *purusa-pradhana*, or male-dominated. The material basis of this (patriarchal belief), as we shall see, was their pastoral economy" (1978 a: 232, bracket added). Discussing the contemporary folk ritual of Ganesa Caturthi Vrata, Chattopadhyaya points out that the male deity Ganesa is given a minimal role representing the new moon of the sowing season and in some parts makes way for the female deity Gauri, not according to the Puranic pantheon, but represented by a bundle of plants and her human representative, a virgin (1978 a: 233). He sums up his interpretation of the foregoing relation between gender, socio-culture and productive relations within changing historical contexts in the following manner, "The social importance of the sexes is correlated to the development of the economic life. The original pre-hunting stage was characterised by mother-right. With the development of hunting, however, the social supremacy was shifted to male. In the post-hunting stage, among those peoples that developed the pastoral economy this male-supremacy came to exercise even greater hold: among those, however, that discovered agriculture, the situation was reversed. There was a revival of mother-right among them. With the further development of agriculture—more specifically, with the introduction of the cattle-drawn plough to the field—this agricultural mother-right was finally overthrown. Gods and goddesses are after all created in human image; these shifts in the social importance of the sexes were naturally reflected in the form of parallel shifts in the celestial sphere. Deities representing the hunting and the pastoral stages are predominantly male, whereas those representing the earlier stages are of agriculture were predominantly female" (1978 a: 241-242). The sudden and relatively violent overthrow of mother right resulted in the Indian context, especially in non-adivasi societies, in the establishment of the institutions of hypergamy, child marriage and sati. The foregoing would need to be interpreted in a contemporary contextualized manner in the case of the adivasis of Palghar district where there has not been any significant influence of the pastoral economy, there has been a strong practice of bride price as opposed to dowry and a dominant role of the female at the time of birth and marriage within the life cycle, as different from the predominance of the male bhagat within the rituals of the agricultural cycle and at the times of illness. The social historical factors mentioned above could explain the ambivalent status of women in the adivasi communities of present-day Palghar district.

A predominant feature of Tantrism which emerged from early pre-Vedic tribal practices was the relation between Purusha, the male principle, and Prakriti the female principle. "There are two basic trends in Indian culture, the Vedic and the non-Vedic. A predominant, if not the most conspicuous feature of the latter is Tantrism, with its supreme emphasis on *prakriti* or the female principle" (1978 a: 269). At the time of the discovery of early agriculture by women with a lack of knowledge of the apparently mysterious process of the growth of plants from sowing to reaping, it was understandable that there was a strong faith in magic especially in the context of the fickle process of cultivation. "Magic rests on ignorance. But it would be wrong to view it as mere ignorance. For it is also a guide to action, though a psychological one. At the initial stage of agriculture, at which this psychological guide is most needed, we naturally find a peculiar intensification of magical beliefs and practices. If agriculture was the invention of women, then it is only logical that agricultural magic in its origin should belong exclusively to the province of women....To sum up, agriculture was the discovery of women. Agricultural magic, from which the ancient religions originated, belonged exclusively to the province of women. Later, in order to adjust the religions to the patriarchal conditions, these functions began to be transferred to men. Even then, the male as male could not discharge these. They could become priests only by changing their sex to that of females" (1978 a: 272, 277). Ancient practitioners of rituals had to dress as women during the ceremonies. Primitive tribal belief saw a strong relation of mutuality between human reproduction, especially the role of the female, and the productivity of nature; early agricultural operations that were anyhow primarily discovered and conducted by women. "The main point is that human fertility, particularly female fertility, and natural fertility belong to the same order of existence. In other words, human reproduction and agricultural production are linked up. Therefore, by contagion, or by imitation the one can influence the other. In Frazer's terminology, the former would be Contagious Magic and the latter Homoeopathic Magic" (1978 a: 286-287).

Chattopadhyaya draws attention to the significance of a contemporary Durga Puja practice of placing an earthen pot, the Purna Ghata, with leaves and a coconut at its mouth smeared with vermillion at the time of the ritual; a practice which one also observed to the present day at the time of the Khali harvest festival among the Warlis in Palghar district. "We may now easily see the significance of the *purna ghata* being placed on the *sarvatobhadra mandalam*. Plants and fruits are brought into contact with the female reproductive organ. The same idea is repeated in the *purna ghata* itself. The vessel is the female womb; that this womb is with a baby is indicated by the picture of the *sindura puttali*. It is, thus, an enactment of human reproduction: the symbolic significance of the use of vermillion only confirms the point. But why this enactment of human reproduction? Obviously to ensure the multiplication of the fruits, plants and leaves. That is why these are brought in contact with the female reproductive organ. We are thus back to the magical belief that the productivity is ensured or enhanced by the imitation of contagion of human reproduction or, more particularly, female reproductivity" (1978 a: 295-296). Citing Thomson, Chattopadhyaya provides a telling illustration of the conversion of a positive symbol of female fertility to that of a negative view of pollution, where the external symbol of vermillion in reality representing menstrual blood is retained in a valued manner over time in ritual practice while transforming social practice to the subordinate status of women post puberty in the context of the rise of patriarchy. "From one aspect the woman who may not be approached is inviolable, holy: from another aspect she is polluted, unclean. She is what the Romans called *sacra*, sacred and accursed. And hence in patriarchal society, after woman has lost her control of religion, it is the negative aspect that prevails. Not only are her sexual functions treated as impure in themselves, but the same condemnation attaches to her feminine nature as such. She becomes the root of all evil, Eve, a witch" (1978 a: 305). This historical process is relevant to our interpretation of the present role of the male Bhagat in identifying a witch, a Bhutali who is generally a destitute female, as the cause of illness when all his ritualistic endeavours have failed due to lack of medicinal plants resulting from deforestation or ignorance of adivasi traditional medicinal practices as a result of transmission losses over time. Chattopadhyaya sees a similar role for the persisting use of liquor, traditionally representing blood, in tribal rituals at the time of illness towards overcoming death and at the time of birth towards ensuring life (1978 a: 309). *Tantric practices that believed in the equality of all humans may be traced back to five thousand years ago among the ruins of those that built the Indus civilization as well as in highly modified forms among contemporary adivasi populations and among despised caste and occupational groups. "Tantrism, in its original form, therefore, is not merely ancient; it is also modern, even contemporary. The problem of the survival of Tantrism, however, is more complex. There survive not only the original beliefs and practices underlying Tantrism among our backward tribes, but the very culture of India bears deep marks of Tantrika influence" (1978 a: 323-324, italics added).* Chattopadhyaya cites Needham to elaborate an understanding of the close relation between magic and science in ancient thought and practice. "If science be based on an instinctively materialistic outlook, and if magic be originally next of kin to science, magic too must have been originally based on an instinctive materialism. And there is no mystery about it, because this instinctive materialism is itself generated by the labour process. Primitive society was yet to witness the degradation of the labour process: magic, its characteristic outlook, had to remain instinctively materialistic, and as such closely akin to science. It is from this point of view that we are to understand Needham's bold formulation: 'magic and science were originally united in a single *undifferentiated complex of manual operations*' " (1978 a: 351). The foregoing throws some light on the emotional desperation that underlies the ritualistic practices and incantations of the adivasis in Palghar district in their attempt to make some sense of their struggles for livelihood and to comprehend the relation between their life cycles and the annual agricultural cycle; the primary source of life giving grain. Several of the ritualistic practices by the bhagat as a cure for illness suggest traces of Tantrism, though in a perverted form over time (Chapter 4).

The Lokayata world view of the primitive tribals is understood to have passed through Tantrism to original Samkhya philosophy and Yoga practices, with its a-theism, materialism, and its opposition to the Vedic tradition that culminated in the Upanishads. Discussing the original significance of Yoga practice and the desire to control nature through magic, Chattopadhyaya writes, "The magician had accordingly, to work himself up to a point of delirious frenzy and ecstasy. He had to feel a super-normal power within himself, with the aid of which alone he could hope to bring the forces of nature under his control. Such a super-normal power could not be a material reality; it had to be a psychological one. The primitive magician had to feel that he possessed it. He tried various techniques to acquire a sense of the most stupendous power. Such techniques included various physical exercises, the control of breath, abstinence, withdrawal, self-torture, narcotics. These did induce 'morbid nervous and cerebral exaltation' and sometimes even a 'cataleptic rigidity and insensibility'" (1978 a: 444-445). The induced trances of the bhagats of Palgar district appear to have more to do with the belief in spirit possession, relics of the Tantrism of the past, where elements in nature and human existence take the form of spiritual deities. This is different from the Shamanic practices of ecstasy, which might include spirit possession, but is essentially a mode of 'rising up' and experiencing the ultimate. However the trances of the bhagat have in common with the mystical practices of shamanism in that, "The shamans have played an essential role in the defence of the psychic integrity of the community...In a general way, it can be said that shamanism defends life, health, fertility, the world of 'light', against death, diseases, sterility, disaster, and the world of 'darkness' " (Eliade 1964: 499 and 508-509).

Chattopadhyaya sees the traces of the ancient tribal thought and practices even within early Vedic ritual and incantations, given their own tribal origins. There is an underlying statement of the unity of humans with the deities who were in effect great humans who were venerated; unity in labour and ownership of cows in a pastoral economy; unity in the distribution of shares in the early agricultural produce, and finally; unity in thought within the early Vedic collective (1978 a: 564). He sees the Vedic

Yajna having an origin in early tribal society where rituals had a make-believe, psychological significance in controlling nature and early agriculture. It is only later when a priestly Brahmanical class develops in a differentiated Vedic society under the hegemony of religion that rituals take on a supernatural and other worldly character and also herald the dominance of an idealistic philosophy (1978 a: 604-605); which may be seen in the difference between sacrifice and magic, the former serving to propitiate the gods and the latter serving as an instrument to control the natural course (1978 a: 615). Magic also passes onto witchcraft, the former serving the community and the latter being a misapplication by individuals of magic (1978 a: 620).

While acknowledging that there are no original writings of the materialist Lokayata philosophy that are presently available, most probably as a result of being destroyed by its dominant opponents, ironically access to this thought may be found in a reverse interpretation of the writings of idealist critics such as Madhava. The following are a few extracts from what was known as 'authentic popular verses' (pramanika lokgatha) of the ancient materialist philosophy that has been cited in Chattopadhyaya (1989: 44, 45). They have an eerie resonance with our contemporary observation of the existential experience of the adivasis and their rituals and incantations in Palghar district as discussed in Chapter 4:

> "While life is yours, live joyously;
> None can escape death's searching eye:
> When once this frame of life they burn,
> How shall it e'er again return?"

> "The pleasure which arises to men from contact with sensible objects,
> Is to be relinquished as accompanied by pain, such is the reasoning of fools;
> The berries of paddy, rich with the finest white grains,
> What man, seeking his true interest, would fling away because covered with husk and dust?"

"The fire is hot, the water cold, refreshing cool the breeze of morn;

By whom came this variety? From their own nature (svabhava) was it born."

"In this school there are four elements, earth, water, fire and air;

And from these four elements alone is consciousness produced."

"There is no heaven, no final liberation, nor any soul in another world,

Nor do the actions of the four castes, orders, &c, produce any real effect."

"The Agnihotra, the three Vedas, the ascetic's three staves, and smearing of one's self with ashes,

Were made by Nature as the livelihood of those destitute of knowledge and manliness."

"While life remains let a man live happily, let him feed on ghee even though he runs in debt;

When once the body becomes ashes, how can it ever return again?"

Traces of the materialistic outlook may also be found in the early Rig Vedic songs, precisely because of the shared existential experience of the difficulties for survival for ancient tribal communities, whether invaders or indigenous. As Chattopadhyaya notes, "The early songs of the *Rgveda*, which often surprise us by their primitive vigour and uninhibited imagination, are almost totally obsessed with the problem of physical survival. These express, so to say, without cessation, the desire for food, cattle, progeny, victory, and so on. All this is mixed up with the mythological imaginings of a people, who see deities in many things that they do not understand and which fill them with awe normally passing into reverence. For instance, they see such deities in natural phenomena like the sun and wind, fire and forest, in the extraordinary might of war chiefs or heroes, in the intoxicating power of their drink *soma,* and so on. The deities are important for them, because they are supposed to be aids to the fulfilment of elemental desires. As people with a rudimentary control of nature, the poets see deities in their frankly pathetic wish-fulfilments like those of the prevention of abortion and the cure of pthisis. ...The next phase of Vedic literary activity can be traced to the *Yajurveda.* This reaches its climax in colossal texts called the *Brahmanas.* These texts are characterized by a shift of interest to discussion of the rituals or *Yajna*. The rituals must have originally been something like the magical rites still to be observed among some primitive peoples, surviving in certain pockets of the modern world even today" (D. Chattopadhyaya, 1978: 240). He sees these rituals as an illusory technique that serves as an aid to real ones; a wish fulfilment that brings about an attitudinal change in the struggle with nature. He goes on to add, "As discussed in the *Brahmana* texts, however, the rituals are uprooted from their original context and their function passes to its opposite. These become tools for a new technique—that of man's struggle with man" (ibid: 241). The 'creative role of consciousness' is seen in the later Upanishads, which however were the philosophical speculations of a leisured class that could indulge in a total alienated introversion thanks to the fact that it lived off the labour of the despised Sudras: "'I am the ultimate reality'—declares the Upanisadic idealist. The result is the lofty contempt for the material world, in which the philosopher himself has his being....Consciousness is now viewed as a 'deified absolute'—too mysterious to be grasped by mundane thought and too awesome to be described in ordinary language" (1978: 245). Chattopadhyaya presents in his notes several illustrations from the Brahmanas of the upper castes' contempt for the Sudras, within the context of an evolving four-caste rigidification: "*Gautama* xii. 4-7: Now if he listens intentionally to a recitation of the Veda, his ears shall be filled with molten tin or lac. If he recites Vedic texts, his tongue shall be cut off. If he remembers them, his body shall be split in twain. If he assumes a position equal to that of the twice born, in sitting, lying down, in conversation or on the road, he shall undergo corporal punishment. *Gautama* x. 50: The *Sudra* belongs to the fourth caste, which has one birth only. For him also are prescribed truthfulness, meekness and purity. He shall use the cast-off shoes, umbrellas, garments and mats of the higher castes and eat the remnants of their food, and live by practising mechanical arts. *Manu* x. 129: No collection of wealth must be made by a *Sudra*, even though he be able to do it: for a *Sudra* who has acquired wealth gives pain to a Brahmin" (1978: 268-269).

The foregoing analysis throws significant light on the present-day ritual practices of the adivasis in Palghar district (Chapter 4) that in fact preserve some traces of the past as a sediment of history and has facilitated our interpretation of the incantations of the bhagats. It also draws attention to the persisting social and economic exploitation of the adivasis.

How does Chattopadhyaya analyse the relatively persistent urge, throughout history and to be found even among the contemporary adivasis of Palghar district, for explanation of limited, human, existential experience in terms of beliefs that imply spatial and temporal transcendence? In addition, there is the reality of the fearful and awe-inspiring experience of the certainty of death; the definitive end in the indefinable future to one's present travails; the inescapable finality that awaits one and all. This strong tendency for ultimate explanation may be seen as enduring from the naturalistic, animistic, materialistic and ancient tribal past to the largely ritualized belief systems of the adivasi present. The human urge for ultimate meaning yet emerging from the experience of the limitations of existence and the drive for a more harmonious order is a reality that cannot be denied. Does this tendency contest a historical materialist explanation? Not necessarily so, given that human transcendental belief, including faith, ultimately emerges from an immanent human context; all the more so if it has to have relevance to present reality. It is perhaps for this reason that Joshi (1991) would compare aspects of orthodox Marxism with that of religion. That 'religion is the opium of the poor', that belief in the deified transcendent is an act of projection on and a seeking of solace and remedy from one's desperate present situation, can at best be only a partial explanation. It is important to discover materialist, and not idealist, ways of going beyond crass materialism. Action for social transformation creates a new historical reality away from the present on the dimension of time, and abstracted inference from empirical evidence within the sphere of epistemology may be seen as modes of transcending crass materialism. This is a significant inference from the writings of Chattopadhyaya (1989). Perhaps the experience of the transcendent could be by way of a convergence of action and inferential learning within given materialist contexts, thus going beyond the very limitations of actions and inference; as it were, incarnating the transcendental as immanent to human experience. The foregoing formulation is a way of arriving at a synthesis in a progressive materialist manner and thus transcending the dual tensions implicit in the idealism of ancient Brahmanical thought and the materialism of ancient tribal conscious practice; the contradictions between idealistic oneness and marxian holism; the tensions between the Hindutva attempts to assimilate the Vanyajati and the adivasi assertion of self-identity on terms of distinctive integration; and finally the human experience of the struggle for survival through livelihood and yet the urge for transcendental explanation of limited experience. Ultimately, both the progress of science through seeking evidence based inferences and the commonsense of the adivasis in a ritualized thirsting for an all encompassing explanation are based on the thrust towards the future, in the present based on the past, and the leap towards the whole as an explanation for the sum of the parts.

In addition to the issue of the relative basis for collective identity, the thrust of this publication, raises the question of what is a more basic human need/drive: physical survival, hence issues related to ecology and livelihood; or a quest for explanation, hence a search for meaning. One would consider that generally the latter is closely aligned to the former, i.e. meaning is sought in relation to and within contexts of livelihood and survival. Even the animistic deification of nature by the present-day adivasis could be interpreted as rituals of pacification of nature and spirits in a hostile ecological and social environment.

One might get some insight into these questions from a fascinating analysis where Chattopadhyaya (1976 a) engages in a critical dialogue between the idealistic 'integral sociology' of Aurobindo and the materialist 'dialectical historicism' of Marx towards the possibility of a synthetic forward movement. While the former approach is seen to have an underlying 'spiritual psychology' that drives it, the latter is founded on a sustained materialism. This discussion makes for a fruitful interpretation of the adivasis' animistic rituals and incantations that are firmly embedded in the life cycle and the annual agricultural cycles that cohabit the longer term cycles of generations and that provide the adivasis some security in lineage. The Aurobindo-Marx tension also provides a relevant insight into the resolution of the contradiction/tension between the adivasi yearning for security in long-term existential meaning and ultimate explanation on the one hand and the desperate quest for immediate short-term livelihood on the other. Chattopadhyaya's conclusions are not conclusive and definitive; and perhaps that can never be so while dealing with this relatively intangible sphere of consciousness. Some illustration of his internal struggles of thought might be seen from the following quotations. Regarding the epistemology of science, he writes, "In the name of science he (the 'spiritualist metaphysician') is not prepared to deny 'the profound mystery of the cosmic existence'. The limits of normal reason should not be allowed to define the boundary of reality. Disability should be confessed but one should not make a virtue out of necessity. I find it difficult to express myself clearly on this point. It is not easy to refute the argument of the materialist. The spiritualist's consideration has also a point in it. It would be too simplistic to argue that scientific method is a good instrument to unravel all the mysteries of the world. The true scientist does not perhaps claim it either. In fact he wants to explain facts of experience in terms of assumptions and hypotheses the truth of which is partly unknown or unfamiliar. To avoid the fallacy of positivism we must not insist in trying to understand and explain the known in terms of the known. In that case the horizon of our knowledge does not expand. The gradual expansion of that horizon is evidently a trend of history. What I want to say is this. We *are* expanding our horizon of knowledge relying partly on the unknown. But that unknown is relatable and answerable to the known and there is nothing mysterious about this...The moment we start believing in a community of experience, we go beyond the narrow circle of 'personal experience' disowning at least partially both positivism and solipsism and thereby commit ourselves, may be unconsciously, to a sort of metaphysics, grand or modest. Laws are invariably grounded in metaphysics—the world not immediately given to our experience...Consciousness being a derivative phenomenon of matter-in-motion its character and function on ultimate analysis must be subject to certain laws which are seemingly external to it. Consciousness as consciousness cannot be conscious of the whole Being, matter-in-motion. Similarly, will as will cannot effectively will the whole of Being as its object. This impossibility is intrinsic" (1976 a: 210, 211, 212). So much for Chattopadhyaya's struggles regarding interpreting ultimate explanations at the ontological and epistemological levels within the sphere of consciousness.

One might recall in this context the response of an adivasi from the Bilaspur region of Madhya Pradesh/Chhattisgarh in an interview with Sharma, which suggests an understanding of the limits of science. "Science is moving ahead. It is moving very fast. Its power today is above all things. The entire world is in its grip. For us it is not possible to even truly know the extent of its power. Those who know science do not recognize the existence of any final limits. We do not understand the knowledge of science. And we cannot understand it. We only know its power. Then how can we determine limits for science? They alone can determine the limits for their knowledge. So long as those who know science do not recognize these limits, there are no limits for them. But final limits do exist. A time would come when even they would be forced to recognize these final limits. But until then they would keep moving ahead and beyond. Behind them would remain nothing. And when they would already be far, very far beyond, something would happen. But by then they would already have gone far beyond their final limits. Something terrible would jolt them. Mind would simply 'crack up'. At that point they would recognize their 'final limits'. But those 'final limits' would already be far behind. As to what would follow, no one knows!!" (Sharma 1994: 132).

Regarding the meditative and yogic practices that have more direct relevance to the ritualistic practices of the adivasi bhagat that involve afflatus and 'spirit possession', Chattopadhyaya is of the following view. "Psychosomatic excellence may as well be called spiritual excellence. And one need not postulate a God or an Absolute to explain the supernormal features of the transformation of the normal body-mind complex. Somewhere Sri Aurobindo himself has said that yoga is nothing but practical psychology... The silting process of the normal experience of a particular cultural milieu over the years results in what is called *community of experience*, an objective situation, which provides the necessary background for the understanding of supernormal experience" (1976 a: 220, 221). Our own tentative interpretation is that the adivasi nostalgia for the distant past and hope for a more just future—the Lokayata materialist belief system of the ancient tribal past and its traces in the immanent adivasi present and yet the ritualistic urge to seek a transcendent explanation—can be resolved within an interpretation of the adivasi All-Theistic, animistic belief (as different from both a Theism as well as an Atheism) in the potential harmony of nature-human beings-community engaged in a struggle for livelihood towards a possible just social relational order; rather than by an explanatory framework that takes recourse to orthodox, hierarchical, Brahmanical, scriptural and religious belief in the divine. The adivasi need for the sustainability of present life into the future is met by remembrance; a recollection of past ancestors and a recognition of clan lineage through the communal celebration of Pitra Baras, ancestor worship, and a veneration of the dead through wooden markers/images (Viras) on the boundaries of fields that also serve as an assertion of territorial rights. The satisfaction of the need for continuity does not require the Brahmanical belief in the Karmic reincarnation of the afterlife and the retribution for past deeds through variable status embodiment. However, there appears the need to placate the spirits of the dead during death ceremonies and anniversaries. This spirit veneration is part of an animism that is rooted in a symbiotic relation with nature in the present and that encompasses the lives of humans, both past and future. Religion is the sublimation of the deepest yearnings and aspirations of humans. However, for the adivasis it takes on naturalistic or anthropomorphic expressions so that the objects of veneration can no longer be seen as transcendental, the totally other, the incomprehensible, and hence, the divine. On the other hand, while spirituality has a materialistic basis in human consciousness, relatively isolated from nature and social relations, it has the capacity to reach out to transcendence. For the Warlis, it was their naturalistic spiritual experience that got formalized into a ritualistic 'religion' as it were. While there was no religious hierarchy, no formal priesthood and sacred text prescribing specific forms of ethical behaviour; their place was taken by lineage, by tradition passing down through bhagats and women agents presiding largely over domestic rituals, and a ritualization of beliefs through content encoded in incantations. These ritualistic incantations while being true and salient to the past, presently have an added function of an escape from the struggles in ecological contexts and social relations of seeking livelihood.

Chattopadhyaya (1989: 84-85, 126, bracket and emphasis added) concludes his assessment of the Lokayata popular worldview with the following statement: "The attempt to develop a unified view of man and nature on the basis of such knowledge (then existing, limited, ancient knowledge) appears to be a remarkable performance. No less remarkable was the way it was often a pointer to further research to understanding man and nature. Much more remarkable appears to us the way in which it tried to evolve a philosophical alternative to the views that wanted to dope people for exploiting them with deceptions and falsehoods—with the fiction of scriptural authority, senseless rituals and all sorts of empty talks of the other world, etc. Here, at any rate, our ancient Lokayatas or Carvakas are not in need of any concession, especially in the Indian context, where the same or similar deceptions are still going...*we have to admit that the Lokayata view is not fully extinct even today. This does not surely mean that there is any question of returning to their primitive materialism, mixed up as it is inevitably with all sorts of primitive imagination and also later superimposition on their basic outlook of all sorts of religious and quasi-religious hotch-potch. But the fact that the people- particularly the lower rung of the people- still instinctively stick to some form of materialism is not to be overlooked.*"

How is Chattopadhyaya's foregoing analysis of the origins of tribal beliefs related to contemporary ritual practices and associated incantations among the adivasis in Palghar district? An important basis for the perpetuation of ethnic identity is the memory of emotive experiences of the past, related to physical and economic survival in ecological and socio-economic contexts, articulated in belief systems, crystallized in rituals and associated incantations, that then have a life of their own and continue to provide security and some explanation; even though the existential contexts might have changed as well the popular interpretations of the rituals whose original significance may not be generally known and may have undergone transformation in the context of adivasi relations with non-adivasis.

The primary traces of the original tribal belief system persisting among the contemporary adivasi rituals and incantations during the life and agricultural cycles as interpreted from our field work (Chapter 4) may be seen as follows as aspects of adivasi perceptions:

The persistence of a proto-materialism regarding the close relation between the human body and the earth/nature,

The perceived parallelism between human reproduction/fertility and the productivity of nature/agriculture,

Similarities seen between the birth of humans and the origin of the universe,

The fundamental valuation of human manual labour in food gathering, hunting and later in agriculture and its contribution to the knowledge of medicinal plants and to survival in very adverse ecological and social conditions,

Ambivalent and contesting relation with Brahmanical rituals and idealistic beliefs such as the existence and salience of the ultimate being, karma and rebirth,

Ambivalent emphasis, significance and awe of prakriti or the female principle, as a result of changing gender relations in close relation to their basis in production relations and modes of seeking livelihood,

The persisting belief in magic and spirit possession—instruments to control the forces of nature through identification/imitation and later as an expression of the pacification of deities—in rituals and incantations related to the life and agricultural cycles,

The deification of elements and forces of nature and the unity of humans and deities or the humanization of deities.

These thematic archetypes of beliefs, also discussed in the concluding section of Chapter 4, are sustained and perpetuated through ritualistic incantations, and hence largely crystallized as an ethnic identity which has a materialistic basis in the search for livelihood primarily through agriculture and labour on land and in the forests. In so doing an embryonic form of identity based on shared economic interests emerges. In addition, these thematic archetypes may be viewed as a link to an ancient pre-Vedic past of the tribals and their Lokayata materialistic beliefs. As Kosambi (2009 a: 30, emphasis added) writes, "*...there exist in India today many tribal peoples whose customs go back to preliterate times. ... These peoples preserve many features—in fossilized form, as it were—of Indian prehistory.*" This reading of the contemporary historical anthropology of adivasis is similar to that of D.P. Chattopadhyaya in his *Lokayata* (1978 a/1959) and other writings, as earlier discussed. While not clearly and consciously articulated among the contemporary adivasis, they may be seen as a trace in the collective unconscious of the present-day adivasis of their early Lokayata beliefs. Sentiments, emotions and solidarities attached to cultural practices, especially rituals and accompanying incantations, are transmitted across time more forcefully and in a sustainable manner than the cognitive rationalizations and explanations for them. The latter may now have been ritualized in a cyclical manner and the meanings of rituals may not be known even to the participants. Collective memory is the remembered history of a people and rituals are one way of reiterating it. Genetics is the embedded history in given social historical and ecological contexts of a people seeking their survival through production. Time is the crystallization of space in motion and religious rituals are different ways of making sense in this space-time context. Identity that is value loaded is the relative objectification and generalization of experience (consciousness in action) on a wider social spatial scale, within given structured contexts and social historical processes. A sense of community, whether ethnic and/or class, is the relative objectification of the relatively subjective processes (experience and identity formation) mentioned above. It would be the creative and empathetic task of social science epistemologies and of ideological mobilization to take forward the ethnic and class identities of contemporary adivasis towards more just political formations, given that insight into contemporary social processes and formations is the recognition of the interrelation of realities in flux.

An early matriarchal organization of society within the adivasis of Palghar district is suggested by the persisting relatively equal status of women as seen from participation in agriculture and the household economy, the free movement of women beyond the household and the village, their participation in drinking alcohol, toddy and smoking of bidis (tobacco wound in leaves). This may also be interpreted from some social practices such as the payment of the bride price by the male to the woman's family at the time of marriage, the predominant role of women in officiating at marriage ceremonies, the gharora practice of marriage when an indigent male unable to afford the bride price can stay and work at the bride's family and work in their fields, the significant role of the maternal uncle in various ceremonies, and the salience of the feminine principle, the interpretation of puberty in terms of human and agricultural fertility and the defining place of female deities during rituals of the agricultural and life cycles.

Seeking the origins of these matriarchal practices, Dalmia refers to Kosambi (1962: 64) who cites a verse from the Rig Veda which speaks about a conflict between Indra, the god of war of the patriarchal, pastoral Aryan invaders and a woman, Ursas the daughter of heaven, "This heroic and virile deed didst thou didst strike down (or kill) the evil-plotting woman, the daughter of heaven. Ursas, verily, the daughter of heaven, the great to be regarded as great didst thou crush, O Indra. Ursas fled from the shattered wagon in fright, when the Bull (Indra) had rammed her. Her wagon lay completely smashed to bits on the Vipas (river), she (herself) fled to the farthest distance." According to Kosambi, "There is no reason or explanation given for this conflict. Indra is the young god, one whose birth is mentioned several times, and who takes the lead over all other gods because of his prowess in battle. In fact, he reflects the typical Aryan tribal war-chieftain, irresistible in strife after getting drunk on *Soma*...But why was it (the wagon) smashed up by the new leader? Her fleeing to the farthest distance is equivalent to her death. She is ascribed only an ordinary horse chariot (*ratha*) in most later hymns. The ox-cart, like the archaism *sim*, must represent great antiquity. At the same time, she is an ancient goddess in spite of her virginity and youth, which are preserved by her being born again and again: *punah, punah jayamana purani*. The only possible explanation lies in a clash of cults, that of the old mother goddess being crushed on the river Beas by the new war-god of the patriarchal invaders, Indra.

That she survives after being 'killed' can only indicate progressive, comparatively peaceful, assimilation of her surviving pre-Aryan worshippers who still regard her as mother of the sun, wife of the sun, daughter of heaven. Her behaviour is reflected in that of apsaras like Urvasi, who degenerate into the witches of the Atharvaveda by natural development of the combined society, which really and finally kills their cult, expect for local survivals in villages and the jungle" (cited in Dalmia 1988: 20-21). However, as Kosambi points out, "The conflict between mother- goddess and father-god could not have been resolved peaceably everywhere. Throughout Indian theological art, from the earliest representation of a horned 'proto-Shiva' on Harappan seals of the third millennium BC to gaudy pictures sold in Indian bazaars today, runs a theme of conflict between a female deity and a 'buffalo demon', in which the goddess is the victor. In Kalighat paintings, for example, Shiva's wife Parvati tramples him. The goddess Durga-Parvati is called 'she who tramples the buffalo demon' " (2009 a: 47).

In the context of the foregoing historical analysis, it may be noted that according to Thapar the Rgveda might be approximately dated to 1500 BC, hence following the decline of the Harappan culture. "The term 'Aryan' in the label Indo-Aryan, refers solely to the language and not to the people who spoke it or for that matter to any imagined race...(the second millennium BC) also sees the arrival of the horse, the chariot and spoked wheel, and the use of iron, all of which are more evident in the first millennium... The identities of the indigene and the alien are constantly mutated throughout history. It is more pertinent to analyse the major historical processes of early times, namely, the emergence of dominant groups—the *aryas,* and the subordination of others referred to as *sudras* and *dasas* " (Thapar 2000: 1127, 1133; bracket added). She acknowledges the tremendous contribution of Kosambi to historical analysis by throwing light on the past through anthropological and ethnographic uncovering of the differentiated and layered present, almost as an archaeological exercise (2000: 53 and 2008).

To continue with the historical trajectories of the ancient tribals one might consider the writings of Gadgil and Guha (1992: 82), who hold that "the belief system of food gatherers, with its conservation orientation, saw spirits that were respected in trees, groves, ponds, rivers and mountain peaks. In contrast, in the belief system of food producers conquering new territories, worship focused on elemental forces such as fire and water, and the great god of war, Indra. As the frontier receded and there were no longer large fertile tracts to move towards, there emerged the belief systems of Buddhism and Jainism, which rejected the supernatural and advocated a rational arrangement of human affairs. These belief systems included an important element of conservation: they advocated that resources should not be used wastefully." They go on to suggest that by the time of Gautam Buddha, around the sixth century BC, the topography of social organization emerging from livelihood might have been settled agriculture and pastoralism covering extensive parts of the country moving from the Gangetic plains into the drier tracts of western India and then encroaching onto the central parts of semi-arid peninsular India along the tributaries of major rivers. Hunters and food gatherers would have persisted in the hilly areas of the Himalayas and the north east, on the Western and Eastern Ghats and in the central Indian plateau. The chiefdoms of agricultural-pastoral and the incorporated food gathering communities could have persisted in their heterogeneity based on endogamy and cultural differentiation corresponding to the needs of specialization and division of labour in a diversified economy, in contrast with more homogeneous communities of hunting and food gathering tribal groups. The conquered food gatherers would have been assigned the menial tasks as Sudras and Panchamas (untouchables). During the Gupta and the post-Gupta period between the fourth and the ninth centuries AD, the varna system got concretized into caste society. The new system drew on the ecological basis of the belief systems of food gathering societies assigning a subordinate place to them as associated with the key gods of the Hindu pantheon such as Shiva, male phallic worship, and Parvati, female fertility worship. The related rituals were meant to ensure the fertility of the fields and the regulation of the use of natural resources. For example, Shiva as Pasupati is seen as the lord of the beasts who rides a male bull, Nandi, and has a cobra around his neck; all symbols of fertility. Elephant worship is imbibed as Ganesa, one of the sons of Shiva and Parvati. Devotion to deities as bhakti served to strengthen the relations between various endogamous communities in a prescribed cycle of festival occasions (1992: 103-104, also Kosambi 1965: 49-50, 170). Kosambi states that, "This Brahminization reflects the underlying change from food-gathering in independent tribal units to food-production in a society that preserved endogamy and a (hierarchical) commensal tabu as features of its caste system. This preservation is due primarily to the fact that food-gathering remained a powerful supplement to agriculture till the forests disappeared, while clothing and shelter are not physically indispensable over most of India" (Kosambi 1985: 20). Aryanization is seen by him to be primarily in terms of the spread of plough agriculture with fixed land holdings among the relatively technologically advanced invading groups and the later adoption by tribals of Brahmins who made their dwellings in forested areas and facilitated the incorporation of tribals within the agriculture-based caste system (Kosambi 1985). He further elaborates this point, "A predominantly pastoral, tribal society of bronze-age marauders settled down to agrarian peasant life made possible by the discovery and availability of iron. The iron age led also to a change in the centre of gravity because the Gangetic plain was first cleared for plough-farming only when cheap metals were found" (Kosambi 2009 c: 81). He attributes the persistence of the food-gathering stage with its accompanying belief systems among tribal populations to the extensive availability of staples and a variety of other edibles in a natural state in the forested regions. The process of mutual acculturation with the non-tribal settled agriculturists was based to a great extent on religion and superstition, thus reducing the need for violence (Kosambi 1965: 34). The industrial mode of exploitation of natural resources introduced much later by the British had a significant impact, "For the elevation of commercial over subsistence uses, the delegitimization of the community, and the abandoning of restraints on resource exploitation—all ran counter to the experience of the vast majority of the Indian population over which the British were to exercise their rule. This was a clash, in more ways than one, of cultures, of ways of life" (Gadgil and Guha 1992: 116).

The foregoing suggests that a significant feature of Indian society as underlined by Kosambi was that: "*The entire course of Indian history shows tribal elements being fused into a general society. This phenomenon, which is at the very foundation of the most striking Indian social feature, namely caste, is also the great basic fact of ancient Indian history. The different methods whereby the tribal elements were formed into a society or absorbed into preexisting society are prime ethnic material for any real historian" (Kosambi 2016/1956: 15, emphasis added).* If this be true, then an important direction for future analysis would be the nature of this tribal-non-tribal interface, with all its variations over space and time, over the broad sweep of phases of Indian history as suggested by Kosambi: "The urban but stagnant Indus valley culture (3000-1500 BC) which left its mark on later technique, iconography and probably social institutions. (2) Aryanization, i.e. later bronze and early iron age pastoral-nomadic tribal organization over the two caste system, developing into four caste-classes by 800 BC. (3) Clearing and settlement of the heavily forested Gangetic alluvial basin with Sudra labour, mostly under Magadhan state enterprise (from 500 BC) ending with the first empire over the whole country by 250 BC. (4) A primitive feudalism whereby the peninsula was properly developed for trade and agriculture (say the Satavahana period), but with far less production in cities. The *emergence* of private property, even in land, began earlier than 400 AD, before the prime of the Gupta empire. (5) 'Pure" feudalism, beginning in the later Gupta period but enormously stimulated by Muslim trade and military penetration after 1200 AD. (6) Modern capitalism, culminating with the rule of a new indigenous bourgeoisie that came into being less than 100 years ago, through European trade, factory production, and share capital under British colonial rule" (Kosambi 2009 b: 58). Such an historical analysis of the tribal interface with mainstream non-tribal society would need to uncover the varying consolidations of the caste system in that society as a result of the subordinated assimilation of tribal communities. As Kosambi suggests, "Caste is class at a primitive level of production, a religious method of forming social consciousness in such a manner that the primary producer is derived of his surplus with the minimum of coercion" (Kosambi 2009 b: 59). The present-day adivasis may thus be seen as those that were confined to generally hilly, forested and marginalized regions or as being those who resisted an incorporation into Brahmanical caste society so as to consolidate a distinct identity. Underlying this entire process is the reality that the present diverse communities of the subcontinent have all emerged from the unitary original eco-cultural 'Adi-Vasis' who for want of a better term might be called the 'original, early humans', given the concept of tribe did not exist at the time.

According to Thapar, "The known history of the Hindu religion begins with Vedic Brahmanism from the late second millennium BC and winds its way through a variety of sects, belief systems and ritual practices to the present" (2014: vii). However, in this entire historical process it needs to be pointed out, as Thapar states, that the term Hindu as signifying a religion occurs in Indian texts only in the fourteenth century when the entire range of non-Muslim sects were designated as such to differentiate them from Islam, a distinction later reinforced by colonialism; dharma being used previously to indicate ethics rather than religion. The term Hindu emerges from a geographical designation, initially with reference to the Indo-Aryan/Vedic Sanskrit name for the river Indus, then in a similar manner by the Achaemenid inscriptions of Iran, later by the Indo-Greeks and later still by the Arabs with reference to the people who resided beyond the Indus river.

The historical processes that defined the social transitions taking place in Indian society, especially the political economy of caste formation and the incorporation of so-called tribal groups, is described by Misra and Nagar in the following manner, "Until about five thousand years ago, all of Indian society consisted of tribal people living by hunting-gathering-fishing. The caste system came into existence only after the setting up of permanent farming-based settlements and specialisation of occupations, necessitated by the rural and urban way of life. With the emergence of agriculture, the transformation of hunter-gatherer-fishermen into farmers, artisans and manual workers started. Society became divided into occupational groups and classes based on wealth and political and priestly power" (Misra and Nagar 1997: 155).

Beteille in his useful overview of the concept of tribes appears to favour 'the historical' to the 'evolutionary' approach in the definition and identification of tribes, given that in the Indian context tribes have been visualized as more or less outside Hindu civilization at given historical periods, and their multiplicity of economic formations makes it difficult to group them within singular modes of evolving systems of livelihood (Beteille 1992: 76). One would, however, appreciate the view of Godelier that tribes might be viewed as both a 'type of society' and a 'state of evolution' (Godelier 1977, cited in Beteille 1992: 62). The supposedly negative aspects of valuation implicit in comparison (e.g. between the adivasi and the non-adivasi) on an evolutionary scale is not only substantive, rational and suggesting the extent of promotion of well-being at similar points of time in different contexts, but also of contexts at different points of time on an 'evolutionary' scale involving criteria of value; for example, the foraging of body parts of the clinically dead for medical purposes with the prior consent of the diseased in the current context is justifiably valued higher than the cannibalism of the living and the dead among some societies in ancient times. The principle of evolution need not to be seen in a linear, teleological manner given that its complexity at any given point of time draws attention to the dynamic historical relation between modes of acquiring livelihood and social relations. Some characteristics of the material basis for tribal identity have been one or all of the following: endogamy, cultural ethnicity, lineage, mode of acquiring livelihood and geographical distance. The principle of endogamy ensures lineage and the continuity of a distinctive ethnicity within tribes and clans which are continuously undergoing occupational changes as a result of internal or external social relations. Ethnic identity is socially constructed as a self-conscious distinctiveness from the felt other: that is at the same time an identity that is identified as the 'other' to mainstream 'civilization' and often by anthropological discourse. Hence, it is an intra and inter socio-political relational and socially constructed phenomenon. Beteille justifiably points out that "both detribalization and retribalization occurred in the distant as well as the recent past. But they did not alter everything for collective identities, often outlived changes in economic and political fortunes" (1992: 70).

4. Multiple Levels of Identity in Process

Identity for the purposes of this study is seen in collective and in terms of process; as an inclusive and integrative concept that is subjectively perceived through individual and collective socialization. It bridges and articulates the tensions between the economic, political and the socio-cultural as objectively constituted through historical processes and as subjectively experienced. It indicates the collective self in relation to the other, and is expressed through cultural and linguistic practices, belief systems and values and at times through political organization and ideology. The economic basis of ethnic identity as emerging from the struggle for livelihood in given ecological contexts might often be latent. Perhaps at a more individual level and at a given point of time, identity may be seen "as the set of points of personal reference on which people rely to navigate the social world they inhabit, to make sense of the myriad constellations of social relationships that they encounter, to discern their place in these constellations, and to understand the opportunities for action in this context. It is, in a certain way, a kind of social radar, a perceptual device through which people come to see where they stand in relation to the human environment" (H.E. Hale 2004: 463). In an earlier article, C.R. Hale draws attention to the tensions within scholarly writings in Latin America between a materialist approach tending towards a more holistic analysis and analyses that are more discursive in character that emphasize the multiplicity of particularism within identity politics. "The phrase 'identity politics', will refer to collective sensibilities and actions that come from a particular location within society, in direct defiance of universal categories that tend to subsume, erase, or suppress this particularity. 'Location' in this sense, implies a distinctive social memory, consciousness and practice, as well as place within the social structure" (C.R. Hale 1997: 568). Regarding ethnicity as identity, we are close to the understanding of Sloan (1979: 124) who is of the view that ethnicity "might be defined as an identity claim which, relying on the manipulation of cultural and sometimes of genetic and/or geographical symbols abstracted from some distinct reality that characterizes the group, is advanced by the members of a social group in a given situation of structured interaction with members of another group". According to Malesevic (2004: 3, 4), drawing on Barth (1969), it is the ethnic 'boundaries' or the interactions between groups rather than the internal characteristics that define ethnic identity and leads to its manifestation to a greater extent. Underlining the significance of political action in this process, he writes, "Sociologically speaking, despite its obvious diversity, ethnicity is in the last instance a political culture". One has found the concept of dominant hegemony as quite relevant to an analysis of ethnic identity in this context, as discussed. Jenkins (2008: 14) summarizes his understanding of the 'basic social anthropological model of ethnicity' in the following manner: it involves cultural differentiation, hence relation; shared meanings or culture; it is in process; it is individual and collective, internalized and externalized. He tends to neglect the aspect of the exercise of power in the process of ethnic identification, as mentioned above.

The concept and term 'tribe' first came into prominence in the context of conquest and colonial subjugation as a way of recognition of difference and making sense of the altogether different other, at the same time differentiating the hill and forest people from the larger caste society. This designation has been generally carried forward uncritically in post-colonial society by social scientists and administrators, despite the growing peasantization of the 'tribals' (Pathy 2005: 32 in Chacko ed. and Pathy: 1984). Considering the tribal as an ethnic minority, Pathy states that an "ethnic group is a historical entity whose members in large part conceive of themselves as being alike by virtue of certain common stable features located in language, culture, stereotypes, territory, ancestry-real or fictitious, specific nomenclature and endogamy and are so regarded by the members of other ethnic groups. None of these components however can be regarded as indispensable differentiating ethnic features" (1988: 19). We are in agreement with Dube when he observes that there have been endless and sterile debates on the definition of a tribe/adivasi and that "it may be best now to view it as an ethnic category defined by real or putative descent and characterized by a corporate self-identity and a wide range of commonly shared traits of culture" (Dube 1977: 4). It is important to emphasize the importance given to self-identification in the description. He recognizes that racial, religious and linguistic groups can also have an ethnic character. Sahay (1977: 8) provides an overview of the tribal situation in terms of what is considered to be two related concepts, the self-image of the tribals and their identity, or the ways in which they identify themselves both in a distinctive manner and in relation to others. The names given by tribals to themselves might range from simply human beings or people, or names derived from their ecological setting, the region of origin or present location, occupation, association with ruling dynasties, social characteristics, derivation from deities, the position once or presently held. For Xaxa, as well as for several other scholars, tribe was a colonial construct used to differentiate these communities from the rest of caste and so-called mainstream Hindu society. Tribe came to be used as a residual category rather than in terms of the distinctive features of these communities. For people at the mass level it was cultural ethnicity that was the distinctive feature. Contrary to the colonial position that identified tribal communities as animists and hence distinct from Hindu society as well as the views of Ghurye (1943/1963) who would see them as 'backward Hindus', an understanding that has been fostered by the contemporary Hindutva assimilationist ideology, Xaxa emphasizes the constitutional perspective that, "These groups or communities are categorised as scheduled tribes not because they practise a particular religion but because they constitute a particular community distinct from the dominant regional community" (Xaxa 2005: 1365). One would agree with this position except that in the case of some adivasi communities such as the Warlis, animistic religious practices as a component of a broader cultural and ethnic identity do constitute a self-defining distinctive feature. Xaxa maintains that the social science understanding is that it is possible for a tribal community to be absorbed into the caste Hindu fold. But it would thus lose its tribal status and have to adopt a caste one, given the intimate connection between Hinduism as a religion and the caste structure. The discourse of integration of communities provides space for diversity, unlike the ideological perspective of assimilation by the dominant that would tend to artificially erase distinctiveness and impose a cultural homogeneity in an arbitrary authoritarian manner.

Adivasis need not necessarily in effect be 'original inhabitants' in all the regions that they presently inhabit, as the term suggests, but possibly early migrants or recently dispossessed as well as an object of a colonial construct to create the 'other' as differentiated from the mainstream in the context of modernity; as suggested by several scholars (Bates 1995, Beteille 1998 and others). However, what is not adequately underlined is that present-day adivasis were possibly, in terms of their eco-cultural identity, constituents of the progenitors and ancestors of the multi-ethnic civilization of the Indian subcontinent; a section of people who were generally relegated to the hilly and forested regions or a section of the general population that resisted assimilation within the mainstream caste society. This is a position that appears to flow from our analysis in Section 3 of this Chapter, especially as seen in the writings of Chattopadhyaya (1978 a).

Our attempt in this study of cultural identity has been to identify what Bose (1975, cited in Mehra 1977: 64) calls "the constellation of ideas and emotions which form the core of a community's culture". According to Karna, "Ethnic identity is a subjective articulation of beliefs, values and symbols of culture by a group of people to differentiate themselves from others. It invariably involves claims to a higher status as a collectivity in relation to other collectivities. Obviously such groups evolve their own criteria for inclusion into and exclusion from the group. Thus initially primordial elements are mobilized to consolidate the ethnic but in subsequent phases the same identity turns into an instrument to derive political and economical benefits. It is in this context that we find two different views of identity-formation, they are primordialist and instrumentalist approaches of ethnic identity-formation...It will not be out of context to indicate here that some social scientists have used the concept of community to explicate the idea of ethnic identity" (Karna 2007: 50). Communal identity is viewed as closely related to ethnic identity in academic discussions (Singh 2016: 95). Some scholars see them as undifferentiated concepts. Others consider ethnicity as based on multiple indicators, reserving the concept of communal (religion), caste and language to identities based on single markers. Considering our conceptual framework of multiple identities coexisting at different levels within individuals and collectives at a given point of time and differentially called forth to consciousness and salience to action within processes of social transformation according to context, as will be discussed, ethnic identity may be seen as an overriding and inclusive concept for identities that are primarily expressed in cultural and symbolical terms.

The foregoing section would have drawn attention to the historical basis for the multiple and overlapping character of the identities that one encounters among the adivasis in our study in the contemporary context. Our studies among the adivasis in Palghar district (Saldanha 2015 a and b), including the illustrative ones with an emphasis on culture provided in this publication, suggest that the following may be considered as the major levels within the segmentation of adivasi identity: Language; Region; Religious/ritualistic/animistic; Clan; Tribe; Dalit, oppressed including SCs, STs, OBCs and NTs; related to livelihood and the economy, Class; Political Party and Mass Organization Affiliation; Nationality.

Certain characteristics of collective identity among the adivasis may be specified. Identities are multilayered, structured and relational to the other. They are assumed independently or given by the other and accepted as such (introjected) at each level. Identities are in process, the dominant identity in the foreground of subjective consciousness changes with time. Hence, identities are always contextualized; the dominant identity being called forth to consciousness according to context and changing circumstances and in response to political mobilization. A relevant question is whether the intervention of the political activist as well as that of social science mirror and hence reproduce and reinforce the segmentation of adivasi identities? Class, as seen in the context of collective identity, is not a macro entity comprising micro entities in contractual relations with each other. Nor is it an aggregation, a serial collective of so many mutually contracting 'potatoes in a sack'. Rather class is a collective constituted by the accumulation of shared intra class social relations that result in shared, not even commonly held, interests that move the collective to action against a countervailing collective comprising interests that are in contradiction. Social relations, collective interests and action in favour of those interests are key terms in the constitution of class. Class then may be seen as a community of shared socio-economic interests in a manner similar to or that builds on a community of shared cultural and ethnic interests. Class identity is then a community in process, in the act of formation, never fixed and permanently crystallized into a fossil; but in close relation with cultural/ethnic identity whose formation predates that of class identity.

To revert to the question of the multilayered character of identity, one might consider whether every analytical category dealing with a collective identity that is socially constructed is overloaded with an element of material reality whether it is biological, ecological or the economic; as well as an element of the cultural, whether it be the symbolic or the ideological. These two major sources of identity are symbiotic and mutually penetrating in character. Political mobilization draws on these elements of identity to varying degrees to thus give it the nomenclature and semblance of the socio-economic or the ethnic, to varying degrees depending on the context. Class, professional association, race, gender and regional identity tend to the ecological, economic and material; and language, tribe, caste, religion, political, ideological, affiliation and nationality tend to the cultural and political, with several overlaps. So the real question is why mobilizations and identities of the late twentieth century and the early twenty-first century tend to take on a religious, ethnic colour which is only apparent given the claims made, the banners that are waved and the slogans that are articulated, when in reality the driving forces may be political and economic. Could it be because within the larger political economic context of the authoritarian and militaristic trends within neo-liberalism there has generally been a defeat of mass organizations based on the economic interests of the industrial working class and the peasantry and because oppression, while felt, tends to lose its immediately perceptible human face and takes on a systemic character that is not easily identifiable and recognizable? One has observed that the reality of multiple, coexisting and overlapping identities generally creates no problems to adivasi individuals and collectives, so long as there is a material, contextual and community basis for each identity and there is a clear movement of the interaction of individuals giving rise to collective identities with the introjection of the collective within the individual. It is only when the community basis for identity collapses and individuals are atomized and reified that anomy, opportunism and schizophrenia prevails as in the relatively new liberalized and privatized economy that engulfs the adivasis with industrial serfdom in the informal sector as the only alternative.

The foregoing analysis of multiple identities might be illustrated in the following manner:

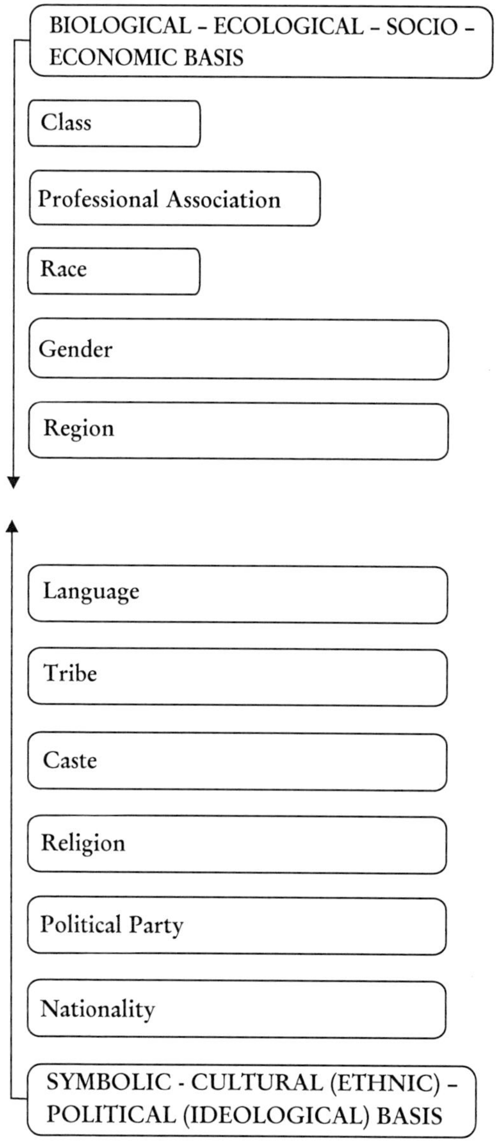

In some senses the adivasi households in our studies, and especially in the present context, have reverted in conscious experience to the reification of the feudal past. This is with the major difference that in the past during British rule they were forced to endure relations of feudal exploitation in a state of 'deprived dependence' as tenants and bonded labourers, while in the present they are free from feudal oppression but are compelled by a new set of economic circumstances that result in dependence emerging from deprivation; forced to seek employment beyond agriculture in the informal sector wherever and according to whatever terms that exist. The new circumstances are the alienation of adivasi lands, population pressure on agriculture, its non-viability and non-sustainability in the present economic dispensation, and ironically the acquisition of education resulting in rising expectations that makes the young psychologically unsuited for agriculture. Within the new political dispensation of ritualized electoral participation and the entry of relatively new political actors such as the BJP, Shiv Sena and the NCP in the region, the adivasis seek out individuals from parties in an opportunistic and instrumental manner who can 'get their work done'. Individualization as a process accompanies this new process of reification.

At a more general level, the networked, globalized universe in India—and as impacting on the adivasis in Palghar district—is that of approximately 30 per cent. Of the rest, the majority are undergoing a transition from presently unsustainable agriculture within precarious ecological conditions to an industrial serfdom in the informal sector away from community, cultural practices and natural environments that provided some solace in the past. While positive, progressive identities tend to get reified; the negative identities are increasingly getting fundamentalized. The country is moving towards a great divide where the few are networked into a national and global industrial order with ancillary service sectors and the many are struggling to find a foothold for their livelihood. What we see is an attempt at inclusion through various schemes that provide fuel for a propaganda machinery through the media and that serve to provide legitimacy for parties in governance (for example, reservations, bank accounts, insurance, employment guarantee, digital India, digital governance, elementary education);

only in practice to effectively exclude or to include at the bottom through deprived dependence and to offset potential protest. The nation state and late capitalist development is swamped by globalization processes; as minimal illustrations, climate change, and trans-border financial flows define the economy, images and messages of the internet pervade the cultural and communicational sphere, and terrorism and fundamentalism impact politics. The nation state is caught in a schizophrenia of reaching out, despite the need to heal within.

Saul (1979) provides several insightful illustrations of researches on the dialectics of class and tribe in Africa that would be relevant to the Indian situation. I will draw on some of these conclusions, most of which have been independently discussed in the foregoing analysis, without reference to the authors cited that are too many for our purposes. It is found that class formation and tribalism are intimately articulated in neo-colonial Africa. Ethnicity is situational in character and can be called forth to consciousness and action through political mobilization. Thus tribalism may be seen as a dependent variable rather than an independent primordial one. The tasks of the 'new nations' which have been the outcomes of colonialism can be one of a differentiated response to imperialism, selective resistance or drawing benefits from the new global order. The so-called 'superstructures' are articulated with the modes of production to a greater extent in pre-capitalist social formations than in advanced capitalism. Saul (1979: 36) concludes his review of literature with respect to Africa in the following manner which might also be a fitting conclusion to one's discussion in this section, "Perhaps enough has been said, however, to suggest that Marxist scientists and African revolutionaries can only make progress when they take ethnicity (and, for that matter, nationalism—though that would be the subject of another essay) seriously as a real rather than ephemeral and /or vaguely illegitimate variable in Africa. This essay argues that this is more likely to be done when the simultaneity of class and centre-periphery contradictions is placed front and centre as a key factor within our analytical framework". One would add that centre-periphery relations, both within and between nations.

5. Ethnicity and Class: Solidarities and Action in Political Process

It would be useful to draw on some other empirical and historical studies that address this issue. One is attempting to primarily explore intra nation state processes of identity formation within social movements. Hence the conclusions from these discussions would be more directly applicable to movements for social transformation within nation states; though some relevance might be seen for broader processes of nation formation. The latter has been comprehensively reviewed with a focus on language and region by Karna (1999). Dube recognizes that while the main thrust of ethnic movements was political, a competition for power, the direction of change and loyalties were largely influenced by cultural factors (1977: 1). Interests, which one might view as meaning economic interests of a class character, are seen as having a relation of mutual reinforcement with ethnic identity. The question of nomenclature for social formations with its implications of ascribed identity, whether this process of defining the other is enunciated by dominant political and economic powers or by social science that generally tends to follow in their wake, has been a significant unresolved issue. Singh elaborates on the historical complexity of the question: "Pre-colonial India was a land of many communities organised into categories which were known by such native terms as *varna*, *jati*, *quam*, *kabila*, *biradari* and so on. There are about 400 terms denoting exogamous units before the notion of clan was foisted on the people. There were many processes of interaction at work. Tribe and caste had not emerged as dichotomous categories. The cognitive perception of communities changed in the colonial period. The colonial system introduced the binary perception" (Singh 1997: 33). As Xaxa points out, "Today, acculturation for tribes means adopting the ideas values and practices of the dominant community rather than being part of that society by assuming a caste status...Tribes can still move in the direction of the peasantry without losing the social attributes of tribes" (Xaxa 1999: 1521, 1523). Hence, as also other social scientists have emphasized, a term that for practical purposes suggests a social formation/community like a 'samaj' might be a more relevant term to identify the identity of the tribal. "Yet the term by which they were known to the multitudes of people were not 'tribes' but 'janas' meaning 'communities of people' (Xaxa 1999: 1524). Guha (2015) on the basis of historical evidence is of the view that the terms and caste and tribe should be discarded because of their colonial origins and their lack of significant material basis except that they served an administrative purpose of defining the other. He suggests that these categories might be replaced by the indigenized term 'khum' which might be applicable to all ascribed social categories. From an outsider social science perspective during one's fieldwork in a contemporary context one has found the term 'samaj'(society, community) to be a relevant generic concept that conveys meaning to the insider (religious, caste, adivasi group) and facilitates a more specific depiction of perceived identity. In the final analysis the concerned social formation should provide an answer to this question. This is because identity today is largely a self-identifiable, political description, even though at times an ascribed one. The terms dalit and adivasi carry significant political salience for the concerned sections of society and serve as distinctive markers for political mobilization.

Steur discusses the rise of an ideology based on adivasi ethnicity during the 1990s in Kerala, in some ways distinct from the predominant communist ideology (Steur 2011). An important element in defining their lives was their situation of poverty, which suggests an economic identity wider than the adivasi ethnic identity (ibid.: 61) She suggests that "the AGMS (Adivasi Gothra Maha Sabha) is transformative precisely because it advocates a broader more universally applicable agenda and suggests a reworking of the received wisdom of Adivasi needs...it is a more 'autonomous' vision of empowerment rather than being able to integrate in society through stable employment and secure rights to education, the ideal of owning a piece of land is that of no longer being dependent on such social institutions for one's emancipation and goes hand in hand with the many (often state-sponsored) 'self-help initiatives' among subaltern populations" (ibid.: 64, 66).

Another useful study which elaborates "the relationship between historical structure, human experience and social consciousness in the constitution of ethnicity" in the state of Jharkhand is that of Devalle (1992: 10), ethnicity being seen as a process rather than a description of fixed ethnic forms. Ethnicity is considered as possibly supportive of dominant hegemony or as a counter-hegemonic force, especially where ethnic ascription overlaps with economic and political subordination. This was also the case of the adivasis in Thane district from 1944 to 1948 and for sometime thereafter. Referring to attempts made to destroy adivasi languages, she writes, "Language is a people's particular code, a field where collective identity and the perception of reality are constantly reformulated, hence a terrain difficult to conquer by those external to it" (ibid.: 17). The diminishing use of the Warli dialect in Palghar district, Maharashtra as a result of education in the dominant Marathi language and growing contact with non-adivasis has been at a cost to adivasi identity. She understands the complexity of using an analytical category such as class to describe an ethnic process in transition and a situation of diverse labour relations and occupational patterns, in a manner similar to the situation of our study (ibid.: 18, footnote 5). In the Jharkhand, as well as in Palghar district, the tribals who were essentially a colonial category persisting during the post-independence period are seen to be presently 'basically peasant societies inserted in a class society, portraying at the same time specific ethno-cultural styles' (ibid.: 53). From the perspective of the adivasi Jharkhandis, "There is no demarcation in their perception of the situation between economic and socio-cultural issues, but a globally experienced reality. Grass-roots struggles precisely show the present class contradictions in the configuration of ethnic differentiation in Jharkhand" (ibid.: 101). The overlap between the ethnic and the class identities are brought out most clearly in what she calls moments of 'high density', where tensions are sharpened. For the adivasis engaged in the movement "being a Jharkhandi came to mean not just a way of life but a way of conflict...Thus, oppression is expressed in a comprehensive way: as being an object of racism, as belonging to a subordinate ethnic group and as being a dispossessed peasant" (ibid.: 166, 170). The importance that Devalle attributes to cultural expression as a political act may be seen from the following, "In situations of oppression a great part of culture continues developing as *lived culture* in the frame of social and political processes, with its own motivations, continuities and contradictions. As such, this vitality of the cultural field in the context of domination may be seen in itself as the most significant act of resistance and defiance to an attempted hegemonic order" (ibid.: 197). Clandestine cultural protest in Jharkhand expresses itself through symbols, work, oral history, and literature and leisure. One does not have the space to go into all these forms, but the expressions in song is worthy of note and have some interpretative significance for aesthetic expression among the Warlis. "For the adivasis in Jharkhand, a *life-song-community-history complex* is practically synonymous with life, both in personal and in social collective terms. There is a saying in Mundari that explains: 'Walking is dancing. Saying is singing' (*Senge susun, Kajige duran*). The community is implicit in all references made to music, song and dance, since all these three develop on the basis of collective participation" (ibid.: 222). Devalle sums up a position on the relationship between ethnicity and class and the epistemological approach to this question in the following statement, "By placing Jharkhand's adivasi societies in historical context and in Jharkhand's present social formation, it becomes evident that *ethnicity cannot be understood unless issues of social differentiation, processes of class formation and the development of class conflicts are considered in the context of articulation with the processes of ethnic differentiation.* Adivasis live in a class society and in an economic formation where the capitalist mode is dominant" (ibid.: 234; see also Corbridge 1988: 37).

Ismail and Shah undertake a comparative analysis of the Maoists in Nepal and in India on the question of identity in processes of social transformation, whether it is with an emphasis on indigeneity/adivasi identity or on class. The interventions in Nepal are seen to underline elements of ethnicity while those in India tend to focus on class. In the view of the authors, "...to think in a strategic manner about indigeneity means thinking through class-as-it-actually-exists, and ensures it remains central" (Ismail and Shah 2015: 119). In an earlier publication, that discusses the situation of the struggles of the Mundas in the Jharkhand region, Shah is concerned that, "This class dimension to the indigenous rights movement is likely to get erased in the cultural-based identity politics its produces" (Shah 2010: 12). However, a suggestion that a future alternative direction to the struggles of the adivasis in the Jharkhand region might be found in a reinstatement of their traditional institutions of political governance appears idealistic given that there is no elaboration of how their livelihood concerns relating to land and forests would be resolved: "Unlike the secular structures of indigenous governance that the activists are trying to reclaim for the new state, institutions such as the parha and authorities such as the pahan and paenbharra have legitimacy for the Mundas because they represent a cosmology in which the sacred and the secular are intimately connected, even identical. This sacral polity embodies a moral politics endorsed by the sprits that is neither self-interested nor divisive, and that is under-pinned by the values of egalitarianism, consensus in decision-making, and mutual aid. This is a final aspect of arcadian space of the Jungle Raj, which should not be reduced to a superstitious belief in ghosts but which might inspire a new kind of concept of democracy emerging from a sacral polity" (ibid.: 190). The slogan of indigeneity and of the rights of indigenous people while having some value for political mobilization, is seen to have a 'dark side' in that it promotes an essential and undifferentiated notion of the adivasi and tends to leave out the voices of the poorest among the adivasis in Jharkhand (Shah 2007).

Baviskar traces the trajectory of tribal mobilization in south Madhya Pradesh bordering on the river Narmada. In the 1990s the Bhil and Bhilala adivasis were mobilized under the Narmada Bachao Andolan and against the displacement caused by the Sardar Sarovar dam. This was preceded during the 1980s when the adivasi peasants were organized under the Khedut Mazdoor Chetna Sangath for access to forest lands and government services. She writes, "The Andolan and the Sangath together defined adivasi identity as informed by a history of dispossession, with their distinctive cultural practices beleaguered by secular and Hindu modernity. Adivasi claims to lands and forests, and their opposition to displacement, were legitimized in terms of class and citizenship, as the right of a subordinate people to, at the very least, not suffer further deprivation. But also woven into these claims were ideas of ecological virtue—that, as autochthons, adivasis were better stewards of the land than the government who displaced them in the name of 'national development'...Adivasi claims to social justice are made not only on the basis of shared experience of oppression, but also with reference to a special culture" (Baviskar 2005: 5109). However, this secular struggle of the adivasis was threatened in 2002 by a potential contagion from the Hindu rightist forces in the districts of neighbouring Gujarat where adivasis were mobilized under a supposedly common identity in a communal conflict with Muslims, and was offset by systematic state interventions in Madhya Pradesh. Baviskar underlines the fact that "the claims to indigeneity of the Hindu Right are starkly different from the claims to indigeneity made by adivasis fighting against displacement by a large dam. Hindu indigeneity legitimizes the violent exclusion and subordination of religious minorities. Adivasi indigeneity is a demand for inclusion in the Indian polity, a claim on resources unjustly denied and alienated" (ibid.: 5110). She does see the danger of a culturist argument based on adivasi indigeneity as disrupting potential alliances with other vulnerable groups within a more inclusive opposition based on citizen rights, and suggests that, " we cannot assume that indigeneity is intrinsically a sign of subalternity and resistance" (ibid.: 5111). Kulkarni also sees a movement towards a more inclusive organized approach of all the oppressed while being based on adivasi identity in Dhule and the then Thane districts of Maharashtra during the 1970s (1979).

Doshi (1990: 169-170) in his concluding analysis of the interplay of state, class and ethnicity among the Bhils of western India finds that a historical and religious-based ethnicity contributes to a significant solidarity around core values, despite the impact of non-adivasi religions and the process of class formation as a result of political processes and state intervention. The scattered pattern of habitation generally in isolation from non-adivasi communities, bride price, status of women, the significance of alcohol, and ritualistic practices and related belief systems based on animism constitute some of the core values. Discussing the adivasi struggles in Thane district, among other movements, Prasad (2014) sees the need for a consolidated approach, given changes in the political economy, that would integrate concerns of ethnicity within the peasantization of the adivasis with organizations of adivasi and other workers in the informal industrial sector.

The foregoing analysis suggests that the movement from a predominant ethnic identity with an underlying, covert class identity (class-in-itself) to an assertive class identity (class-for-itself) would depend on the convergence of three dimensions (see diagrams in Section 2 of this Chapter): the vertical economic and ecological dimension of livelihood in given contexts; the transverse cross-cutting aspect of culture, consciousness and symbolic systems in a community, especially when they have a basis in livelihood; and perhaps most importantly the horizontal socio-political dimension of whether the sense of community can move beyond distinctive culture to embrace the diversity of similar interests of economic survival. The latter is a matter of ideological and organizational mobilization according to contextual circumstances.

One might conclude from the foregoing studies as well as our own that a sense of community based on ethnicity or common cultural practices does not necessarily contradict class awareness, understood as a perception of shared economic interests closely related to ecological conditions, when it comes to a stimulus for political action. In fact, ethnic community consciousness especially when based on community organization can act as a major driving force for action on economic and livelihood needs in semi-feudal societies that may lack political, class organization and ideology. The crucial element appears to be the sense of community and solidarity, whether based on common cultural characteristics and practices or shared economic needs and collective interests. These overlapping identities can then mutually reinforce each other and at times contradict each other depending on mobilization, the formation of solidarities and the ideological thrust of political action. Kannabiran in her constitutional analysis of the status of human rights for adivasi society writes, "If we use the frameworks of popular sovereignty as our point of departure, it can scarcely be contested that *pluralism* and *diversity* (of all life forms) should lie at its core. A close look at the struggles for survival and dignity by constitutional collectives like the STs underscores the indispensability of imagining lifeworlds of freedom and dignity even while reckoning with practical unattainability of justice as its core problem in the troubled present" (2016: 99).

The solidarity emerging from cultural/ritual practices and contributing to a sense of community identity, especially seen in Chapter 4, may be summarized as follows:

The rituals and incantations, even the ones based on the indefinite life cycle, are closely related to the struggle for survival and the quest for livelihood through the insecure annual agricultural cycle involving labour and production on land and forests in an ecological context. Grains are a recurring theme. Human fertility around the life cycle is seen as closely embedded in the fertility of the agricultural cycle.

The rituals involve at least the immediate community from the hamlet and clan members, if not the entire village community of adivasis. This is by way of participation, contributions in cash or kind, sharing a meal and importantly in alcoholic drinks, mutual appreciation and acknowledgement by a symbolical holding of hands and crying out 'ye'.

The rituals serve as annual time markers and sign posts of shared historical memory; reminders to the community through repetition that reinforces recollection, discussed in Chapter 2.

The traditional systems of collective governance still persist by way of recognition of the head of the first/principal clan in the hamlet/ village, the patil, and the main executive, the karbhari; though these roles are being quickly overtaken by the institutions of local self-governance from the village to the district and electoral participation in the state and national legislatures.

The rituals serve as a mark of ethnic distinctiveness from the 'other' for the majority of the adivasis who take pride in this distinctiveness, thus strengthening the identity of the 'self'.

The actual adivasi community could thus be seen as a collective of shared economic, political and cultural practices that reinforce beliefs norms and aspirations.

We will turn to features of the ethnic identity of the adivasis, the Warlis in particular, in the region. This could be analysed under two dimensions: the political culture of largely individualized resistance that characterized the pre-1944 period which might be termed as a 'weapon of the weak' given the lack of collective, organized mobilization. And the more specific aspects of cultural intervention of the Kisan Sabha, especially during the early period of its mobilization. There were several forms of resistance to exploitation by the state and non-adivasis despite the conditions of reification of the adivasi existence during the pre-1944 feudal period, when ethnicity might be interpreted as the 'primordial', felt identity; even though severe sexual, physical and economic oppression was experienced. In marxian terminology the adivasis might be viewed as a class in itself and the later Kisan Sabha mobilization against feudal exploitation during the militant highpoint of 1944 to 1948 built on this ethnic identity carrying forward the process into an identity of a class for itself with shared interests, organizational solidarity under the Lal Bavta (the red flag, as popularly termed), ideology that was gradually imbibed at the mass level, and collective action. The revolt of 1944 to 1948 was marked by a series of actions and has served as an indelible marker in the minds of the adivasis despite the passage of time (Saldanha 2015 a). An event is a point of convergence of structure and social action, imbued with an ideology. This configuration and conjuncture of forces is powerful enough to facilitate recollection and illuminates the possibilities for future trajectories. The Kisan Sabha assumed, did not generally address directly, but built on the ethnic identity and gave it a politico-economic, organized and ideologically inspired class identity in opposition to the dominant landlord, moneylender and trader class and the state machinery that supported it.

It might be observed that the earlier forms of resistance prior to 1944 were very often perceived as prejudiced stereotypes about the adivasis on the part of the oppressive 'other'. It may also be noted that these stereotypes were sometimes introjected by the oppressed 'self' which then provided grounds for legitimization of and reconciliation to one's position in society. The following forms of everyday resistance may be extracted from the narratives provided by G. Parulekar (1975):

Silence: The silencing of the senses, especially one's hearing and speech in the context of verbal threats to one's self-respect and identity, or selectively listening to what one finds convenient.

Stupidity: A pretence of lack of understanding of verbal commands.

Laziness: Execution of commands in a disinterested and slothful manner in order to conserve one's energy and labour power.

Dirty and shoddy work: Due to lack of personal involvement and gain from the task.

Obsessive compulsive behaviour: The ritualization of routine actions as part of the oppressive labour process without investment of thought and involvement.

Indiscipline: Lack of punctuality and absenteeism from work.

Living in the present: An apparent forgetfulness of the past with very little hope in and aspirations for the future.

Drunkenness: An escape from harsh realities through inebriation accompanied by song, music and dance.

Arson: The conscious burning of forest lands, apparently as a mistake, especially when denied access to this natural resource.

Avoidance: Bypassing laws which are then registered as 'offences', especially regarding encroachments on forest lands for purposes of cultivation.

Flight: Deserting one's employer where one has been a bonded labourer and attempting to migrate to another region.

Banditry: The creation of small gangs that live in the forest and swoop down occasionally on the planes of cultivated agriculture.

Strikes: Withdrawing labour and services.

Rumour: Spreading false information through word of mouth in order to create an atmosphere of panic and possible revolt.

Satire: Especially seen in stories and folklore that run down the oppressor in a comical and less threatening manner, which yet creates critical awareness.

Petitions: To the administration or the judiciary with the assistance of non-tribal sympathetic mediators.

Falsification of records: The creation of alternative evidence so as to cover up offences.

The foregoing forms of resistance were generally passive, covert and reactive in character, rarely taking on violent and proactive forms when provoked beyond a point of endurance. They were generally individualized, given that there was no sustained, organized, political mobilization. The forms of resistance may be conceptualized and classified along the following dimensions:

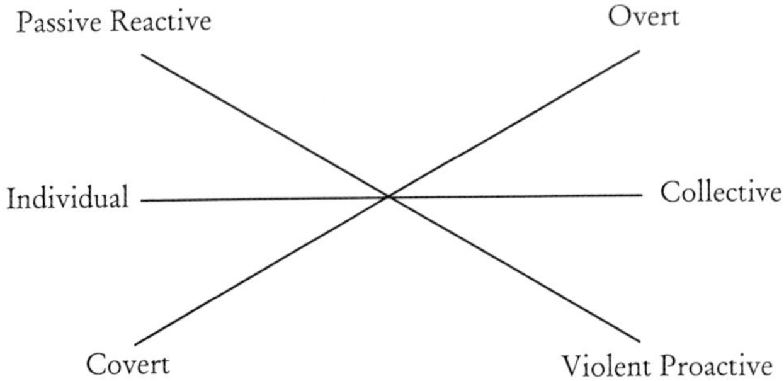

The foregoing forms of resistance may also be seen as coping and defence mechanisms and reaction formations. Coping mechanisms are in effect an indirect critique of present realities through repression through the unconscious, which needs to be uncovered. This is undertaken in circumstances where very little can possibly be done, individually or collectively, to change situations. The tangential relation to the immanent results in a reaction formation. There is a neglect and non-acknowledgement of an unbearable present condition and a repression of the reality that defines livelihood.

Regarding more specific cultural interventions of the Kisan Sabha, especially during the early period of the 1940s, we find from the writings of G. Parulekar (1975) and discussed in greater detail in Saldanha (2015 a), that these were generally sporadic in nature and having to do with dress and external appearance: shorts and shirt instead of the traditional 'langoti' (loin cloth) for men, getting rid of the heavy metalic bangles that women wore and that drew attention to their vulnerability to sexual oppression and the tuft of long hair (shendi) that men wore and that had become a symbol of oppression. Reducing marriage expenses and settling disputes by the elders served to reduce indebtedness and needless litigation. Ideological education, travel and participation in conferences across the country facilitated the widening of horizons of the middle peasant and party activists. The solidarity in action during the early period drew on the ethnic base and the stated identity of 'garib adivasi', across the status hierarchy among the adivasi tribes. Participation in rituals and inter-dining, if not inter-marriage, encouraged cultural solidarity. The observation of Zania, a 45-year-old Warli middle peasant as stated to us in 1980, had its roots during this early phase of mobilization:

> The Dhodis, Dublas, Bharwads (the popular term for the non-tribal, pastoralist adivasis), the Kathodis also have similar problems. Their condition is also the same. Adivasi means, all are adivasis. Even though we are Warlis and they are Dhodis, Dublas, they are also the same. Some of them have to work at the Seth. Because they have no lands they have to do this. They were also exploited in the past (Saldanha 2015 a: 428).

However, during the post-1970 phase of economic differentiation among the adivasis, with the weakening of ethnic bonds and class solidarity as a result of participation in the rituals of participatory, electoral democracy, the entry of new political actors in the region and changes in the political economy, briefly described in Chapter 1, Introduction, there is a growing anomie, individualization and an instrumental approach to electoral actors as best described by Marlu, a perceptive middle peasant party member:

> Everybody doesn't understand the real conditions. If it is night and one has to drive a cart, the people will just drive. One has to drive, so let's drive. Where lies the path, that's not seen. Some even get old and die, but still don't understand (Saldanha 2015 a: 472).

In the present context, one might see elements of sublimation in the ritualized appeal to the 'transcendent' during current cultural practices and incantations as described in Chapter 4 relating to the rituals of the agricultural and the life cycle. Attempts are made to placate spirits that have taken the form of deities and the rituals do provide some explanation and foster elements of fragile collective solidarity. The rituals are a formalistic, ritualized carryover of practices that had content and meaning during a pre or early settled agricultural society which was relatively autonomous from the relation to the 'outsider', whether the state or the non-adivasi. The only desperation appears to be coping with the uncertainties of settled agriculture as a result of transiting from an earlier experience of hunting and food gathering in the forests. The transcendent and the altogether other has a qualified significance in a society that continues to be largely animistic, based on the relations of humans to the community, nature and the spirits; as different from in a religious hierarchical society with the worship of gods and goddesses, in prescribed places, through the mediation of a hierarchical priestly class, following sacred texts. The transcendent is immanent in animistic, adivasi society; in nature and the annual agricultural cycle with symbols of fertility, the role of the feminine principle of productivity, and the overwhelming significance of grains that sustain livelihood. The immanent presence of spirits may also be found in the life cycle of individuals—birth, illness, marriage, death—and the veneration of ancestors which provide some sense of permanence to individuals and to the community as a result of the assertion of lineage. The transcendent can take any form: stones, chains, coins, animals, human functions and can be cajoled or placated and even sworn at. The divine can also be possessed in moments of spirit possession and trance. Elements of sublimation through wish fulfilment may also be seen in aesthetic expressions of painting, music and dance which will be discussed in Chapter 6. Escape is also sought through the process of cooption by and conceding to the 'other' as a result of adopting religious and social practices of dominant hegemonic religions and thus attempting to enhance social and economic status, as discussed in Chapter 5.

It is an irony of history that a belief system that was in ancient times taken from the tribals through a process of violence and/or 'seductive subordination' of the defeated communities, and incorporated within the Brahmanical Vedic Varnashrama system, is presently being offered back in a changed form to the adivasis through a process of 'indulgent inclusion'; that matriarchal materialism which initially was the tribal's 'matrimony' (matriarchal inheritance), is now offered in a regurgitated manner after a process of patriarchal transfiguration as a Brahmanical 'patrimony' (the patriarchal inheritance of the other). It is not surprising, given the foregoing, that the adivasi ethnic cultural consciousness is marked by a certain schizophrenia within the context of dominant hegemony. The adivasi present self is torn between the existential present and the recollection within a collective unconscious, recalled through ritualistic reiteration of an ancient historical past self. Both selfs have been hegemonically subordinated through a process of 'indulgent inclusion' within the Varnashrama system at the lowest level; in the past by an alien, militarist, patriarchal, pastoral economy that prevailed over a matriarchal, hunting gathering economy that had discovered early shift cultivating agriculture; dominated during the British and post-independence period by an exploitative landlord-moneylender-trader economy that was in alliance with the state machinery; and in the present enticed by a growing parasitic capitalism that promotes 'industrial serfdom' in the informal sector. The economic and social relational subordination of the adivasi self in the past and the present by the 'other' lead to their own subjective splits in consciousness, as different from yet corresponding to the cultural ones. This schizophrenia in alternative hegemonic, subaltern consciousness in the present is manifest in thought and behaviour, as discussed in Chapters 4 and 5, through some major expressions:

The selective introjections of dominant ritualistic beliefs and practices,

The view of the self as backward,

The tendency towards sancritized incorporation for enhanced social and economic status,

The practice of attributing causality of evil in a selective manner to the feminine principle as seen in the phenomenon of bhutali, identifying witches,

The ambivalent love-hate relation with Kansari Devi, the deity of grain,

The diminishing sense of community solidarity.

In their extensive review of different aspects of the status of adivasis in the country, Xaxa and others come to the conclusion as regards state policies that, "What the State is actually pursuing in tribal areas—apart from North-East India—is assimilation rather than integration, contrary to what is claimed. A policy of integration would provide space for protections and safeguards for their distinct identity, as enshrined in the Constitution. However, these provisions are precisely what are under threat of erosion through the process of cultural domination and more importantly, the prevailing development paradigm" (2014: 28). And Sundar in her wide ranging edited collection of articles relating to the politics, identities, policies, and work relating to adivasis, comes to the conclusion that, " It is the 'mainstream' which needs to be radically rethought and not the margins who need to be 'mainstreamed' " (2016: 16). The country's national identity has been the product of the convergence and divergence of multiple cultural forces. These have been brought together at times through hegemonic tendencies that have been subordinating and exploitative in character or harmonizing influences towards syncretic integration, led primarily by subaltern communities. The latter process of pluralistic flowering will decide the positive future of the nation. India is a constitutionally created unity of its diversity. A tribe today is that community that is constitutionally defined as such, largely due to distinct ethnic identity that has not been assimilated into caste-based Brahmanical society. It is only just to protect this distinctiveness under the pluralistic ideology of the Constitution.

Section 2

Practices

CHAPTER 4

Rituals and Incantations: The Life Cycle and the Annual Agricultural Cycle

The following is not primarily an exercise in folklore and ethnography. While such material may be found in this chapter, it is used primarily as the basis to uncover their contribution to the understanding of adivasi ethnic identity and to interpret their significance in providing existential meaning to the lives of the adivasis and their struggles for livelihood in contemporary structured contexts. Detailed ethnographic accounts may be found in Enthoven (1922), Save (1945), K. and V. Nargolkar (1955), Dalmia (1988), Dandekar (ed. 1998) in the main, and have been referred to together with one's own fieldwork in order to meet the stated objectives and to trace scenarios at different points of time. The last mentioned, in particular, is a good anthology of some of the myths, rituals and incantations and their primary agents. We have, however, concentrated largely on our own fieldwork.

The interpretation of Warli rituals and the incantations associated with them in terms of their inner meanings and their salience to the everyday lives of the adivasis is fraught with several issues. Several questions immediately arise: How far back in time can one trace the origin of these rituals? What are the changes that have taken place over time and changing contexts? Would there be variations across different geographical spaces within the region of the present Palghar district at the same time and what contextual relevance do they have? Given the real possibility of individual elaborations, additions and subtractions by the major actors in the incantations, the transmission losses and memory lapses over several generations, what is their salience in terms of the reliability and validity of the accuracy of the recitations; or is this question at all relevant in the context of subjective experience and articulation? And finally, and perhaps most importantly, what is the relevance of these rituals and incantations for community solidarity, ethnic identity, collective action and explanation of the experience of everyday life?

In addition, there is a need to understand cultures both distinctively and comparatively. The criteria for comparisons made across cultures that are coexistent and in interaction at a given point of time are fraught with relative judgments. Apart from the question of the substantive valuations of different cultures, there is the underlying issue of chronological change and progress, i.e. what is considered to be a representation of an earlier mode of economic and cultural organization and what represents 'advancement'. The yardstick used is often ethnocentric, i.e. what is considered rational and civilized is often relative to one's own culture, one's own needs and aspirations; in accordance with dominant and majoritarian trends. If comparison is inevitable then one needs some independent principles that would facilitate distinctive analysis as well as comparison. Some of these principles could be based on the following normative criteria. Human action is functional, purposeful and meaningful. It is action accompanied by a cognitive element; action aimed at satisfying perceived needs and/or towards definite ends. A culture of greater relevance and perhaps of higher value is one which is able to satisfy the largest number of needs of the widest possible sections, in a just and sustainable manner. In a dynamic perspective, the very satisfaction of needs give rise to further needs over time. But for purposes of comparison, some degree of analysis at stationary points of time might be needed.

Apart from the content and the context of the rituals, we will focus on the emotions expressed in the incantations of the adivasis on ceremonial occasions as an avenue for the interpretation of meanings that are subjectively held. Emotions understood as powerful expressions of experience provide some insight into the sub/unconscious that might be collectively experienced and retained as a residue from past historical contexts and oral transmission. They also signify what might subjectively be considered as salient to survival. There are two cycles that embrace the survival strategies of the adivasis and that feature prominently in the rituals and incantations of the male bhagats who preside over present-day rituals related to the human- nature relationship, the fertility of the lands, over illness and death; and of the female davleris, savasinis and midwives that preside at marriages and at child birth, the fertility of the male-female relationship. The agricultural cycle broadly corresponds to the public, economic sphere of hunting, food gathering and agricultural production for livelihood and tends to be presently dominated by the male bhagat, whereas the life cycle primarily covers the private, domestic sphere of the individual household and is presided over by female agents. However, there are significant overlaps between these two spheres as well regarding the roles of the major protagonists; for example, the bhagat being called upon at the time of illness at home because this might have to do with the evil spells of female bhutalis and for the veneration of the family/clan deities because this has to do with clan lineage. As a general analytical principle, it is important to recognize the significant role that is given to the male bhagat over the sacralization of the agricultural cycle and the propitiation of related deities. This may not have been the case during the years of hunting, food gathering and shifting cultivation preceding the nineteenth century when gender relations were more equitable. We shall pay special attention to these two cycles in an attempt to interpret the significance of the rituals in fostering cultural identity and in providing meaning to the lives of the adivasis.

1. Spirits, Deities and Their Human Mediators, Bhagats

The following is an attempt to integrate and place in some order the adivasi belief in a multiplicity of adivasi spirits and deities. This is based on our own fieldwork, interviews and observations and the scattered references to them within Enthoven (1922), Save (1945), K. and V. Nargolkar (1955) and Dalmia (1988). There is a need for this inferential ordering because of the at times contradictory statements. In addition, it provides some guidance to the reader for the analysis that follows.

Adivasi Deities

The Sequence of Ceremonial Occasions with Deities

Narayan Dev, god of rains celebrated at the time of the first paddy,

Kul Devs (Clan Deities): Jhotinga, Himai, Narayan, Hirva,

Gram Dev (Village Deity), Vagaya (Tiger), venerated after harvesting,

Ras Khali, Kansari Devi, celebrated after harvesting and before threshing,

Dhartari, earth deity,

Kansari, corn deity, Ihu bai: sister of Kansari,

Gavatari, cow deity,

Other Deities

Maha Deva and Ganga Gauri, original ancestors,

Isar = Shiva (according to Save) = Maha Dev,

Indra, deity of thunder/rains,

Naran Dev (deity of rains?) and Brahma Deva, Pandu given the kingdom of death,

Hiroba, Chitoba and Hirva,

Palaghata, female fertility deity, cross-legged position, symbolizing child birth and intercourse, marriage,

Panchasiriya, male deities, kept by Bhutalis,

Vira: Family/clan ancestor,

Cheda: Pada/hamlet ancestor,

Makar: Village deity, venerated at times of illness.

Pawas (rain) is considered Paramesar (Supreme Deity). The rain god is generally omitted from the death list in the ritual songs and is considered not to be controlled by human beings together with death. The sun and the moon are worshipped as the two eyes of the deity, the former being one who always reveals himself. The Warlis worship natural phenomena such as clouds, wind, lightning, the sea, storms; the four female deities that are considered to have real power during the kalyug are the earth (dhartari), cow (gavatri), corn (kansari) and woman (astari). "It is but natural that as a tiller of the soil, a Warli should have high respect for the Earth. It is the source and reservoir of all life, since trees and vegetables come out of it. A medium while invoking any spirit, first looks up to pay his respects to the Sun God and then bows down touching the earth with his hand as a salutation to it...Waghya is the lord of tigers and is chiefly the god of cowherds. He is supposed to protect the cattle grazing in the forest...Waghoba is worshipped either on the twelfth day of the second half of the month of Aswin or on the fifteenth day (Purnima) of Chaitra. The former day is known as Wagh-baras... The bhagats invoke Waghya in their varen (afflatus). It is also one of the spirits invoked in rawal, a training camp for bhagathood. The rawal is brought to a close on the Wagh-baras day" (Save 1945: 48, 49, 50). The trees that are venerated by the Warlis are the bel, considered as the residence of the first creatures and associated with Isar Dev (Shiva); pipal, considered as the residence of Barambha, a tribal spirit; umbar, also associated with Isar Dev and required at the time of marriage.

The principal Warli family deities (Kul Devs) are the following:

Naran Dev, a male family deity, is generally worshipped also by contiguous adivasis. The image of Naran Dev in the form a stone or an areca nut smeared with red lead is kept together with the main family deities in a basket in the house of the principal family of the clan. The deity is venerated in the month of Magh (February). It is believed that Naran Dev provides rain.

Hirva, a male deity, is another family god of the Warlis represented by a small silver piece covered with red lead. Pardhi (hunter) is considered as the lieutenant and the companion of Hirva, together with his seven naris (women) who are represented by areca nuts. At times an image of an ordinary human figure on a silver piece in a bunch of peacock feathers represents Hirva Dev given that there is a belief that Pardhi killed a peacock for his master. Hirva is venerated during or after the harvest season, and on special occasions when a family member falls ill. Hirva is considered as the deity of wealth and hence represented by silver. The following narrative relating to the tensions between Hirva Dev and Kansari, the goddess of grain, provided by Save and as reported to him by a bhagat, illustrates the material basis for the worship of deities who are closely connected with the struggle for livelihood. "A controversy was going on between the two as to who was the greater of the two. They started on a journey to see the world. During the journey, Hirva felt very thirsty, but had no means to fetch water from a well nearby. Kansari like a wise woman had taken a pot with a long string with her. Hirva admitted the greatness of Kansari and begged for the pot and string from her to draw water. Kansari thus proved greater of the two. It is because of this superiority of the corn that Hirva always seeks protection of the corn. There is no wealth without corn" (Save 1945: 60-61).

Himai, a female deity, is considered as the object of worship for women, in particular. The image of Himai is a waghol, a yellow pigment fallen from the mouth of a cow. Sometimes a brass image seated on a horse represents Himai. She is seen as the deity that oversees cows and cattle, as well as an earth goddess and one who supervises the grain, Kansari. The deity suggests a Dravidian origin according to Save.

The Warli conception of the divine is very flexible given that any strange object may be considered to have divine properties. Commenting on the marriage incantation among the Warlis, Save observes, "Narandev is a tribal god but never styled as Naran Barambha elsewhere. Perhaps Barambha may be the corruption of the Hindu Brahma. Himai is the tribal goddess and Vajrai is a local goddess in the Thane district in whose honour a big fair is held annually at Vajreswari" (Save 1945: 141). The Viras are the family ancestral deities placed in the fields. The main ancestor of the hamlet is represented by the Cheda. The Gram Dev is Vagaya, the tiger deity that protects the village. All three images have relations to ancestors and are made of roughly hewn stone or wood which stand erect at different locations.

Adivasi Deities and Their Possible Relation to the Brahmanical Trinity

Shiva = Isar Dev—Consort Ganga Gauri,

Brahma = Baramba—Consort Sarasvati,

Vishnu = Naran Dev—Consort Mahalaxmi.

The possible correspondence of this contemporary adivasi trinity with the Brahmanical trinity is noteworthy. Could this be the influence of the belief systems of ancient tribal communities that were primarily matriarchal in character and engaged in hunting and gathering in the forests on the invading pastoral, patriarchal communities of invaders with a distinct linguistic affiliation and that had recourse to a more advanced technology and military strength based on the use of horses, chariots and iron weapons and implements and were ready to take to settled agriculture in the cleared forests of the Gangetic plains and were open to incorporate tribals within a fourfold caste structure? This is discussed in greater detail in Chapter 3. Or is this phenomenon of similarities in belief the result of more contemporary adivasi-non-adivasi interactions? (See Chapters 5 and 6). It is quite possible that the divine trinity that is subliminally and very indirectly mentioned in contemporary adivasi incantations could represent a primitive archetype, deeply embedded in the collective unconscious, that has also quite independently influenced Brahmanical and Christian belief, and even secular epistemologies in the social sciences, given a common ancient tribal heritage. We thus have a fundamental principle of ontological being that in social science terms could be translated as structured existence within the material economy of wealth; the principle of becoming, of agency in process, of economic and social reproduction; and finally the aspect of seeking wisdom in truth (See Chapter 3, Section 2).

Dalmia records the incantation by the bhagat at the time of the death anniversary which strangely begins with the narration of the creation of life, suggesting a conception of the circularity of life and death. We cite only the initial part of this detailed narrative which indicates a strong parallel between the main adivasi deities and the Brahmanical trinity of the divine. We would suggest, based on D.P. Chattopadhyaya (1959/1978), that these similarities may be interpreted as pointing to an early historical absorption of tribal world views within an increasingly dominant Vedic Brahmanism, rather than the contemporary influence of caste Hinduism on the adivasis. "The original self-created couple are Mahadeva (Shiva) and Ganga Gauri. They created the universe. Mahadeva created many gods like Moon, Sun, God of Lightning, God of Thunder and God of Clouds. They were allotted different kingdoms. Once Mahadeva told Naranadeva (Vishnu) and Brahmadeva (Brahma) to tour around the universe and invite all the gods to his court. But no one was eager to come. Mahadeva on hearing this insult from the gods was angered and submerged the whole universe in water. He himself swam in the flood for 12 years. In the process he collected the *jiva* or spirits of many living beings. The Kingdoms of those Gods who had insulted and disobeyed him were, however, destroyed" (Dalmia 1988: 25; brackets suggesting a relation to the Brahmanical trinity are inserted). The entire narrative suggests a strong tribal world view as regards the order of things as a cycle of birth and death, creation and destruction. The tension between the feminine and the masculine principles is palpable throughout the incantation which may be interpreted as a historical carry over; oral record and recollection within the collective sub conscious through reiteration of the victory of an alien patriarchal, pastoral society over a matriarchal, tribal community that had already been engaged with early agriculture. Dalmia summarizes the narrative in an insightful manner: "The song conjures up images of the cosmic cycle of creation, destruction and re-creation. It begins with the creation of elemental gods like the Moon, the Sun, God of Clouds and others and goes on to destroy this world. Yet another aeonic cycle of time begins with the sowing of seeds, from which emerges the whole of creation beginning with vegetation and going onto humans and animals. With their natural instinct for ecology, however, the Warlis realize that there cannot be endless creation and death enters to lighten Mother Earth's burden. But Pandu's death is also the beginning of life as symbolized in the song by the bumble bee and its desire for blossoms. Thus begins another circle of creation and destruction reminding us of the grandiose structure of epic time.

"But once the death of Pandu is introduced, time becomes irreversible and irretrievable. Before that 'human beings were like snakes—the old skin used to disappear and the new skin used to come up.' Henceforth concrete or chronological time enters the consciousness of the Warlis, never to leave them. Within the constantly revolving cycle of infinite life and death the fact of individual death pierces a permanent wedge. That the event is of monumental significance can be judged by the elaborate death rites meticulously observed by them. If the death rites are similar to the marriage rites, it is because a wholly new, unknown journey now begins, both for the dead and the living partner which is both fertile and propitious. For the dead is now free to wander from place to place seeking new knowledge, allowing the living to do the same.

Interestingly enough, it is Pandu who is given the Kingdom of death. If *pandu* is taken to mean 'white' or 'fair; in Sanskrit (and Marathi) it could well stand for a superior, white race. Bearing in mind the depiction of Pandu as arrogant and self-absorbed, the induction does not seem far-fetched. Death then enters with the humiliation of the dark race of the Earth Mother by a superior, white race. It pursues the arrogant invader no matter how hard he flees, to avenge the invasion of the dark race. But the tribals too seem to have humiliated their Earth Mother, for death in pursuing Pandu, comes to stay with them forever.

The fact that Pandu is the first man to be visited by death is significant for it speaks of an elemental truth. Pandu does not respect life; therefore he has to die. In his self-absorption and arrogance, he humiliates the Earth Mother, the goddess of life and is in turn pursued by death for that is the basic principle of life" (Dalmia 1988: 30-31).

Evil Spirits

These are propitiated with view to turning away from their evil eye.

Barambha, a male spirit residing in the papal tree, considered fair in complexion.

Sanvari, a female spirit living in a big stone in the forest, who threatens the grain on the threshing floor.

Girha, a water spirit living on the bed of the river.

Cheda, the spirit of a male who dies with unfilled wishes during the lifetime.

Hedli, a woman who dies in advanced pregnancy and is cremated with an embryo.

The long training of the bhagat, raval, begins with the start of the rainy season and lasts for about four months with intervals.

The main raval begins on Dussehra, the tenth day of the first half of Aswin or later and is continued till Wagh-Baras, the twelfth day of the second, dark half of Aswin. It was reported that for special training the main bhagat takes the ones to be initiated to caves in select hill sides which are called Bhoi Ghar, the house of the Earth Deity. The bhagats generally specialize in particular ritualistic incantations. For example, Dhak bhagats officiate at the time of death and marriages; Utare bhagats perform at the time of the Gav Dev, Vaghdev, the tiger god; Ghangli bhagats are well versed in the rituals in honour of Kansari Devi, the deity of grain during the Khali household post-harvest celebration.

The Warlis observe the festivals of Shimga (Holi), and Diwali the 14th day of the second half of Aswin, which are connected with the vernal and autumnal equinoxes, respectively. The Warlis follow the Hindu lunar calendar for these festivals which are considered as auspicious days and are also maintained by caste Hindus. Save summarizes the objects of veneration for the Warlis, based on his observations in the 1930s, which we also had an opportunity of observing in the 1980s and after in a relatively unchanged manner, as follows: "As a tiller of the soil, a Warli has the greatest reverence for the earth. He pays equal respect to corn, the product of the soil and to the cow which gives him bullocks to cultivate the soil. Corn is associated with wealth and Hirva is regarded as the god of wealth, because he always seeks protection of corn. Nay, Hirva is even inferior to the goddess of corn. The Sun is god to them, since he 'shows himself' every day. Rain is god because he grows corn. Naran dev is their greatest god as he is the giver of rain. Rain, corn and cattle are the three greatest necessities of these people; and Warlis have three deities presiding over them. Naran gives rain, Hirva is associated with corn and Waghoba protects cattle. Their life is thus identified with their gods" (Save 1945: 80). Most of the Warli deities have been and continue to be venerated by other adivasi groups as well as by lower caste Hindus, which suggests a strong continuity as well as a syncretism of beliefs among them.

A secondary source, *Jungle Che Raje* (Nargolkar, 1955), and our own observations suggest that there are several Deities/spirits venerated by the adivasis. These sacred manifestations represent the mutual influence of a hunter, gatherer, earlier forest dweller adivasi society and a caste Hindu society of settled agriculturists and migrants to the region from other communities especially during the nineteenth century. The former are primarily animists and their deities are a manifestation of the divinification of nature and the flora and fauna of their natural habitat, whereas the latter objects of worship are an attempt at the hominification of the divine and the divinification of major historical humans that have achieved mythical proportions through narratives over time. The adivasi deities may be seen as ways of coming to terms with a very insecure agricultural cycle in a sharply changing social and natural environment and as emerging from the existential experience of the life cycle with the need to ensure the continuity of the clan and the tribe through rituals of fertility.

Vagaya (the tiger deity) may be considered as the principal deity of the Warlis, closely related to the agricultural cycle since it is venerated after harvesting and before threshing operations around the time of the household Khali festival. Savri Dev or Mavlya, associated with the Dagli musical instrument, is also venerated for good crops. The spirit Ran Bhut may be encountered in the jungles and in isolated places. Faltani Cheda and Gupit Cheda are warrior deities that ensure the protection of the tribe and could possibly have some relation to generational history and lineage. Bahram Dev is venerated by the adivasis as the brother of Mahalaxmi Devi and may be seen as one of the most significant aspects of the adivasi non-adivasi interactions, as will be described separately.

Every clan has a Kul Dev and the Kul Dev of the Vartha clan in Kulambi village, for example, is placed at the police Patil's house who is a Vartha. The Kul Dev is significant in terms of an iconic indicator of clan lineage and generational history. One might view this ritualistic practice in a manner closely connected with ancestor worship (Pitra Baras) and acknowledgement and veneration especially of the dead heads of households (Divas Pani). There are two major sub groups among the Warlis: the Dawars are towards the north of the present Palghar district and the Neeri towards the south. According to one of our adivasi informants, the different households within a clan, say bearing the name of Vartha, were one and had a common Kul Dev. With the increase in population and with the coming of the British and the non-adivasi outsiders the clans broke up; so that today the households within a clan, especially in different villages, might have different Kul Devs that are of different shapes and forms. Hirva, Joting and Chita are family/clan deities invoked at the time of marriage given that they are viewed as contributing to fertility and the continuity of the race. Images are made with sindur (vermillion powder) and are kept in a basket covered with a red kerchief (sarposh). Himay and Jada Dev are also family deities that are held in reverence for their capacity to ensure the fertility and abundance of the crops. They are represented by the damru, musical instrument. Vir and Supli are deities in honour of the ancestors, the former representing the male and the latter the female.

2. The Life Cycle

Birth, the Varsa Ceremony

A midwife who is an elderly woman from the same tribe is generally called for deliveries. The umbilical cord is cut by a sharp chip of the boru tree. The midwife officiates at the Sat ceremony which is observed on the fifth or the sixth day in honour of the controlling deity of the child. In the Dev ceremony, the child receives a name from the bhagat who takes an afflatus after he receives rice that has been waived by a male relative around the child. A male child is generally named after the paternal grandfather and the female after the paternal grandmother. The Warlis believe that ancestors are reborn in the same family (Save 1945: 117). The two Sairins (midwives) who were in attendance at the birth are the ones who perform the rituals on the day of the Varsa ceremony. The bhagat is also invited. Kulambi village has at least one Sairin in each hamlet. On April 28, 1977 at about 8.30 pm we went with Ramji Vartha to attend the Varsa ceremony of Devaji Dadodha's sister's daughter, a clan member. She stays in Devaji's house with her mother. We found the men seated outside and about 50 women old and young seated along the walls inside the hut. The Sairins occupied a prominent place. They were two old, emaciated, wrinkled women, dressed in red with heavy bangles. The child was cradled in a piece of white cloth tied at its two ends from bamboo sticks stuck in the ground. Bombils (a dried fish) and some rice and a few notes and coins were below the child. In a corner there was some rice with sindhur marking on it. We sat outside together with the men. Servers went around serving boiled gram, pieces of chicken and toddy. Devaji told me that the next day the mother would go to the well in the morning, place the bombils against it, mark them with sindhur and leave. The water is expected to carry away the bombils. We were introduced to a famous adivasi bhagat from Varvadha village. He narrated how he cured a Pakistani and his wife and he were invited to Pakistan as a result.

Puberty

Puberty is considered as an auspicious occasion and called Padar Yene given that the girl used to place the ends of her sari over the breast and the left shoulder after puberty in the past. The first menstruation is called Palav Yene, getting new foliage. Puberty is considered as a sign of fertility and if it is attained when the grain is being threshed it is considered as an auspicious sign for rich crop. However, this view is not held by all Warlis and a contrary one may be found in the Warlis towards the forested areas in the east (Save 1945: 113).

Marriage

Marriages are generally held in the months of Magh (February) and Phalgun (March).The marriage ceremony starts with a few men going to the bride's place with sheaths of grain which have to be husked by the bride and the bridegroom after the marriage ceremony is over. Together with this corn which is called ghan, the bridegroom's party has also to take the dej which consists of about 12 faris of paddy and two seers of wal (a bean), about ten gallons of toddy, a bottle of liquor, a bundle of tobacco leaves and Rs 15. The dej is offered to the bride's father to help meet the marriage expenses. Apart from this there are other expenses by way of cash to the bride's mother and to the adivasis of the hamlet. Marriages may be performed at any time during the year except during the rainy season, the months of December and January and a day falling on Amavasya (the last day of the Hindu month) (Save 1945: 85).

The Palaghata is a female deity drawn at the time of marriage with rice flour on the inner wall of the hut within a square, a Chauk, made up of four parallel lines on each side, by generally young married women, the Savasinis. Palghata is represented in a cross-legged position, a symbol of sexual and agricultural fertility. The limbs of Palghata are represented by harrows, perhaps signifying the use of this implement for cultivation by the Warlis in their earlier shifting cultivation in the forests and once used in the Indus Valley Civilization; an interpretation provided by Dalmia (1988: 147) based on Kosambi (1975: 68). A smaller square called the Deva Chauk is drawn and contains the five-headed male deity Panchshirya, the guardian of Palghata, who looks after the welfare of the family. Like a number of realities that have a dual character in the lives of the adivasis, an image of Panchshirya as a source of power is believed is kept by witches, the bhutalis, who can cast an evil spell on others. The image of Palghata has a parallel with the 'pal-ghata' or 'punna ghata' representation of a water pot overflowing with plants, symbolizing agricultural fecundity and human fertility represented by the womb. The round-bottomed pot is also used for containing water, toddy and for cooking rice (Dalmia 1988: 180). We have, in addition, observed this type of pot being used at the time of the ritual for the Khali harvest festival. The central features of the painting are embellished by drawings of animals, humans and trees. Dalmia describes the process of painting the marriage Chauk in great detail since she considers it the primary illustration to interpret traditional Warli painting. She concludes her description with the following observation, "It was interesting that the act of painting itself was always seen as 'writing' (*cauk lihane*) for it was the primary means of expression for the artists. The visual forms and sometimes non-forms were the only means that the artists had for mirroring their own well of experience, knowledge and emotions, as well as that of the community. Just like the artists everywhere else, however, we found it difficult to talk to them, to make them put into words what they felt while painting....If the *savasinis* did the actual work of painting, their counterpart were the *dhavleris* who animated the painting with life, by their singing. It was also their songs which brought the marriage couple together. Not anyone could be a *dhavleri* but only those who had 'dreams'....When asked what their art signified the *savasinis* always pointed to the process which they employed while painting. It became clear that art and in fact their own identity is seen by them as a process rather than as something conclusive. It is the very act of creating which is important rather than the completed work. For into the making of it goes the entire world of experience striving for coherency. Once finished, the painting is animated, capable of magical powers, fully potent. The painting serves a ritual purpose: that of enabling a marriage to take place. But marriage, for them, takes place not merely in the ordinary sense: it implies the union of the entire cosmos. In a way, then, it is their own world of experience which on acquiring an order, is considered the potent force of life" (Dalmia 1988: 136, 140, 142, 143). A regional trend in the qualitative content of the paintings was observed; from more traditional forms in the north of the district among the Davar Warlis moving to the south among the Nihir Warlis where stylized decorative designs and the decreasing significance of Palghata may be found, influenced by caste Hindu society and the urbanization of the Greater Mumbai Metropolitan region; as well as from the west of the district towards the east impacted by other sanskritized adivasi communities such as the Malhar Kolis and the closeness to the caste Hindu areas of Jawahar taluka and Nashik district. Brahmin priests presiding at weddings replacing the Dhavleris is a corresponding phenomenon. Dalmia raises the question of the relation between artistic expression in consciousness and its relation to material culture within the agricultural economy. Her tentative conclusion is, "A question that arises is: can the process of a developed self-conscious be deciphered in greater material development? And why has this led to a depletion of artistic values in the east? In the paintings we find evidence of an increasing self –consciousness as we reach areas where there is greater material development. From this it can be concluded that as the Warlis learn to harness the energies of nature and thereby become more self-reliant, they also attain a greater sense of their own identity by becoming more self-conscious. Progressively towards the east, however, this identity is subsumed to that of the caste Hindus. While this seems to result in more efficient material development it has also led to an alienation and neglect of their own culture illustrated by the poor quality of the paintings" (Dalmia 1988: 176).

Approaches to Illness

Illness, whether that of the individual in the family or collective when it affects large sections of the adivasis in the village or on a wider scale covering the region in the form of a mini epidemic, is met with fear as an intimation of mortality. It calls for the propitiation of the spirits and explanation by the bhagat; and in the latter cases of wider coverage of the illness it serves as an expression of collective solidarity in the face of calamity. The bhagat addresses the issue by way of a ritual accompanied by incantations, and/or prescribing herbal medicines or failing which attributing the cause of the illness to evil spirits in the form of the spell of the bhutali (witch). Illness is attempted to be cured by the bhagat by a process of divination. Rice grains are waved over the sick person and taken to the bhagat who then decides whether the illness is due to internal or external causes. If the former, he prescribes some herbal medicines. If the latter, then it is attributed to the evil eye, at times that of a bhutali, and the bhagat has to perform a counter ritual of utarne (removing) (Save 1945: 245).

Near the Patilpada school in Kulambi village, Talasari taluka, on either side of the path leading out of the pada (hamlet), there are poles tapering at the top. It is in honour of Makhar Dev. The poles are coloured red with geru (a paste) and have little lamps on them and an image of Makhar Dev. Puja (ritualistic worship) is done at the time of illness. On March 16, 1977, during one of the spells of our fieldwork there was a havan (sacrificial offering) with a jagran (staying awake all night) because govra (small pox) illness had spread among the villagers. Five children had died. About 200 children in the village had been affected by the illness. The villagers gather in the evening in front of the poles. Each family brings along a little rice. This rice is ground into flour and a statue of Makhar Dev is made. The bhagat performs the havan and the rites. The people sing religious songs all night. In the morning the rice flour idol is thrown outside the limits of the village symbolizing the freeing of the village from the illness. We were told that Makhar Dev is invoked for Govra illness, in particular, as well as any other illness.

A doctor is generally consulted in addition, except in the case of Govra and Devi illness. It is only then that Makhar Dev is invoked. Illness, apart from death, is a sad occasion in the life cycle and the spirits are propitiated at these times. Collective contributions, community participation and propitiation of the deity mark these moments of village level apprehension and grief.

We were told during the field visit in 1977 that though the belief in bhutali had receded, evil spirits (bhuts) were still feared. There is a tradition that women should not serve food to strangers or guests or even water for fear of transmitting evil spirits. Bhuts may be present only in women. In a house under construction when the wooden beams that support the roof are put up then a white cloth is tied around it to ward off the evil spirits. The cloth contains a coconut, coins and rice. It is kept there till the day of the puja. Relatives are called, a chicken is cut and food is given. The mistry (carpenter) performs the puja and takes away the cloth. No cooking fire is lit in the house till the day of the puja. When we were staying at an adivasi's new house the puja had not yet been done, so all the cooking was done outside the house. This custom is to ensure the longevity of the house.

Bhagat for Bhutali, Illness at Mohankar's House, Kulambi Village, October 1979

The bhagat is generally called during Deevas Pane Karne at the time of illness and is done generally for internal illnesses. Allopathic doctors in the region, we were informed, generally advise adivasis to go to the bhagat first. The bhagat Mohankar talking about the role of the bhagat in various rituals, says,

> All the people of Pada come at the time of Khali. We've not seen God, but we say the words of gods. We learn from bhagat gurus; others learn from dreams. We do not know what gods appear in dreams. If we don't bring the bhagats and do the rituals of Khali then there will not be enough grains. This has come down to us from generations. If we don't do this, even though the crops look good, then there will not be enough grains at the time of malni (threshing); one will get half of what one expects. The grains grow even on the Khali threshing floor. There is a brief ceremony, when people fall ill. The grains get burnt and we have to protect the

crop against fire. The gangli (musical instrument) is played by the main bhagat. One sits in front and gets possessed as a result of the recitation. 'Let there be a good crop, I beg you'. He puts rice in the hands of the young one, sitting in front and to all the family. There is a ceremony prior to moving the plough. The farmer puts sindhur to the plough, bulls, to himself and makes promises. Leaves of the kunbi tree are tied to the plough. From the time of ploughing to Khali the head of the family cannot eat coconuts, sugarcane, muli, kothmir, aal, lasoon. Before kapni (harvesting), some people cut a kombdi (chicken).

The following is the recitation to remove the bhut (evil spirit) at the time of illness:

> The Devi went for a bath, had a bath, changed her clothes, and dressed up. The big god saw her. She had her meals and went ahead. The gods ate, went up and came down. All the gods are awakened. If there is a curse of the bhutali (the female who casts an evil spell) on the body that has been buried or on the body that has been burnt, then I will remove it. If there are any curses from the bhuts in the forts of the rajas (the old gods who were kings), then I'll remove them. The Dev Bhagat has released the Randi (the bhutali) from the stone and she goes to the sea. And she is drowned in the sea.

According to Mohankar, the Devs (deities) can do evil if the sacrifice is not made to them. They are stronger than the bhuts (evil spirits) and live in the hills. The bhakti (devotion) that the bhagats get with the grace of God cannot just be given to others. All cannot learn the bhagat practices. The possession and shaking is not put on. It is an expression of the Dev. The bhutali cannot bear to see the greatness of others, so she casts a spell of the evil spirit. He states:

> If someone amongst us goes ahead then the bhutali does not understand it. She feels that all must move together. She will not allow anyone to go ahead of the others. That is why she puts a bhut. If someone puts up a big house, has good fields, the children are fine and go to school and get educated, then they don't like it. All must be as we are in one house, they feel. Men cannot be bhutali. Only women do this; others don't know who the bhutali is. Even the Dev does not know who is the

> bhutali. Only women can learn about bhutali. We don't know from whom they learn.
>
> Mohankar claims that he cured a cow of a broken leg when the vet had failed. The bhagat gets toddy, liquor, handmade bread in return for his services and sometimes money. The kamla illness which causes red eyes and red urine is caused by the bhut and can only be cured by the bhagat.

In response to our questions, Mohankar continues to explain his understanding of the role of bhutalis.

> Men cannot become bhutalis. Bhutalis learn how to send bhut. The men who learn bhakti (devotional practices), become bhagats. The women who learn bhut, become bhutalis. Woman can get possessed at temples like Mahalaxmi. Women cannot do Kul Dev, Khali work. They cannot become bhagats. They can do only what is in their capacity. People do not as yet understand that everyone must live in peace. The women are less educated. The Anvir village incident happened in about 1970. The bhagats make these rice flour images when there is bhut and throw them in the river. If anybody says or does some harm to a woman then the woman might say, 'I have drunk toddy and daru. You wait and see what will happen to you'. Then certainly something will happen to that person his wife or his children.

An incident that took place some years ago had caught the attention of the adivasis and the public at large. According to Mohankar,

> There was much unhappiness in Anvir village. People, especially the young, used to fall ill. The people went to a good bhagat with rice, etc. The bhagat gave the names of the bhutalis. You must do something. If you can't, I will do something, he said. All the women of the village Pada were called. People decided to beat up the two bhutalis. They were beaten so badly that they died. The bhutalis would deny that they were bhutalis. But people persisted. People intended to put them to death. They placed them in a bullock cart and buried them in the jungle in one hole. The brother of the bhutalis got upset. Their husbands had already died. The brothers complained to the Patil. The bhagat was called. 'The government is not dead. The government is still alive. Let's make a search', said the Patil. The complaint reached the Police

DSP. People were beaten and acknowledged the murder. The women were dug up. They were taken in a cart to Talasari. The people got sentences for three years. Some of them were of the Lal Bavta (the red flaf of the Kisan Sabha); they are now released". Mohankar approves of the murders and believes in bhutalis.

Apart from indicating the ambivalent status of women in Warli society, the practice of naming a bhutali which has been considerably reduced was generally done for old and destitute women who could possibly have staked a claim to inheritance. The interpretation of envy and jealousy towards those who have experienced economic advancement is, in a negative sense, a sign of adivasi solidarity where the general expectation is opposed to individual competition and individualistic economic enhancement, especially at the cost of the rest of the community, and where progress is viewed as a collective enterprise. This is especially true in this village where a few middle peasants, thanks to their political connections, had acquired lands and had begun to engage in economic enterprises such as acting as labour contractors and taking toddy trees and grasslands on rent from poorer adivasis.

Bhagat Barga, March 13, 1980, Removal of Bhut Ceremony

A bhagat, according to Barga, might also know 'jungli dawa' (herbal medicine). A bhagat when ill goes to another bhagat. Barga knows 'jungli dawa'. We observed the cure for a hand swelling of Arvind's mother and also of Devaji's wife who suffered from red eyes at Garud Pada. Eight rice flour images are made and the bhagat gets possessed accompanied by chanting and the beating of the leaves of the umbar tree. He says 'choo' and throws the leaves into the river.

When the patient was asked to whom she attributed the cure, given that she had been to both the doctor in the dispensary and to the bhagat, she says to both. Arvind's mother's swelling of hand continued for three days after this ceremony. The fourth day she went to the Talasari dispensary and came back with a bandaged hand. She applied the doctor's medicines for two days. The swelling went down and then she applied jungle medicine for another two days. The swelling by then had almost subsided. Rahya bhagat had been suffering from lack of appetite, weakness and fever for about a month. He had gone to a bhagat when I met him but to no avail.

A week later, I met him. He had taken injections and tablets from the malaria doctor and was up and preparing baskets for fishing. He said he was fine and attributed his cure to the malaria doctor. He appeared not to see the contradictions of his faith in his bhagat profession and taking the assistance of 'scientific' medical practice. The adivasis in general appear to see no contradictions in this overtly schizophrenetic existence.

Bhagat Vartha, Police Patil, Khadi Pahane, Kulambi Village, March 14, 1980

The diagrams that are shown below are made with moistened rice flour and grains of rice. The explanations of the items in the diagrams as provided by the bhagat are given below.

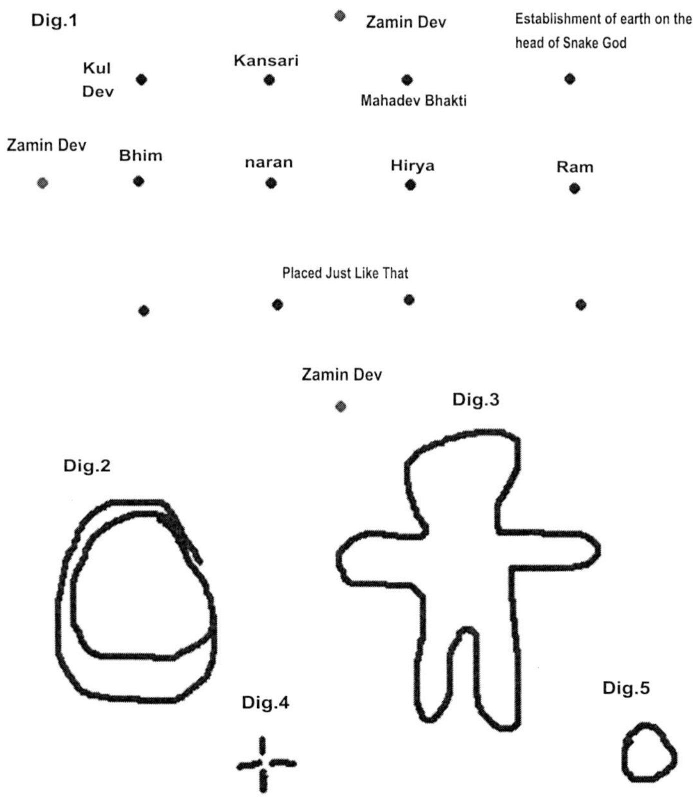

Zamin Dev: At the three corners of the **Dig. 1,** piles of grain are placed. This represents the poles of the earth. The **Dig. 3** represents the sick person; in this case a child.

The bhagat takes grains from the **Dig. 2** pile and puts them into the **Dig. 4** pile. Sometimes the grains are pushed forward to the **Dig. 1** piles, sometimes to the **Dig. 5** pile.

Dig. 5 below **Dig. 3** is formed from the collection of grains from each of the other piles. The remaining grains are pushed together and with some other grains the following design is formed:

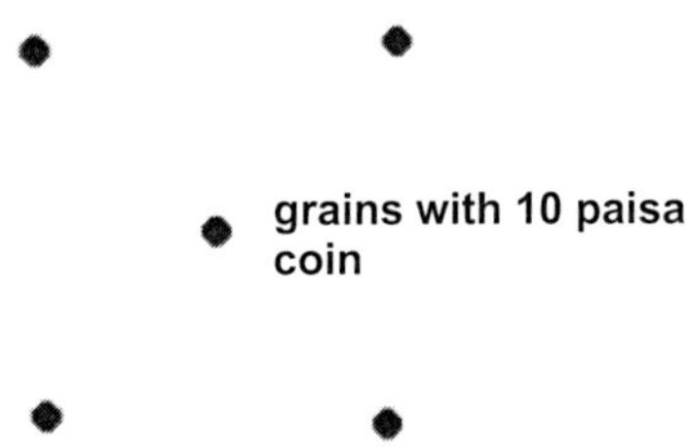

The bhagat recites with grains collected in hand over the new formation. Grains in hand are tied with a cloth. The cloth with grains is then tied to the left hand of the sick person till he gets well. After the person gets well the 'pahne' are done. The foregoing ritual could well be the result of a transformed Tantric practice over time with some Brahmanical additions (see Chapter 3).

Bhagat Vartha, Police Patil, Stages of Learning of the Bhagat Practices

The following stages are not necessarily sequential.

Visari:	Snake poisoning, 3 Kandi, i.e. 3 stages	
Mothi:	Pain in stomach, 3 Kandi	
Khadi Pahne:	Seeing in rice at the time of illness/misfortune, 2 Kandi	
Gav Dev:	Awakening (zagran) Kamai Karne Motra Takne	3 Kandi

Kul Dev:	Zagta Karne (Awakening)	Kandis are the number of incantations
	Khasoba Dev – Keeper of house	
	Hiroba Dev – Peacock feathers	
	Zoting Porvari Dev – Peacock feathers	
	Valo Dev – Image	
	Chita Dev – Image of tiger	
	Baman Dev – Gods of Brahmins	
	14 Sisters of Khasoba Dev – Image	
	Godni Dev – Image of wood	
	Pardi Dev – Hunting God	
	Image of gun. Prayed to before a hunt.	
Khali:	1 Kandi	
Lagna:	Wedding. Kandis are according to number of Kul Devs	

Regarding the payment for teaching-learning, bhagat Vartha says,

> "The bhagat to be, goes to another senior bhagat and gives him daru (liquor) or toddy for each kandi (stanza) learnt. He may also give him a kombdi (chicken). Cash payment consists of Rs. 10-15, as asked for. They go away from the village to some quiet place to learn. Learning all the kandis of the various rituals lasts for about four months". "If the bhut is adani (uneducated), the situation does not improve in spite one doing bhagat work", according to Nathu Bhimsa, a bhagat. According to Vartha, "Even if one goes to a doctor, one has to do bhut first just in case the problem is of the bhut; if not it gets worse."

Death

The Warlis perform the ritual of Divas during the death anniversary of the dead to settle the restless spirit. They generally cremate the dead, but if a person dies of a contagious disease the body is buried. Burial is generally carried out during the day time with the sun as witness. As part of the observance of the anniversary for the dead, human blood is offered as a result of a small cut on the back of the head carried out by a clan member. The blood of a cock or goat is not offered on this occasion considering that human blood is considered as the greatest offering and perhaps suggesting that the tribe at sometime in the past practised human sacrifice (Save 1945: 134). Kosambi suggests that while human sacrifice had been rejected by Hindu practice by about the sixth century BC, it persists in various forms among adivasi society even to the present indicating a living prehistory (2009 a: 44).

The circularity of the life cycle may be seen from the following death incantation:

> The soul has no death; only the body dies (Jivata maran nahi, kay komate). This body (chest) is the home of life (soul). As a fruit is plucked from the tree, so is life plucked from the body. This soul gives up its outer form like a snake giving up its outer skin. Death is inevitable. God giveth and He taketh. (Paramesar detu na toch netu). A man should neither fear nor hate death. This circle of life and death is eternally going on. The body is like a lac-dye melting away by fire. It is like a full-moon setting all of a sudden and like a plantain stalk breaking in the middle. An earthen pot can last at least a few days, but none can predict how long the body can live (Save 1945: 137-138).

Nature and other tribal deities are considered exempted from death as they are considered responsible for keeping the cycle of human existence in motion.

It is possible that ancestor worship and more so the possibility of reincarnation, according to Chattopadhyaya (1978), was not intrinsic to ancient tribal materialist belief. It appears to have been the influence of Brahmanical rituals propitiating the spirit of the dead; Pitra Baras and the Shradha ceremony, respectively. Surely the conception of Karma, a retribution for past actions through reincarnation in various earthly forms, is not held by the adivasis as part of their materialist world view, though a spirit existence in the afterlife is recognized. Ancestor veneration, on the other hand and what might correspond directly to adivasi practice, might be seen as a way of recognizing and asserting lineage; an important principle in the adivasi belief system. It might also be interpreted as a way of establishing territoriality—the land of the forefathers, the land where the ancestors were buried—in the context of the introduction of private property rights by the state and the outsider and given the illiteracy of the adivasis and their lack of familiarity with scripted contracts. Wooden markers of the dead, the Viras, on the boundaries of one's land perhaps served this purpose and acted as a protection against possible encroachments on land for cultivation.

The Practice of Bhutali

Nathan illustrates the gradual encroachments of patriarchy within the adivasi society of the Santhals in relation to the practice of witch hunting and the identification of bhutalis. This has special relevance to the situation of Warlis in Palghar district. "Witch-hunting then was the form of the internal (class) struggle through which the shared authority of women and men in the swidden-cum-gathering economy was sought to be changed into the sole authority of men in plough agriculture with patrilineal descent. Witch-hunting is a form of what Engels called 'the first class struggle'...The destruction of widows' life interest in lands is then the immediate economic objective of the struggle reflected in witch hunting" (Nathan 1977: 255, 256. See also Nathan, D. and others 1998).

Only when sufficient attention is paid to the linkages of deprivations and neglect with witch-hunting, will the practice cease to be 'othered' as barbaric, and seen as an outcome of marginalization and institutional failures, according to Mehra and Agarwal (2016). Our observations and discussions with contemporary bhagats in Palghar district suggest that instances of identifying a particular bhutali, which is rare, might have more to do with 'reciprocal violence', violence against women where there is a perceived cause such as a family feud or for want of a better explanation for illness, rather than a matter of a more generalized 'gratuitous violence', violence that is arbitrary and apparently without cause, as discussed by Skaria with respect to the Bhils in South Gujarat during the nineteenth century. What appears more appropriate is the interpretation that, "In the *adivasi* societies of western India, the image of women as *dakans* (the bhutalis of Palghar district) was simultaneously an acknowledgement of their power and a reflection on the fundamental illegitimacy of that power" (1997: 132, bracket added). Our field observations and the interactions with bhagats mentioned in this section suggest an ambivalent status of women in Warli society. Some of these contradictory positions are as follows. One might note that bhuts can be given only by women, i.e. the bhutali. Men just can't, men can become bhagats. The bhut removal recitations by bhagats reveal a fear and awe of the sexual powers of women. Women can, however, receive bhuts and fall ill. It is considered inauspicious for the guest to be served cooked food by the woman of the house for fear of the bhut given by the bhutali. However, women generally participate in toddy drinking together with men on ceremonial occasions and during daily life. They go to toddy pattas (the local community bars) and drink. A bride price is given at the time of marriage, divorce is permissible with community approval and retribution and there is a well balanced sex ratio. On the other hand, women generally receive lower wages for the same work as men. They are not permitted to participate in the Gav Dev ritual in honour of Vagaya which is the main communal agricultural ceremony after harvesting. The Cheda Dev ritual is done only for males and heads of families. Women carry the primary burden of housework and child rearing. The foregoing contradictory status of women within the Warli community might be attributed to historical changes in the social relations of production and to the varying interface with non-adivasi society.

The Use of Alcohol in Rituals and Daily Life

Alcohol has traditionally held deep significance in the life of the adivasis. It has a meaning of establishing community bonds and solidarities related to class and ethnicity. It has been observed that the act of drinking together signifies a community of equals and the establishment of bonds of friendship in everyday life and on ritual occasions. Goshti karne is understood as to engage in easy conversation and gossip related to events in the village, planning work, exchanging notes on prices, produce, on the behaviour of government officials and even teasing each other. This is generally indulged in at the village bonga; a depot on a hillock which puts up a white flag when toddy is available. Drinking alcohol, generally toddy or sometimes distilled liquor from jaggery, has an entertainment value perhaps the main one for an adivasi. Payment for labour can also be partly be made through the exchange of alcohol, especially if it is within the adivasi community. Alcohol also has significant ritualistic significance, with almost all religious practices being accompanied by the use of alcohol.

However, alcohol also has an oppressive character. A major reason for indebtedness is addiction to alcohol apart from domestic expenses for grains at times of scarcity and marriages. It has presently taken on an impoverishing character, as one adivasi said,

> It is true that most adivasis are addicted. Money in one's pocket does not stay in the pocket. We spend on toddy, daru, then no work the next day. The Seth Savkars (landlords, moneylenders) used to bring Bhandaris from Nargol and Maroli to take out toddy. Adivasis used to purchase and drink toddy from the Seths. Earlier the adivasis used to drink mahua (alcohol distilled from flowers). Now there are very few mahua trees. We can stay without food the whole day only if we get toddy.

It also takes on a dimension of escapism from the drudgery of everyday labour. According to Roopji, an elderly adivasi with whom we interacted in March 1980,

> It was the Seth Savkar who introduced the habit of daru and toddy to the adivasis. Before the Savkars, the adivasis would steal 'mahua' from the forests and prepare its drink. With the coming of the Seths the forests were destroyed; the Bhandaris from Gujarat came in and started taking toddy from the trees and the Seths opened up daru shops. During prohibition we fought for the right to drink toddy. Toddy gives us nourishment; we can do without food if there is none and spend the whole day only on toddy.

Hardiman (1987, especially Chapter 7) provides a comprehensive picture of the role of alcohol in the lives of the adivasis in South Gujarat during the nineteenth and early twentieth centuries, which broadly corresponds to our area of research in north Maharashtra, based on primary, secondary and archival sources. Munshi, Saldanha (1995) and Hardiman (1985) draw attention to the devastating effects that the British Bombay Akbari Act of 1878 and the Mhowra Act of 1892 had on the lives of the adivasis; the former restricting the natural resource of toddy, the fermented sap of the date palm, and the latter banning the use of the flowers for fermentation. While there was an increase in revenue for the British government and indebtedness and land alienation to the outsider trader in alcohol, there was no significant reduction in alcoholism.

3. The Annual Agricultural Cycle

3.1 Ather, a Form of Mutual Self-Help

The adivasis, especially the poor peasants and the middle peasants, can get help from other villagers in their cultivating activities, i.e. harvesting, carting rice stalks from the fields to the khali (threshing floor), etc. when they are in need of labour and there is shortage of family labour. This help is given mainly to village leaders and the more affluent adivasis for the following reported reasons: they have larger fields, are in greater need of labour and they command respect and people are ready to help them. The payment made consists in serving toddy to all the labourers. According to Ramji, this is a big 'saving' for those who are assisted in this way. The cost of toddy comes to Rs. 50 and the wages would have come to Rs 150. The villagers, especially the agricultural labourers, give this service only when there is no other work and they are free from their own work. The help lasts a couple of days. During our fieldwork in December 1979, we saw an ather being done for harvesting by about 15 labourers for the Sarpanch (village head) and for the deputy village head and leader of the local CPIM, for cutting the paddy from their fields and carrying the stalks to the Khali, involving about five labourers. The practice of mutual self-help serves as an expression of strong community bonds and is an old tradition among the adivasis not related to the CPIM influence.

3.2 Gav Dev, Kulambi Village

Somewhat beyond the poles in honour of Makhar Dev, on the side of the road on a raised stretch of land is the place for the Gav Dev (the village deity). The Gav Dev is represented by Vagaya (tiger). The place is fenced off on one side by cactus plants with an entrance and is dotted with trees which may not be cut. This place is also maintained as the sacred grove by the adivasis. Beyond the location of the Gav Dev on the other slope of the hillock is the place used for the burning of dead bodies and the place for the burial of the dead during the rains. If a person is buried during the rains then later on a rice flour figure is burnt instead after the rains. We took off our slippers at the entrance at the request of the accompanying adivasi and proceeded to a spot which had a spherical stone pointed at the top jutting out of the ground. The place was walled in by single bricks and bore the marks of oil lamps. At a distance from the spot was a carved stone block resting on the side of a tree. According to the adivasi, the villagers believe that the spherical stone spontaneously emerged from the ground and displaced the carved stone to where it lay. There is also a stone standing in honour of Makhar Dev. There is a belief that should a passerby rest at the place at night, or a drunken person fall by it, a tiger sits by the side of the person and protects him during the night.

The collective celebration of Gav Dev and the individual household ritual of Khali on the threshing floor that are held during harvesting and before threshing are important markers during the annual agricultural cycle. These two occasions bring out the entire range of sentiments of the adivasis as associated with grain, food security, climatic and social insecurity and livelihood. Once a year, after harvesting at the time of Khali the villagers gather at the place of the Gav Dev, on the day of Vagh Baras in the second fortnight of the month of Kartik (November), offer a cock and goats through the bhagat, recite songs and have a communal meal for which there is a collection of Rs. 2.

On December 1 and 2, 1979 we had an opportunity to participate in the Gav Dev rituals. The ceremonies begin with the veneration of the Kul Dev of the Vartha family. The Varthas and the Dhombres were the earliest residents of Patil Pada, Kulambi village, and are considered as the founding fathers of the village and the leading clans. On the 1st after the ceremony for the Kul Dev the bhagats with Rahya as leader sit at the Gav Dev place around 8 pm and perform the incantations accompanied by the dhank musical instrument.

The incantations begin with the story of *Brahman Dev and the Bhil People's Song*. On the night of the first day, on December 1, 1979, a narrative is recited which suggests the influence of non adivasi, Brahmanical society. The song also suggests the possible geographical and historical origins of the Warlis since the song is considered to be that of the Bhil adivasi community who are concentrated to the north east of the present Palghar district in Dhule and Nandurbar districts and in South Gujarat.

> In the beginning there was the Cow. The Brahmin had gone to beg in the village. He was then cooking his meal. A Bagla bird sat on the tree. It shat on the Brahmin's food. The next day the Brahmin began cooking again, climbed the tree, caught the Bagla bird, ate his food and began to continue his begging rounds.
>
> The Bagla appealed to the keeper (shepherd) of the cows. The shepherd tells the Brahmin to take with him a 12-year-old bullock or a 12-year-old cow. The Brahmin leaves the bird and takes the cow from the shepherd and goes to his home. He ties the cow.
>
> The next day the Brahmin goes to beg. The cow eats the rice that the Brahmin's wife had been pounding, while she went to get water. One day the Brahmin's wife hides and knocks off the top teeth of the cow (even today the cow is without top teeth). The Brahmin's wife tells the Brahmin to take away the cow. The Brahmin takes the cow to the jungle with some of his things. The Brahmin leaves the cow in the jungle. A tiger arrives and says that it will eat the cow. The cow appeals to the Brahmin's things which are left there. The tiger throws away all these things. The cow finally tells the tiger that they can live peacefully together. Both get pregnant and deliver.
>
> One day they find kakdi (a vegetable) and decide to share it without giving it to their children. But the cow brings it out and gives it to her child. A fight breaks out, the tigress kills the cow. The child of the tigress gets upset and kills her mother. The younger tigress promises protection to the young cow/bull by putting a bell round its neck. (The cow becomes the bull. Why? There is no reason given for this change). The bull one day dances with joy. The tigress comes and says, "Don't do this".
>
> One day the bull encounters the Bhil people. They kill the bull and eat it. A bird takes the bell to the tigress. The tigress drives away the Bhil people and finds them eating the flesh of the bull. The tigress sets fire to this flesh and herself and burns in it.

The bhagat who recited this song mentioned that, "The cow/bull represents the Warli people and the tigress, the Gav Dev, the protector of the Warlis. That's why this song is sung". The Warlis respect the cow to the extent that there is generally no practice of drinking its milk. It is believed that the milk is for the calf alone. This could explain why the cow that is venerated by the Brahmin is changed to a bull later in the narrative and is killed by the Bhil adivasis. The recitations continue for the whole of the next day with breaks in between for getting invigorated with toddy.

The ceremony at the Gav Dev spot continues at the time of sunset on the second day. Rahya, senior bhagat, sits with another bhagat and places rice around the conical stone representing the Gav Dev. Sindur is applied to the stone, a burning wick is placed next to it in a broken coconut shell as well as a sheaf of paddy, a wicker basket with rice and a brass pot with water. Four elders representing the clans of the village sit around. The bhagats shake as if possessed with the sound of the recitations. After some time the main bhagat drops some grains of rice into the pot and shouts at the grains saying 'ulhasman' that they may rise and sink in the proper manner without touching the sides of the pot. According to him this decides whether the grains at threshing will be full or only small. He shouts at the rice and is accompanied by encouragement by the village elders. This is repeated three times. Then a cock is brought and the elders with the bhagat accompanied by the village Patil pull out its feathers and throw it around the Gav Dev spot. The cock is then taken away and slain. Sindur with oil is then applied to the stone. The bhagat takes away the sheaves of paddy and shakes with the reciting at the same time. Sindur is then applied to the foreheads of all present around. Rice is then presented with the coconut which was broken and shared with the heads of families. The adivasis then move away and have a community meal with toddy, chicken and mutton with potatoes. No women are allowed to be present throughout. The heads of families sit together, the younger people on one side and the boys on the other side. The meal ends with the elders applying tilaks on each other's foreheads, led by the Patil, embracing each other on either side with arms held saying '*Ye! Ye!*'. The elders and the other adivasis then proceed to the outskirts of the village on the banks of a stream and finish the rest of the toddy and the meal with a send off.

Several significant factors might be interpreted from the nature of the ritual and the incantations. The exclusion of women might be seen as a mark of the increasing dominance of males over the economy and the agricultural cycle as the adivasis moved from a predominantly hunting, food-gathering and shift-cultivating economy in the forests that was marked by more egalitarian gender relations to settled agriculture over the nineteenth and early twentieth centuries as a result of British policies of land revenue and reservation of forests. The insecurity of land holdings as a result of the sharply changing social relations of production with the coming of non-adivasi commercial interests in the region, and the uncontrolled environmental and climatic forces that influence the cultivation of paddy, the now increasingly significant food crop that gradually displaced hunted animals, coarse varieties of food grains, roots, tubers and leaves as means of subsistence, may be interpreted from the pleadings for a good crop, the almost desperate invocations of the spirits in order to pacify them and secure a good harvest. The incantations also express a strong sentiment of positive affirmation and wish fulfilment. The special significance of this traditional harvest ceremony within the agricultural cycle that is held before the Khali ceremony that marks the start of threshing operations within each household, may be seen in the very detailed incantations of the coming of paddy to the village that is projected onto the deities to ensure an element of sacredness through divinification and thus ensuring wish fulfilment. The ceremony of the veneration of the clan deities that precedes that of the Gav Dev, the participation of the heads of clans and other male villagers, their mutual greetings and expressions of goodwill, the sharing of a common meal that was preceded by monetary collections from all the households, represent a persisting solidarity of the tribe around the cultivation of grain, the primary means of livelihood. The social need for affiliation through community solidarity is an important contributory factor to identity.

One had an opportunity for interaction with the bhagats who officiated in the ceremonies. When asked about the direction that they were facing during the rituals we were told that it was the direction of the sunrise.

> At the start of the Gav Dev ceremony we salute the sun. This tradition has come down from generations. This is the big god. Different songs are sung during the two days at different times. On the first day the songs are about the sun. On the second day it is about the gods and the harvest. We ask for grains, coconuts, onions, chilies, all that we need for our lives. In the song we say that in Kulambi village the people who are peasants are in a bad condition; we are broken '*Modoon Gela, Todoon Gela*'. We learnt these songs from our fathers. The tradition carries on in the family. A new person can also learn. Some learn through dreams.

The following are extracts of the incantations of the bhagat, to the extent that we were able to record and translate them. The principal bhagat, Rahya, is accompanied by two assistants with beats on the dank musical instrument on the second day from 11 am, onwards.

> Take out the 'vak' of the sun and throw it in the water. The Kave Vanjaras (names of gods) will come and weave the bags for the paddy. The 'phale' of the sun (a tree which gives strings meant to weave bags) are taken to the water to decompose. The threads are then taken by the Sukh Vanzar (name of god) and dried. The threads are taken by Tage Vanzar (name of god) to make bags. And the remaining threads are sold to Nalya Masi (name of god). The lengths of the bag are being woven. The bags are made. The Upza bag is brought. The Desha and the Vesha bags are brought. The Satike Vanzar (a god) is in a hurry to fill the bags. The bullocks are brought and the bells are put on them. They are ready and decorated. The Upzai Mavli goddess has opened the godown. The makhul flowers are lit as incense and the bags are offered. The bags have been filled to the brim. The Seva Vanzar god has sewn the bags. The beams of the wood are placed under the bags and they are lifted and put in the tangad (a vehicle).
>
> All the bags are placed in the tangad and a message is given by the Upzai Mavli goddess to take the bags carefully to Vagaya Dev, the Gav Dev. Kansari (the goddess of grains) is sitting on the bulls. Vihaya Kothari, sister of Kansari, sits on the red bull. Hiroba God is seated on the horse. Narayan Dev is seated on the tangad. Hiroba Dev is checking and going in the front and back. Kani Ghat is where the grains have arrived. The Kanhai Mavli

> sees the grains approaching the Vagh Dev. Kanhai Mavli asks Vagaya, "Where are you going?" He says, "I'm going to Kulambi where farmers are in trouble. They have little grains." Kanhai Mavli opens her own godown and gives her own contribution of grains and places them in the tangad. Kavli Mavli sends the tangad onwards. Alphai Mavli goes ahead and asks the same question and gives her own contribution. At Shishola Ghat, Shishola Mavli gives her contribution. They reach Shendad Ghat and the story repeats itself. They reach Sona Ghat and the story repeats itself, but Gira is placed on the tangad. The tangad reaches Muli Ghat (radishes), Naral (coconut) Ghat, Lasun (garlic) Ghat, Sopari (a nut) Ghat and the cotton Kasi clothes Ghat. The Khali time is here, the Gangli will be played, may we have plenty.

Despite the exclusion of women from the Gav Dev ceremonies, it may be noted that the role of the female in fertility rites related to agricultural production is maintained; even though projected onto female deities as may be seen in the contributions of grain by various deities in the above narrative. One might also observe the absolute reverence that is paid to Kansari Devi, the female deity of grain, during the threshing ritual of Khali described below. The various ghats (hills) that mark the countryside serve as major landmarks and are given names of food items associated with female deities.

At around 5 pm in the evening of the second day the following incantation is made. Warlis have a way of giving a wedding invitation by placing rice at the entrance of the house. This is called 'notra' and the same process of extending invitations to deities for the harvest festival appears to be followed below.

> The day is ending. We invoke the sun and moon. The sun has climbed the seven steps, the earth has awakened, the entire earth. The gods are awake. Seven rays have been held by the sun god and seven rays given out to the world. Upze Ghat, Dese Ghat, Vese Ghat, Alphe Ghat, the God (Gav Dev) have called you all.
>
> Kani Ghat, Jire Ghat, Mire Ghat, Lasai Kard Ghat, the Gav Dev has called you here.
>
> Sopani Ghat, Nagoli Ghat, Naroli Ghat, Bagdi Ghat, Tachkadi Ghat, come to this place.

Mule Ghat, Dhane Ghat, Shende (Sugarcane) Ghat, are called.

Kapri Ghat, Gaude Ghat, Kopar Ghat, come to the Gav Dev.

Bhat Khala, Dev Khala, come to the Gav Dev.

Kinbi Dhrang (Hill), Bimbi Dhrang, come to the Gav Dev.

Thapesar Dev (who placed the earth), Lipesar Dev (who flattened the earth), Tipesar Dev (who fixed the earth) are invited.

Unhai Savri, Tanhai Savri, Dudhai Savri, come.

Tumrai Sonar from Varoli village, come to the place.

Barham Dev, Phool Wadi, come.

Hindoli Savri, Gurai Mavli, Supai Mavli, Karogi Mavli, come.

Borimala (a resting place of gods), Binbai Mavli (umbilical cord), Lohar Mavli, come to the wedding (celebrations). Do not refuse the invitation.

Sambrai Mavli, Kothai Mavli, the Lion God (Sivha), i.e. the boundary of the village, invitation has been given to you.

Gav Mumbya (small gods of village), Vagoba Dev, Sathai Mavli (the overseer of grains), Bhikai Savri (the goddess of the Bhils in the hills), come to the wedding.

Zugmadi (a hill), Ayar (near Daman), Mil (a Devi related to Mahalaxmi), come to the wedding.

Tambia Rani (red mud hill), Patai Mavli (name of hill), come to the wedding.

Kuvli Mavli, Gidadi Savri, Kilai Mavli (a fortress hill), come.

Goteri Mavli (Varuada Hill), Dahmnai Savri, Baghdai Savri, Usar Vohra (name of well in Sutrakar), Pasla Vagaya, come.

All the above deities related to hills and fortresses are named after actually existing places that mark the landscape. The names of the hills have special significance to the adivasis. According to Rahya, the bhagat, "The gods had established the earth. Water with great force started coming out in places. To stop the water the gods put mud. These became the donghars (hills).

"Bharanath Dhodi (Bordi village), Bhuingar, Taro Khand (near Safala station), come.

Vagh Deva, Sakhli Vagh (hills at Mahalaxmi), come.

Mahalaxmi, Vajrai Bai (temple near Charoti), Balsa Mata (all temples), come.

Gambid Ghadia (a hill), Chand Mata (a temple), Hale Mata (Devi), Narain Dev, Gada Lot, come. (Dev Raja tied Narain Dev and threw him down a hill. This place is called Gada Lot).

Udhava is considered as a capital city of the Gods. The following are all fortresses which may not be seen today. According to Rahya, the gods built these forts in British times.

"Kohji and Mohji Kile (near Manor), Aseri Kile, Maholi Kile, Munlia and Adsu Dhongars (beyond Charoti), come.

Alna Dhongar, Satchi Varhadi (range of hills, like crowds), come

Navlakh Deva, Ishwar Pendi (gods), come

Keval Bhata (sound in seas), Tivrad Zad (trees near sea), Pohni Nal (bushes with big leaves near the sea), Bhatar Vel (creeper with leaves near the sea), come.

Dhage Samdev(S), Moje, Halphe(S), Bolha(S), Bhovre(S), Hade(S), Zade(S), Thine(S), Gore(S) (all names of seas), come.

Ranchesar Dev (who set the building blocks of the earth on the waters), Sanchesar Dev (fittings of earth), Thapesar Dev (fixing the earth), Lipesar Dev (spreading mud), Tipesar Dev (flattening the earth), Khambesar Dev (pillars for the skies), Nimbesar Dev (beams), come.

Singal Dipi (Kansari lives in this place), Ahya Pangla (Kansari), Narain Dev, Phudle Dare (front door), Vihe Kothari (sister of Kansari), Magle Dare (back door), Sonai Hindole, come.

Kansari is sitting in a place called Singal Dipi, with Narain Dev guarding the front door and Vihe Kothari, the back door.

Kamari Bala, Nagli Bala (Nagli grains), come.

Daso Ghat (G), Vesu and Sathe (all hills), come.

Dese Samudra, Vese Sumudra (seas) and Hire Lakhmane, Rahya Lakhmane, Narain Baramba (Brahmanical gods), come.

Varcha Raja (Deities from above are of the Gods), Khalche Raja (Deities from below are of the peasants), Kathya (Kotwal) and Patil (Vagh Dev), come.

Peasants of the village come.

The invitations to the various deities to the Gav Dev ceremony are an act of pacification and invoking the blessings of the divine that adds solemnity to the occasion and makes it sacred. The deities represent in general a process of deifying the physical and natural surroundings, trees, hills, fortresses, villages, historical and pilgrimage places, as well as the sublimation of the aspirations of the adivasis for a good crop and food, the basis of their survival; a projection of these deeply felt needs onto the divine. However, the transcendental is always immanent within the struggle for livelihood in the context of the animism practised with respect to natural and social relations.

At around 6 pm on the second day the following incantation is made. It symbolizes a ceremony of returning the goods that had been borrowed for the occasion from the various deities. The ceremony ends with an act of tribal solidarity, recognizing the presence of the heads of the various clans and offering salutations to them.

> Chandar (moon), Surya (sun) have begun to rise. The four corners of the earth have become awake. Surya has begun to rise. The four corners of the earth have awakened. Navkhand Dhonia (the entire world) is awake.
>
> Navla-Tangad (the vehicle) is awake. Hake Vanzara, Bombe Vanzara, Lavni Vanzara, Dange Vanzara (all vehicle drivers), get ready to unload the grains. The empty sacks are prepared. Hold the reins of the bullocks. The empty sacks are put on a cart and they are ready. Come on let's go. Don't throw the sacks anywhere. Take them carefully. The tangad moves out. Hake-Vanzara calls out. Sumare Vanzara shows the way. The vehicle goes by the Dohri way, the main road.
>
> Kathya Mavli, we return you your sacks.
>
> Sunge Vanzara, shows the way.
>
> Pande Vanzar, directs the way.
>
> Vale Vanzar, turns the vehicle.
>
> Ikhal Vira, has returned his empty sacks at the Khali of the gods called Bhat Khala. His bulls have been returned. Farewells are made.

Mithai Mavli, your bull is returned, as also your sacks. Farewell.

Mor Mavli, Supai Mavli, the empty sacks are returned to you. Your bull is returned. Farewell.

Arkholi village, Suthai Mavli your sacks are returned, bulls as well. Farewell.

Kavdas village, near the trees of the Kavda variety, O Vagoba God, your sacks are returned. Farewell.

Nagar Village, home of Bahman god, your sacks are returned. Farewell.

Varoli village, home of Tumbda Sonar, your sacks are returned. So also your bulls. Don't forget that they are returned. Farewell.

Ghoda Bhavi O God, your sacks are returned. Farewell.

The tangad vehicle moves along the Dhori way. Then passes Jawahar Ghat.

O Jowar Mavli, your bulls, empty sacks are returned. Farewell.

Mukhod village, Dev Khala, Kopar Ghat, Govandi Ghat, Rupoli Ghat, Shisholi Ghat, Samouli Ghat, Dese Ghat, Vese Ghat, Upje Ghat, Vanzar Ghat your bulls, your sacks are returned. Farewell.

Hargi Bhagat, Saya Pakhela, Maya Pakhela (bhagats of the primitive times), sit down in peace.

Dev Kotwal, Dev Patel, the Dev Kharbari, the Dev Kulambi (peasants), sit down in peace.

Vartha, Rahya, Bhimra, Dhombre, Vasavla, Dhulsada, Irim, Singda (names of some of the major clans whose heads were present), sit down in peace.

A significant observation might be made regarding the foregoing ritual and the accompanying incantations. There appears to be no reference to one of the most important reasons for present food insecurity and an uncertain livelihood, even though the abiding hunger and desperation for a good crop is an underlying theme. The real reasons have been the history of alienation from the forests and their lands especially over the nineteenth and twentieth centuries as a result of British and post-independence policies and the intrusions of outsiders. Could it be that these recitations of the bhagats belong to an historical period of hunting and food-gathering, prior to settled agriculture, or to the stage of the early nineteenth century of coping with the insecurities of inputs in settled agricultural lands together with the climatic changes and the sharply evolving social relations of production with the non-adivasis. The incantations appear to have been handed down over generations of bhagats with their substantial content remaining essentially the same; aspirations for grains and appeals to the deities for satisfaction, and with minimal adaptation to the changed circumstances of the adivasis. There would certainly have been changes as a result of memory lapse and loss in transmission, with the addition of elements from the local contexts of particular villages. The relatively static nature of the content of the recitations might have been ensured by the sublimation of desires and their projection on to the transcendent; the deities being given an immanent character through the process of providing a sacred character to the physical and natural environment. The past of hunting, food-gathering and shift cultivation before the nineteenth century had its own dangers and uncertainties, but there was an essential harmony of nature, spirit and one another within the tribal community.

In October 2016 we paid another visit to Kulambi village at our request and at the invitation of the local Kisan Sabha, Lal Bavta (red flag) leader. The purpose of this visit, other than some others, was to observe changes in the Gav Dev ritual, if any, after a period of close to forty years. The leader was requested to meet the villagers at the Gav Dev site for a consultation related to our visit. The gist of the lengthy discussion to which we were not present, and as reported later, was that a small section of the villagers who were not present and who owed allegiance to the NCP (Nationalist Congress Party) might object to our presence at this solemn occasion, given that the matter had not been raised at the earlier planning meeting. The outcome was that we could not participate in the Gav Dev this year and were promised a more appropriate process the following year with the consent of all adivasi village representatives. The significance of this incident was the upholding of democratic norms of common consent, the growing assertion of political power over even ritual practices and the emerging divisions in the village along electoral party lines after what had been an earlier solidarity under the Lal Bavta.

3.3 The Khali Household, Post-Harvest Ritual

Considering the significance of this festival for the adivasis during the annual struggle for livelihood over the agricultural cycle, we have discussed it based on secondary sources and our field observations, at different times and at different locations. The following are some illustrations. One might wonder why the deities are venerated when all is said and done with respect to the agricultural season, i.e. after harvesting and before threshing, given that do not appear to be sentiments of thanksgiving expressed in the incantations. What one could gather from several inconclusive discussions, apart from the general refrain that this is what our forefathers have done, is perhaps the unarticulated foreboding of the future which is expressed by the Kabele in Bourdieu's fieldwork, 'Don't count a good harvest before threshing'(1990: 226). Could this timing of Khali also have something to do with the recollections of the claims made by the landlord-moneylender on the adivasis' produce during the pre-rebellious 1944 to 1948 period, exactions which continues in some places to this day?

The Khali Ritual in the 1930s

The following is a narrative of an incantation during the 1930s, provided by Save (1945):

> Oh, mother corn, I bow to thee at dead of night. This man of black head seeks your protection. Where was the corn deity born and where was she brought up? She is the creation of God and moves in the eight worlds (*khanda*)...'I am not willing to follow you to the kingdom of gods,' said she to Naran. 'But I will give you five drops of my blood.' Naran Dev accepted this proposal. Kansari cut one of her fingers and gave five drops of blood to Naran. He took it and sprinkled it over the world, (That is the reason why there are five ears to the corn). Naran thought, 'The gods will not take so much care of the corn. If it is entrusted to the black farmer he would certainly regard it as his wealth.' So from that day the farmer was associated with corn. The corn was unknown to the black farmer till then; he was only eating some wild roots (Save 1945: 173, 175).

Corn is portrayed as insulted and attempted to be subordinated by the deities and at times unconsciously neglected by the adivasi cultivator who adopts a tone of self-depreciation. This forms a running theme over this narrative. As a result there are several situations cited where corn is difficult to please and attempts to hide or run away. The incantation also suggests that corn is finally entrusted to the dark skinned, adivasi cultivator and Kansari Devi (the deity of grain) finds herself more at home with him. In addition, the narration does suggest the tensions within the context of the discovery of early agriculture by the female within a matriarchal situation, the attempted dominance by an external patriarchal pastoral society from without over an early predominantly hunting and food-gathering society with some elementary knowledge of agriculture of a slash and burn variety. Save's interpretation of the strong bond between the adivasi cultivator and corn, represented by Kansari Devi, is noteworthy: "This narrative is an indication of the Warlis' devotion for corn. It is believed that telling or listening to this story gives them good crops for the narration is in the honour of the corn-deity. The story gives a detailed account of the corn, how it was the heritage of the gods in the beginning and the circumstances in which corn was handed over to the black farmer. The composers perhaps wanted to emphasize the fact that this disrespect or neglect of the corn meant miseries to oneself. This is amply proved in the case of gods who had to starve because the corn deity refused to favour them. The sub-story of the farmer's son also bears out the same moral. He had to suffer hardships because he failed to respect the corn in refusing to work on his father's field. It is again the corn that rejuvenated both him and his wife and they were transformed into the 'corn-child' and the 'lady-corn'. In bringing about the happy union of the two the story again impresses that a Warli is after all associated with corn and can never part with it (Save 1945: 179).

One has presented the above narrative to draw attention to the fact that some of the underlying themes and existential concerns have persisted over close to a century, as will be seen from the narratives of the incantations and the analysis given below of ritual practices that are closer to the present.

Khali at Baraf's House, October 1979, Kulambi Village, Gurud Pada

The bhagat Shendad performs the ritual. He places sugarcane, paddy stalks, rice in basket, dudhi (a vegetable), a coconut and other vegetables at a spot on the threshing floor. From the start of the monsoons to the threshing of the corn the Warlis avoid eating items such as coconut, bananas, betel leaves and nuts, turmeric, sugarcane, beans and cucumbers. This taboo is presently observed by the head of the family and by young men who are being initiated to being a bhagat, who in addition do not eat non-vegetarian foods and do not engage in sex during their training.

Leaves are tied to the central beam and grains are placed in four corners after they have been held over burning coals and a short recitation is made. Then the bhagat sits in front of the burning coals and starts a long recitation (see tape) and waves his hands over the coals with each stanza. Towards the end of the recitation the head of the family, Baraf, takes rice from a tray and sprinkles it and moves around the Khali (the threshing floor). The bhagat gets possessed. The lady of the house takes rice and sindur in a tray with a lighted wick and applies it to the bhagat, the pole, to the head of the family and to me. Then she kneels and sprinkles rice thrice, each time facing the four corners. The husband places his palms in his wife's hands and they receive rice from the bhagat together. The bhagat tells the head of the family something and he agrees. He then puts the rice near the pillars. Rice is treated with great respect by the Warlis. It is called 'aayee' (mother) and is not wasted. Liquor is not made of rice. The joint participation of both the male and the female in this agricultural household ceremony might be noted, which is not the case in the Gav Dev ceremony.

The rice from the four corners earlier placed on leaves is collected and placed with vegetables in front of the bhagat. The vegetables and coconuts are then passed around by the bhagat to the two sons and the head of the family. The coconut is then skinned and little by little put on the rice. The 'Bhur Kohla', one of the vegetables, is then broken in two and placed on the rice. The coconut is broken. The sugarcane is then split in pieces. Most of the vegetables are cut up and placed on a leaf. The cut vegetables are held over the fire with a recitation and placed under the sheaves of rice. Cooked rice and some of the vegetables are then held over the flame accompanied by a recitation and put into the mouth of the head of the family. The same is repeated with the wife's brother and the other family members.

Another bhagat takes a cock, recites, pulls out the feathers of the neck and places them at the earlier placed rice facing west. He cuts the neck of the chicken with a koiti (sickle). A coconut is then held accompanied by a recitation. The skin is removed, placed over the rice, broken and the milk of coconut is shared with the other bhagat and members of the family. Rice without vegetables is then offered by family members, including women, to each other. A cock then held near the pole with a recitation. Feathers from the neck are removed and put to the pole, the neck is slit and blood mixed with rice is applied to the stacks of paddy and is sprinkled around the pole. The bhagat takes sheaves of paddy, beats them against the pole and recites. The sheaves are then tied to the pole. We were told that bhagat Shendad had learnt the recitations from another older bhagat from Sutrakar village. According to him,

> During three months—July, August, September—the younger bhagats to be would go into the jungles with a senior bhagat and learn these Khali recitations together with other recitations for snake bites, Devi illness, to get rid of bhuts, Gav Dev, Kul Dev. Austerity had to be observed during that period; no onions, no cutting of chicken, no sleeping with women, etc. Whoever among the adivasis wants to learn, can learn. It depends on their desire.

We provide below some of the incantations of the bhagat that have been recorded and translated. The recitations begin with the awakening of the various deities.

> Hiroba, Langiv Mai, Lasenge Bap, the peasants of Kulambi village are worried.
>
> From the Govandi Ghat, Hiroba Dev is seeing.
>
> Tarsu Ghat, he had his bath and wore his clothes.
>
> Kanha Vanzar, Hako Vanzar, where are you going. 'Going to Kulambi village'.
>
> Hiroba Dev is coming over the various hills (the names of the hills are mentioned).

> The head of the family has called Hiroba Dev who crosses the river and comes. He crosses many villages (the names of actually existing villages in Jawhar taluka are mentioned) and comes.
>
> Ranaji Rai Dev sees Hiroba Dev going.
>
> Hiroba Dev crosses caves and comes.

As in the Gav Dev incantations, an appeal is made to the various deities to come and participate in the Khali ceremony. This serves as an act of pacification and seeking blessings. As we shall see in the incantations given below, the normal agricultural activities in the agricultural cycle of the adivasi peasants are projected onto the deities. The rivers, hills, villages and caves serve as markers; landmarks in the adivasis' natural environment. The mention of the landmarks in Jawahar taluka suggests the historical origins of the Warlis from the north eastern districts and further on in Dhule and Nandurbar districts that were relatively isolated and thickly forested as part of the Western Ghats and their gradual migration towards the coastal hills and plains in the wake of early nineteenth century introduction of settled agriculture by the British policies. The fields are called 'Bara Holi' that is, the 12 plots of land irrespective of their actual numbers.

> The Hiroba God has reached the Khali, and why has he come? The bad winds, that is the Bhuts, have affected the fields. Hiroba is seeing this. There has been no good harvest. Rains have been bad. May the crops rise and flourish ('Ulhasman'). All the God peasants and the human peasants are waiting.
>
> The husband and the wife of the house are standing. They had a dream about what has to be done. They woke up, smoked the bidi (a country cigarette), took money in advance, took a stick and set out to Dhodpe Raja. The peasant passes many fields and proceeds further to the Lohar's (blacksmith) house. He asks for all the implements connected with the fields. The Lohar says, 'There is no support to my life. I am confused. I do not know in what direction to set my steps. I have gone to collect mud, but I do not take it. I have taken my tikav (pick axe) and basket but I don't find the right mud. My hands are trembling and my tongue is quivering.'

He throws away the top mud and takes the bottom mud to his house in order to light the fire. The Lohar crosses many places and goes to the well to collect water. He wets the mud. The stove is lit. Thapesar Dev has lit it. Four days passed the stove bursts and he sets out to prepare a stove again. The Lohar goes to the carpenter and pays his respects to the carpenter and collects his tools. He cuts the wood. The carpenter starts to set right the stove and gets exhausted. 'I don't know what to do'. The carpenter goes to the forest and from the skeleton structure of a dead cow gets knowledge about the framework of the stove. He collects the parts, screws, etc. from the hardware seller. The carpenter prepares everything and the Lohar pays him. The Lohar goes to the Manga (the scheduled caste person) for skin. The Manga goes to the jungle sees the eagle and finds the dead animal, a cow. He gives the flesh to the dogs, foxes and flies and takes the skin. He takes the skin to the Mochi (shoemaker). The Mochi prepares the skin, takes it to the Lohar who puts it on to the stove. He fixes all the parts and gets the coal. The Lohar goes to the hardware person to get the metal. He prepares the koiti, kurhad, tasni, vinna, paura (agricultural implements). The peasants come and collect their implements and pay for it. The peasant takes the implements and does an Aarti (a form of worship) and applies sindhur to them. He has a bath, eats, talks to his wife. The next day he calls out to the labourers and says, 'The other fields are ready for rab (preparation of the seed beds), and our fields have remained'. He worships the jungle deities and tells them not to get angry at his cutting the branches. He offers a hen. The peasant's wife pays the labourers with rice. They eat. The peasant says, 'The Chaitra month has come. I have to do the rab. The rab of others has been done. What about mine?' He lights the ground and sweeps, arranges the branches. He prepares different rab places for different seeds.

The Kausi winds, the Kapri winds, the Sawni winds have blown and the rains are due. I have to light the rab. He lights the rab and goes for a bath. The labourers are paid with bhat (paddy). The Jeshta month has come. The rain gods of the black clouds will come. The thunder has come and so also the lightning. The Rahatesar Dev [refers to the rains, that is, at the wells there are the Rahats which cluster up and let it fall] will come down. The rains have fallen, the ground is wet.

The peasant and the wife talk to each other, 'The fields of others will be sown. What of ours?' The peasants have taken the sticks and have tied their head gear. The Sutar (carpenter) deity has been called and he starts to prepare the plough. The Sutar is paid and goes. Now bullocks are needed. He bought the bullocks, good strong ones, he pays and brings them home. The nose of the bullocks are prepared and the strings are tied. The various types of seeds are removed. They go to the rab grounds. He puts the seeds over the manure and says to the seeds, 'Do not be afraid of thunder, lightning. Even if the rain gods take you away in the floods, do not be afraid. Give us a good crop. Do not be afraid of the heat, neither of the jungle gods, not of the Brahmin gods, nor of the Kothari gods'. He begins to sow and says,' O gods do not trouble the seeds. We will call you again at the time of the Khali, now go away'. He applies tilak (a sacred mark with red paste) to the bulls and the plough and to the labourers. The labourers wonder if the shetkari (peasant) has gone mad. 'Why does he not start the work?'. The Shetkari throws the first handful of seeds to the earth, a second to the rains, the third handful to the birds and insects, fourth to the winds, fifth to the Khali Gods. He sows all the seeds. The day ends and he goes home. Cleans the bullocks, pays the labourers well and truly.

The rops (paddy shoots) have come. The crops are even bent. 'Come on let's do our lavni, that of others is over. Come make chikal (soft muddy fields). He takes vegetables, rice, incense, flowers to the field for the start of the lavni. He worships the Kul Dev, Gav Dev, Bahman Dev and starts the ropni. He starts the avni in different beds. On the last day of the avni they put mud on each other and the labourers take chikal and put it on the peasant's wife. He washes the implements, bulls and takes them home. Two months have passed.

The Kansari (grain) has grown big and asks for a husband. The Shetkari says no husband for you. But one night the Bhogesar Dev (the impregnating god) impregnates Kansari and she gets pregnant and the child grows. Days passed, she experienced pain in the stomach. Kansari gets frightened 'Gabri Babri'. 'I need a midwife'. The gods set out to get one. The midwife stands up and is informed. She says, "No". They move on to different gods asking for a midwife. They finally find a midwife. The Kansari is relieved of her fruit. The midwife moved off in the lower world.

She meets a snake. The snake asks the midwife to deliver the cow (make two of one). She does so. The winds had beaten up the Kansari. The midwife comes, but Kansari has already become dry with the heat.

The peasant is disappointed. The peasant swears at the labourers. 'We sweated, ploughed, left our children but still no fruit from Kansari'. The cow has started giving milk, the other cow has given birth to a calf. The cow's udder is caught and sweet milk is got. The milk is taken and thrown into various plots where Kansari is: dangi, bazaari, khadri, kasbai, nagli, wari (various food grains). Kansari becomes cold. Two or three days pass, the peasant moves around, watches Kansari recovering and swaying like the waves of the seas. The grains are ripened as also the leaves. 'Come all labourers. The Kapni (harvesting) of others is over. Ours is left. Let's go to the fields and start harvesting. Worship the gods, rains, winds, jungle, earth'. They harvest all the fields. The sun is setting. They go to the jungles to get the threads of the Nandan tree to tie up the sheaves. The sheaves of the different grains are tied. The new cloth is taken.

Come on let's do the Khali. Call the labourers, clean the Khali place. The earth is scraped and the earth should be thrown on the Ulsan Dongar (a hill). The peasant has gone to get the central beam of the Khali made of sag wood. The peasant's wife has gone to get cow-dung. She asks the flies for good dung. But the flies say that you will get dung with worms in it. The dung is put on the Khali. Water is brought. She goes to get water and meets the frog. 'I want water'. The frog says, 'You will only get ushta (stale/soiled) water of the frog'. The peasant tells his wife to throw away the dung. The beam is put in the Khali. The peasant husband and his wife speak to each other. We need a bhagat. The kulambi (peasant) bathes, dresses, takes a koiti (sickle), ties his turban and sets out to get a bhagat. He lights his bidi and starts. One or all the parts, can't find the god. 'I need a new bhagat as new as the Kamani'. The bhagat says, 'From the time that my umbilical cord was cut I have become stale'. He goes in search since he wants a bhagat who has had no relations with a woman before. He finally finds one. He comes with the bhagat back to his house. Passes fields and reaches the khali. Tobacco and seda leaves to make bidis and, in addition, toddy are given.

> The bhagat goes to the Khali and takes out a sheaf of rice. He gets possessed. He takes a cock. (Generally for the rituals cocks are used, not hens). He takes the names of various bhagat Devs. 'Kansari Devi, I offer you these feathers of the cock. Kansari don't get angry. I am a fool, but you are wise. I don't listen, but you keep your ears open. If anyone puts the mantra to take you away, then don't go away. Don't be afraid of thunder, lightning and the stamping of feet. Let peace be in your mind. Don't get angry. Halpha sea, Moze sea, Daga sea, Olal sea, Olal Mane (all these are seas) rise with the wave, so may you flourish and form big heaps. I may have made a mistake, but don't be angry. As the tide comes in the sea, so let waves of rice come into this Khali. As the hills rise up, so also may you. As the wells, as the tanks get filled, so may you. As the mountains rise, so may you. As the moon grows, so may you. *We have worked in the fields, let not the shackles come on our hands, or chains round our necks as a result of debt. Don't get angry with this peasant. Give him happiness.* Kisola Bhaya, the bhagat, is standing on the fields and is seeing. The people have dreams and have begun their work. The Kul Dev and Gav Dev will tell us if the grains are good or not. (He gives the sheaves of grain to the head of the family). May the 'kar' sound of the grains come. The peasant may be hungry for a day, but please Kansari Devi stay with him. This peasant's wife is a good person. Give her a good harvest. Keep the enemies away. If anyone puts his hands to the grains or eyes to the grains, break the hands and eyes. Here I give you rice. This peasant's wife has suffered for 12-24 years. Don't give her trouble. They have dreamt. May they have plenty (The bhagat repeats the names of ghats, seas). May you also rise.

The previous stanza represents a vivid and desperate plea to Kansari Devi, the deity of grains, to provide the adivasi peasant a plentiful crop of grains. The various insecurities and uncertainties of the agricultural operations as seen in the previous stanzas now reaches a crescendo with the bhagat pleading on behalf of the adivasi household for a bountiful supply of grains at threshing. This has strong elements of self-depreciation in the context of food insecurity and in the presence of the deity. There is also a passing reference to the relations of production with respect to the non-adivasi with the mention of possible chains and shackles resulting from debt.

What follows is that various articles of domestic consumption and usage like kothmir, onions, muli, chillies, coconuts, bukhola (like dudhi), sugarcane, bangles, sindur, most things from the house are brought and placed at the Khali. The adivasis' main meals consist of a little salt fish and rice at the harvesting time or rice and dal; two meals a day. The lack of nutrition is manifested in the eager search for it, especially of the more nutritious foods. A hen is occasionally cut and its flesh cooked and small pieces served to all present. Toddy is had in the morning and in the evening and sometimes in the afternoon, with great relish. Once a 'valin' an animal about one and a half feet long, with the shape and fur of a large squirrel, was caught by a dog and cut and eaten with much fanfare by all present. The hunt is presently an expression of this desperate search for nutrition. The Kul Dev is invoked to keep an eye on the fields and to give a good crop. The bhagat recites, 'May the Shilpi get Khandi bhat and the Bhaval Muda Bhat. Hiroba Dev, I offer you a chicken. Gav Dev, I offer you a chicken'.

Incantations in Honour of Kansari Devi at Kotwal Vartha's Khali, Bhagat Rhaya, December 5, 1979

In this short Khali and in the invocations to Kansari Devi one sees even more sharply the desperation of the adivasis as regards crops and food grains that springs from their food insecurity, as has been mentioned above. The bhagat takes rice in his hand and places it over the fire and recites. He puts rice near the poles at 14 different places. The wick is lit. Rice is placed in four places and a vessel of water is put over it. Sheaves of paddy are placed in front and the recitations are begun. Rice is placed in a vessel. Several attempts are made to ensure that the rice rises in the appropriate manner to the surface of the water and when satisfactory the rice from the vessel is thrown on the sheaves of paddy. A chicken is brought. A coconut placed over a large vessel of water followed by a recitation. The feathers of the chicken are removed and placed on the rice. The neck is slit. Mango leaves are placed under the coconut on the pot. Toddy is taken in a leaf and dropped at several places on the ground. The bhagat repeats 'Ye' and he drinks the toddy. The sheaves are then tied to the beam of the Khali.

The following recitation is made:

It is morning the sun has risen above the seven steps. Land awake, Hera awake, cattle awake, the four sides awake, the whole earth awake, birds awake, different hills (names said with names of eatables) awake. The people awake. Different gods awake. Vagaya awake (some of the gods mentioned in the Gav Dev song).

Fire was in the beginning and the earth caught fire. The sea caught fire. Ram Laxman, Hirva Laxman went to put it out and then the fire ran away and sank in the earth, rocks, trees and the remaining fire was taken by Jagesar Dev, Vijesar Dev. The Toradi Doradi gods took the rest. The rest was given to the Parsi god, who is now at Udhva village in Gujarat (where there is a Zoroastrian fire temple today].

Seas awake. Rain is male, earth is female, and Kansari is born of their mating on the earth. Sisters of Kansari Dev do not trouble these people. Kansari Dev, do not get angry. A mistake may have been made. The sun and moon have risen. Daso, sister of Kansari, mango tree in the front and at the back door plantain trees - do not get angry. Don't get angry if the grains are fallen elsewhere, in the plots of the fields. Come here and gather here.

If you shit I'll receive it with open hands. If you piss, I'll open my mouth. I'm your slave. I'm your bhangi (a Scheduled Caste of the sweeper community). I fall at your feet.

Just as in the Halphi Sea the waves come in, so may the rice come into my Khali. May the cow without milk, give milk. May the cow not giving offspring, give them. (Grains are dropped in water saying 'Ulhasman' and the grains rise in the vessel. 'Sod' and they separate. If this happens then Kansari is agreeable). May the butter and oil flow from the milk. Give us in plenty. Do not get angry. If you get angry, then may your stomach bloat out with the anger withheld, and your mouth held small like that of a needle head. Your hair may have been burnt and your eyes may have been blind. Your nose may be gone, ears may be burned, but don't get angry. In three years the Gangli will be done and all your desires will be fulfilled.

Let the threshing give much grain. Do not give us 'dukh' (sadness). Keep all the children happy. Our peasant is a good man. Give him plenty. The golden beam (that at the centre of the Khali) and the rope (that is used around the necks of the bullocks) are set. Give the 'Kar' sound to the feet of the bullocks so that grains may fall in plenty. Don't be afraid of thunder and don't be afraid of shit in the fields, O Kansari. We've put milk in the vessel for you (in reality it is water). If you keep them happy, then we will do the Gangli in three years (a goat has to be cut then).

The Khali is a significant festival related to harvesting and is conducted before threshing, generally after the Gav Dev is venerated. It is a family and clan celebration when other members of the hamlet are also invited as a mark of solidarity. The role of the bhagat assumes tremendous significance since he gives expression to the deepest desires of the adivasis for grain and acts as a mediator with divine forces, interceding on behalf of the adivasi community. He also stands between human desires and the unknown, unpredictable forces of nature and the adivasi 'other'. Undoubtedly, there is very little mention of the oppressor within the social relations of production which may partly be attributable to the possible origins of the incantations; coping with early settled agriculture during the early nineteenth century. The fact that over the years since then the role of the state and of the non-adivasi outsider in extracting surplus finds no significant mention could be because the rituals are a coping mechanism, involving processes of rationalization, sublimation and projection onto the divine; even thought the animistic and nature-spirit basis of this projection continues in an explicit manner and provides some degree of immanence to issues of livelihood within the agricultural cycle.

The Khali Ritual, December 15, 2015, at Satu Jetya Vartha, Bhagat Baraf

We revisited the Kulambi village after a long interval of time in order to get an update on this significant ritual which is so meaningful to the lives of the adivasis. Khali was being performed at the vacant land in the fields which belonged to the Vartha family. This Vartha family owns about three acres of land and rents in a few other acres. The land helps them harvest about 30 sacks of rice annually. Newly harvested vegetables, including coconut, radish, sugarcane, tur dal, coriander, etc are not consumed until the ritual is performed. The family also sells toddy for about Rs. 10 per litre on certain occasions. The Vartha residence is in Paras pada but the ground where Khali was performed is located in Umber pada. The male and female members of the family usually migrate after the harvest season is over. They had all returned home a day before the ritual. The family members present at the time of our field visit were an elderly adivasi who was the brother of Jetya Vartha, the head of household who was no more. Jetya's son Satu, his wife Bharti and his elderly mother presided over the ceremony. Satu engages in fishing off the coast of Mumbai throughout the year so that the main function of tending the fields is performed by his wife and mother. Satu's younger brother is a driver. There were several children of the family who had missed school for the ritual. The invitees for the communal meal at the end of the ritual were other clan relatives and adivasis from the hamlet

There was a delay as the bhagat named Arjun Baraf reached late by an hour. By the time we arrived, the basic yet important preparations for the ritual had been performed. The family and the bhagat did not hesitate to welcome us as we observed and documented the various rituals involved in this process. The ground where the rituals were being performed was surrounded by ten large circular pillars of haystack and there was a central pole (a log of wood dug into the ground) where most of the rituals were being performed. The central pillar was surrounded by loose hay, vegetables, two sugarcanes and leaves along with some other entities required for performing the ritual. The male member of the family was arranging the grains of rice on the leaves over the loose hay near the pillar and along the different markings made around the ground. The bhagat then started chanting as he held some vegetables in his hand. He then held some leaves in his hand and chanted as he tied them at the top of the pillar. The bhagat arranged some grains on the floor and kept a coin on it and then completed this arrangement by keeping a jug filled with water over it. One by one, he started chanting and putting some rice grains in the jug. The striking feature was that, when most of the grains would drown in the water, some grains would just pop up to the top, when the bhagat would command them to. He would then dip his fingers in the jug and remove the grains floating at the top. This mantra, chanted by Baraf would involve first, inviting the gods for the ritual and later bidding them farewell. Having performed this ritual for about an hour, the bhagat then got a leaf filled with toddy as he first spilled a few drops on the floor and later consumed the rest of it. The male of the family stood next to the bhagat as some more mantras were being chanted and some hay was burnt to produce smoke. Turn by turn, the bhagat and the Vartha spread the smoke first on the vegetables and then on each other.

'Bharati Kunbi' was a term often used by the bhagat during the incantations and on being asked the family told us that Bharati was the daughter-in-law of the family and Kunbi referred to the woman of the household who looked after the farms in general. As the daughter-in-law is central with regard to the fertility of the family, the term 'Bharati Kunbi' was being chanted over and over. Different members of the family keep migrating periodically and are unable to give total attention to the fields, however, they had all arrived a day before the Khali ritual as it was important to take the blessings from the various deities.

After having chanted for over three hours, the bhagat started preparing some threads to light diyas in different places around the ground. The first diya was kept at the bottom of the central pillar without being lit. Bharati brought a plate with grains of rice arranged at one side. After making these arrangements, Baraf started chanting again and after a while, some grains were handed over to Sattu Vartha, who spread it along the haystacks-one by one and then lit the diya placed by the central pillar, following the bhagat's instructions. The husband and wife were then called together, and individually they applied tilak to the bhagat and in turn, the bhagat did the same. The bhagat handed over some grains to them and held their hands as he kept chanting with his eyes closed and after some time, they bowed down to the bhagat, who sprinkled some rice on them.

After a while, three male members were asked to sit besides the bhagat in a circular fashion. The bhagat, picked up a basket of vegetables and cradled it in his arms (thrice) and handed over to the member next to him, he did the same cradle move three times and passed it over to the next person. Once the basket was returned to the bhagat, he picked up the pumpkin, which was huge in size, cradled it and passed it on to the next member and the same act was perfomed. Once all the vegetables were put through these rituals, the Bhagat placed them all in front of him. The bhagat picked up the coconut and peeled it of its fibres, all by his hands and broke it. The water from the coconut was filled in a container. Alongside the bhagat, one of the men broke the pumpkin by banging it on the floor. The pumpkin was cleared of its seeds, all the vegetables were cut into small pieces and the bhagat placed them in front of him. The vegetables were mixed with rice grains and were individually handed over to every member of the family. A leaf filled with water was handed over to Bharati, after the bhagat blessed it with his chanting.

As a cock was being arranged for the sacrificial ritual, some of the children in the family followed a male member in the field, where another cock, much smaller in size was taken right before a totem and sacrificed. The totem was rubbed with the blood oozing from the headless cock's neck. This cock was taken by the children, who arranged a fire just beside the ground where the Khali was being performed. The children, carefully picked out the feathers and dissected the cock so as to separate its intestines and the other parts. All these were cleaned by the children and the cock was roasted in the wild fire without applying any salt or spices, etc. This meal was celebrated specifically by the children as they had done all the hard work around it.

The sacrificial cock was brought around the central pillar, the bhagat continued chanting for about seven minutes as he held the cock by its neck-pressed on to the ground. The cock was stretched out and the bhagat held its lower part, pressed by his knees on the floor. As he chanted, he picked out feathers from the cock and once the chanting was complete, the bhagat cut its neck with help provided by Sattu Vartha. This cock, the bhagat explained, was sacrificed in the name of the god residing in the mountains. The bhagat carried the body of the headless cock around the central pillar and then the severed neck was then touched onto it, enough to leave a stain of blood on the pillar.

After some time, the bhagat returned to his seat and using

a rope, he tied some hay and handed it over to the couple after chanting. The couple moved the hay around in a circle and stuck it on the top of the pillar. The remaining hay was tied together with a larger rope by the bhagat, who after having prayed to the goddess, smashed it on the floor, enough to scatter its seeds around the pillar. These seeds were collected, after which the bhagat held some of them in his hand and started chanting. The hay was horizontally arranged around the pillar and the floor around was swept with a broom.

On the side of the ground, the bhagat started making a rangoli (a decorative desgn) out of newly harvested rice flour, following which he kept a few strands of hay arranged in a circular manner and over this arrangement, an earthen pot filled with water was placed and was completed with a coconut and leaves on top. A diya (lamp) was then lit at the foot of this arrangement. A cock, much smaller in size, compared to the one initially sacrificed, was brought near this setting and was cut. Not too far from this, a coconut was broken and water was collected in a small metal pot. To end the ritual, two diyas were lit and some water was poured around them.

It was already dark by the time the ritual was complete. The cut vegetables and the slaughtered cock were cooked together on the traditional wooden burner available to the family. This was then served with bhakris to all the guests and the bhagat along with toddy, as the day ended.

With great difficulty we were able to identify some of the content of the incantations based on recordings. However, the translation and interpretation of these recordings were contingent on several incoherent passages as a result of the whisperings and cajoling of the bhagat in his desperate address to Kansari Devi for grain, his at times state of inebriation with toddy or 'possession' by the Devi, and the interventions of household members during the course of the long ritual. Some of the themes were the following:

> In ancient times, the Warlis were suffering because the deities were angry with them. To pacify the deities, the bhagats performed a puja. So the deities were pleased and life returned to normal. Since those times when the crop is ready, before bringing it home, the Warlis perform a Khali Puja and invite the deities to the Khali.

Songs which talk about the power and good deeds of deities are sung and as a mark of respect a cock is offered to them.

The puja begins with offering salutations to the main gods—Hirwa/Hiroba, Himay and Narandev. The Bhagat requests them to preside over the proceedings. The main ritual unfolds through the narration of ancient song-stories. The stories are quite long and repetitive. An element of mystery surrounds them. Only those who are trained by the bhagats know these stories.

The Journey of Hirwa and Himay

Riding on a horse, Hirwa and Himay arrive for the puja. It is a long journey. On the way, they face many obstacles. There are thick forests, hilly regions and many oceans. Only Hirwa has the power to withstand such an arduous journey. They have to reach Kulambi village. Finally they arrive and sensing their arrival, Arjun Baraf bhagat heaves a sigh of relief and takes a break for toddy.

Choundya Sutar Prepares for the Monsoon

The monsoon is fast approaching so Choundya sutar (carpenter) is getting his implements ready for the agricultural activity. He checks his saw. To test it out he cuts some wood. Feeling satisfied, he starts gathering other items on his list. He goes to a Chamar (leather worker) to find out the address of the bronze-smith because he requires a copper-pipe. He meets the bronze-smith, gets the pipe and riding his horse cart goes to fetch a whole lot of coal. Bringing it home, he keeps it in his storage-room. Discarding his old plough, he prepares a new one and uses it for farm-work. All this labour does not go waste! Choundya gets a bountiful yield that year.

Panglay Bai's Pregnancy

Hectic activity is going on in the fields because before the rains start, people have to get the fields ready for aavani (transplantation). Amidst all this, a guest Panglay Bai arrives at the Kunbi's (cultivator's) home. She is searching for a groom! Kunbi and his wife get agitated because they do not have time to help her out; they are too busy with the preparation for the cultivation season.

Finally, Panglay Bai herself finds a partner. After a few days, she gets pregnant. When she starts getting labour-pains, she urges the Kunbin (wife of the cultivator) to look for a midwife. Kunbin calls a midwife, gives her a vida (betel leaf) and requests her to help Panglay Bai. As the midwife struggles to help Panglay Bai, a pregnant cow and a hen also queue up and seek her help. The midwife does the needful. Amidst all this chaos the Kunbi family does not get time to look after their fields so they get worried. But since they help others, the gods are pleased with them so they take care of the Kunbi's crop.

At this point, the bhagat calls the host and his wife and guides them through some rituals. He tells the deities that Bharati, the hostess, has followed all the rules and regulations and she has also avoided eating things such as tur dal, carat, chavali, pumpkin, meat which women are not allowed to eat during the cultivation season. He explains to the audience that once the puja is over, Bharati can start eating the above-mentioned food-items. On reaching the last phase of the song, the bhagat invites all the deities from the neighbouring places. Prominent among them are—Mahalaxmi, Jivdani, Tungarli. He also urges the hills from the surrounding regions to safeguard the hosts' family. Lastly, paying obeisance to all the oceans, the forests and the creepers he pleads to the deities to accept the puja and bless the family. The prayers end with a special message to the family:

> *Our mother, Kansari, has come to your place. Please take good care of her. Look after all those who come to your place. If a poor person visits you, offer a chatai (mat) and ask him to relax. Look after the pets; the cat, the dog and be kind even to rats!*

We had an opportunity to interact with the bhagat and other family members during the breaks in the ritual. We enquired about the purpose of the ritual and the bhagat responded,

> On behalf of this family, Hiroba, Narandev and Himay are requested to visit their Khali and look after their well-being. We seek the blessings of the deities and tell them to take care of the legendary seven fields, seven oceans, the creepers in the forests and urge them to increase our yield. During the old times, the community did not know much about agriculture, but later on people prayed, sought the deities' assistance and began to cultivate the land.

One was keen to understand why there were no references in the incantations to the deities to social relational and political issues that defined the present economic problems that confronted the adivasis. The response of the bhagat was:

> Let me tell you that initially the condition of the people was a lot better. The Lal Bhavta was a single unit but then it started falling apart because of which the people have failed to progress. Now some are Lal Bhavta, some are Rashtrawadi, Shiv Sena and other parties. We know that now they can no longer function as a single unit and the important people, like the Sarpanch or any other senior members are unable to provide guidance. So, these different factions do not provide adequate support to any particular leader and even our children are bound to follow that. When one persisted that why such issues are not mentioned in the incantations, his response: "When people themselves are stupid, how can God help them. Even God is bound to be helpless. People run where they reap benefits rather than struggle for a common cause.

While there was a strong element of frustration and cynicism in the responses, perhaps the questions themselves were inappropriate with respect to rituals that had origins in a long historical past and that by their very ritualistic character transcended the details of the political economy of the present, while at the same time expressing a strong aspiration for food security and livelihood. Bhagat Baraf is a non-literate having left school because he was beaten; but is well versed in all the rituals except those related to death and illness. He cultivates his fields and migrates for work in the sand works beyond the agricultural season. He does not believe in bhutalis.

4. Cultural Changes Among the Adivasis

Enthoven, writing in 1922, describes certain external characteristics of dress which the majority of the present day adivasis, at least over the last 30 years, would hardly recognize. "In Thana, the men go with their heads bare, and on their bodies have nothing but a loincloth. The women, except a few of the well-to-do, wear nothing but a robe, one end of which is drawn over the shoulder and chest" (Enthoven 1922: 446). However, the following divisions among the adivasis as described in 1922 persist to the present.

"The Varlis have four endogamous divisions, Shuddha or pure Varlis, Murdes, Davars and Nihirs. Murdes and Davars, who are found in the north of the Thana district, eat and drink together and intermarry, but they neither eat, drink nor marry with the Nihirs, who belong to South Mahim, Bassein, Jawahar and Vada" (1922: 447). It is significant that the ritual practices of the adivasis as reported by an Assistant Collector in 1859 and as cited by Enthoven as continuing in 1922, remain largely the same to the present day: "Their religion consists chiefly in spirits worship. They think that every place is under the care of some spirit who lives in a tree or in a stone. Some they think unfriendly and spiteful, others friendly, and others indifferent, friendly or unfriendly accordingly as they are propitiated or not. They seldom have recourse to these spirits except to escape from evil. They stand in great awe of them. They are much given to the use of charms to turn aside evil caused by ill-natured spirits or neighbours. If any one falls sick they suppose the illness to be the work of an unfriendly spirit or neighbour, and send for some charmer, who either performs certain rites by which he divines the cause of the sickness, and what particular spirit has sent it, or he is himself seized with a shaking fit, and being thus, as they suppose, possessed by a spirit, tells the cause of the sickness and the means of recovery. In such cases medicine is seldom used. The usual cure is the sacrifice of a goat, a fowl or a coconut. The sacrifice is performed by a medium cutting the animal's throat, and then cooking and sharing it with the sick man's friends. At other times a sick person remembers that someone has lately abused him, and imagines his sickness to be the result of his abuse, and consequently charms have to be used" (1922: 450). While Enthoven (1922: 451) states that the only festivals that the Warlis have in common with the cultivating castes of Kunbis are Shimga/Holi and Diwali, there has been a greater imitation of Hindu rituals and festivals in the present.

On March 13, 1980, we had a very interesting discussion on the changes that have taken place among the Warlis regarding cultural practices with Roopji Vartha, an elderly Warli who had taken an active part in the struggles of the Lal Bavta in Kulambi village. He reported that about 40 years earlier, the shendi (a tuft of hair on a relatively shaved head) was worn by most of the men. This had almost disappeared among the Warlis. According to Roopji, G. Parulekar an important leader of the adivasis at the height of their struggles in the 1940s had told them to remove it since it was a symbol of oppression. The landlords would hold it and beat the adivasis. 'You should rather sit on the backs of the landlords and moneylenders'. The adivasi men have generally given up the loincloth (langoti) as a result of travel and exposure to other ways of dress in Mumbai, Thane, Kolhapur, Dahanu and Mahalaxmi. Wheat is eaten more as a result of compulsion than the earlier times when the staple diet was rice and jowar. There is a tendency for the younger, educated generation to go to the doctor at the time of illness, whereas the others go to the bhagat first and then to the doctor, if necessary.

A major change has taken place regarding expenditure for marriages and other ritual occasions. Generally the serving of food for the entire village or hamlet has been stopped. About Rs. 50 is given to the girl's parents at the time of marriage and Rs. 450 is spent on the villagers. A ritual in honour of Cheda Dev is performed at the time of the death of the head of the household. A wooden or stone image is made, sindhur is applied on it and it is placed in the field together with an offering of a chicken, coconut and a lamp. New rice has to be placed at this site at the time of the Khali threshing festival. The Cheda is installed only after divas pani for the dead is performed. Toddy has to be served to the clan members, but expenses on food have been stopped. The ceremony is performed within 10 days to two years' time depending on the economic circumstances of the family. The ceremony of sathi or dholi bharne is performed at the birth of the boy after four days and after three days for a girl. Presently food is given only to a few clan members and toddy is served to the whole hamlet. Rs. 10 for a boy and Rs. 8 for a girl is collected from each household from the hamlet in order to reduce expenses. Before this ceremony the child is not put in the cradle, we were told. These ceremonies may thus be seen as an ongoing recognition of lineage and as an initiation of the child into the clan in solidarity with its members. According to the local CPI(M) leader, "There has been very little impact of the Lal Bavta on cultural life. Rituals continue. Belief in bhuts continue. These questions have been neglected. Scientific and rational outlook has had some influence on party members through shibirs (camps)."

On October 15, 2015, we had further discussions on socio-cultural changes with Dhodia, an important CPI(M) village level leader. Apart from the tribal deities being worshipped and the traditional rituals, other gods like Ganesha were also worshipped. The adivasis also celebrate festivals like Navratri, Diwali, etc. Influence of the Hindu sects like the Nirankari, Swami Raghuvira Samartha, Swadhaya, etc. had increased. Initially these groups would preach under very basic infrastructure like tents and shades, but with more people joining the base has strengthened. What motivates the people to attend these practices or rituals is that alcoholism has reduced among them, which used to be a major social problem. There were about 27 villages in the Talsari taluka and sects like the Raghuvira Samartha and Swadhaya were very popular there, the latter being more popular amongst the fishing group. In Kochai village, particularly, the influence was about 10 to 15 per cent. People still worship the adivasi deities; it is just that they have seen others rising from illness and that is one of the reasons why they do not have a problem in following the alternative Hindu or Christian missionary groups. The adivasis are known for the solidarity they possess and the influence of any other group has not affected them negatively. Lal Bavta, the CPI(M) led Kisan Sabha, is strong particularly in the Talsari Taluka. The people still pursue this organization as they have been able to regularize encroachments on forest land from both the ends; administrative and local. Talsari taluka has also seen some increase in the political influence of the right wing Hindu groups. This can be measured by two popular schools; one in Sutrakar which is run by the Vishva Hindu Parishad (VHP) and the other in Girgao, which is a VHP school and hostel. Vansha Dumada is the Chairperson of the Panchayat Samiti. People believe in the Lal Bhavta as they have supported the Women's Bachat Gat (saving groups) which has made them financially more self-reliant. The Vividh Karyakari Seva Sahakari Society is involved in providing loans to people, apart from the 50 per cent government subsidy, and water facilities are made available. The rate of unemployment is very low in the area as it is close to the industrial belt of Gujarat. The youngsters usually go to Silvasa, in Dadra and Nagar Haveli to find employment on a daily basis, whereas the women from the village go to a company making pens and pencils, not too far away. There are about 15 to 20 concrete bungalows in the village for the adivasis. The government provides cement and asbestos sheets periodically, apart from the money that is transferred to the people's accounts. Practices such as Bhutali have seen a reduction due to improvement in education and employment facilities on the one hand, and due to influence of the Hindu and Christian missionaries on the other. There is a Primary Health Centre (PHC) in the village and the sisters help the patients. Comparatively, the health and medical condition of the locals is much better than before.

On December 15, 2015, we interacted with a few school teachers at the local secondary school which was initiated by the Kisan Sabha. We were informed that the local educated adivasis had begun commuting for employment to the industrial sites along the Gujarat coast and in Dadra and Nagar Haveli. They work as manual labourers, packers and a few with technical training handle machines. They get paid about Rs. 170 for 8 hours of work, Rs. 220 for 10 hours and Rs. 270 for about 12 hours of work, depending on the kind of work they do.

The adivasi youth participate in the adivasi rituals with enthusiasm. The younger children even miss school so that they might participate. Asked about the belief in bhagats and their rituals, one adivasi teacher said,

> There are certain truths in these ancient traditions. It is actually like, if you believe it is true and if not, then it is not. People say that God enters their body, so when you talk about God, if he is adivasi it means that it is ancient (adi), which means that these rituals are very old. Educated people, especially the urbanized or modern kinds, do not know anything about traditional medication. Adivasis reside in the forests which mean that they know and practise some ancient traditions. Some bhagats are very genuine and some of them are dummies. It is true that PHCs have contributed immensely to the health conditions of the village. Major problems like kidney disorders cannot be cured by the bhagats. These days people visit the bhagats for certain illnesses that can be cured by taking some medicinal plants available in the

> forests; but for the life-threatening diseases, people prefer going to the hospitals as they have seen lives being saved. So, it is a matter of faith in the kind of treatment available to the people.

It was mentioned that the younger generation find it difficult to undergo the training of the bhagats.

> The children these days are used to a convenient mode of lifestyle. Even if you ask them to stay away in a forest for a single day, they may be unable to make it. Four to six months is impossible to achieve with all the sacrifices required. It takes a lot of character to sleep without the wife for four months, stay away from meat and stop eating food once an animal faces you while having your meal. We use abusive language in our day-to-day communication, whereas while undergoing the training you have to keep your head calm, not use abusive words, control on thought process and frankly, it is not possible for this generation. The old people have left the world and taken those secrets with them as there was nobody reliable to pass this information on to. Hence, a lot of information and mantras have become extinct since. So all these reasons add up to the point that the will of the people has been reduced and hence the power of the mantras has been lowered comparatively. So the illnesses of the people do not get cured and they have no choice but to visit the hospitals. God will only work miracles if people have the faith in his presence. If the faith has gone down, then why would God be concerned and how would his miracles work?" About the belief in spirits, one of the adivasi teachers said, "There are many supernatural entities around and I have experienced them. If you consider them as being ghosts then your own fear will kill you, whereas if you treat the spirit like God then it can come like a blessing. It is said that there is just one source of power with a number of channels through which it flows. Human beings are all the same, for example, but some of them are a little notorious and others are good. If you treat the notorious ones as being good then they will reciprocate in the same way. That is how it works even with these supernatural entities.

The general impression was that the Christian and Hindu missionaries, such as the Nirankaris, had brought about positive changes among the adivasis; for example, the reduction of alcoholism.

5. Conclusion

It would be useful to identify what might be considered as the principal archetypal themes that serve as a running thread across the ritualistic incantations and provide a rationale from a historical and material basis for them. Perhaps the most important thematic content is the deep aspiration for grains that is still the primary basis for the adivasi livelihood in agriculture. The underlying emotional content of the incantations is full of pathos and desperation, resulting in humble pleading to the deity of grains, Kansari Devi. The incantations take on a character of at times abject self-depreciation in the face of the deity, a desperate recourse in the face of scarce livelihood options and new forms of exploitation. The further material basis for this state of consciousness could only be the uncertainties and insecurities with respect to land and livelihood starting from the early ancient engagement with settled agriculture as a transition from hunting, food gathering and slash and burn shifting cultivation; to the loss of land to the non-adivasi outsider, especially during British rule starting from 1818; the gains from the post-independence struggles and land reforms; and the further pressures on land through alienation and population increase till the present times. As discussed earlier, the adivasi belief in the afterlife of the spirit and the veneration of ancestors through the celebration of Pitra Amavasya in the month of Aswin (September-October) and the placement of wooden images representing ancestors, the Viras, on the boundaries of one's fields might have more to do with the assertion of lineage through the persisting symbolical presence of ancestors and thus also serving to stake one's claim to ownership of land in the context of illiteracy and the lack of access to scripted documents within the new order. These practices apparently do not necessarily represent an influence of the Brahmanical belief in the theory of Karma and the retribution for past ethical behaviour through caste-structured reincarnation.

A second significant theme is one which is especially observed during the marriage rituals and paintings through the veneration of Palghuta Devi, a symbol of fertility and procreation during the life cycle; but closely related to Kansari Devi, the fertility cult of the post-harvest festivals of the communal Gav Dev and the household

Khali. Palghuta Devi, as has been discussed, represents fertility both in humans and in nature/cultivation. She also suggests the tension between the female and male principles, perhaps indicating the transition from a primarily matriarchal community in the forests to one dominated by patriarchy, as a result of the impact of incorporation by ancient tribal marauders from the north west, who had a different linguistic affiliation, a largely pastoral economy and who took to settled agriculture initially over the Gangetic plains and then southwards thanks to a higher technological advancement through the access to iron implements, means of transport and weapons; a process that was reinforced much later when settled agriculture was institutionalized thanks to British land and forest policies starting from the early nineteenth century. The predominant role of bhagats as mediators in the rituals, especially related to agriculture and illness and the relegation of women as presiding agents to primarily marriage practices and some rituals of the life cycle, is possibly the result of the inevitable institutionalization of animistic, naturalistic beliefs and their transformation into a pseudo organized religion with a priesthood that imitates the Brahmanical one.

A latent thematic narrative over the incantations is the ongoing cycles and rhythms of time, interpreted in some detail in Chapter 2. The uncertain life cycles of individuals with an indefinite duration is seen as closely articulated with the insecurities of the annual agricultural cycle which has a relatively defined flow, though with uncertain outcomes due to ecological and socio-economic factors.

What might be seen as a theme that is diminishing in significance and salience is that of a sense of community. The advance of capitalist relations of production, urbanization, the media and strangely enough education, and the encroaching industrial belts that surround this region accompanied by ecological degradation has resulted in a growing individuation of households and persons, an instrumental orientation to the quest for livelihood wherever available and to political allegiance towards whoever can get the job done, imbued with a general reification of existence and a sense of anomie. These factors which might appear as insignificant from an analytic perspective are of great salience as seen from a subjective experience of a diminishing ethnic identity that is largely sustained in a manner of shared rituals. They serve as an assertion of distinct cultural identity. While the basis of community solidarity is still visible, the materialistic ground and meaning of contemporary adivasi beliefs as articulated through ritualistic incantations is obscure and calls for interpretation. This is due to the historical transfiguration of the ancient tribal Lokayata worldview under the enforced cooption by a Brahmanical, idealistic, ritualistic and the hegemonic interface with the non-adivasi caste society over a historical process of inclusive subordination over more than 5,000 years. It is ironical that the immanent social relational and contemporary historical contours of a system of beliefs gets lost in an, almost schizophrenetic, double-edged bind—existential meaning or escapist alienation through ritualism—that, as ritual, was the patrimony of the 'other'. The rituals are presently explained by the adivasis, including the knowledgeable bhagats, as something that has to be done almost as it were for its own sake lest evil befalls the people, as coming down over generations from the forefathers who knew best, as a practice of placating transcendental deities who once were in fact the product of the immanent animization of nature and the process of seeking one's livelihood from land and forests and, perhaps not mentioned, because ritualized festivals offer an escape from the drudgery of everyday insecurities through dance, music, intoxication and trance. *Thus the material basis of the rituals may be seen in the persistence of the themes of the quest for grains that ensures livelihood and food security; marriage, children and ancestors that is an affirmation of sustainable clan and tribal lineage; fertility, both human and within nature and agriculture; the awe of the feminine principle; and the bonds of adivasi solidarity as an ethnic/cultural, distinct community that could possibly be mobilized for political action for their economic, class interests.*

The adivasi identity tends to take on and struggles with several polarities in tension in order to establish a harmonious balance. These are mediated in order to arrive at a balance through various elements in the natural environment, intra-tribal social relations and ritual and cultural practices. These may be visualized as follows:

<table>
<tr><th>Polarities</th><th colspan="2">Mediations/Resolutions Towards Balance</th></tr>
<tr><td>Earth – Sky</td><td colspan="2">Hills, Forests</td></tr>
<tr><td>Livelihood/Food – Starvation</td><td colspan="2">Fasts</td></tr>
<tr><td>Life/Birth – Death</td><td colspan="2">Festivals, Rituals</td></tr>
<tr><td>Health – Illness</td><td colspan="2">Festivals, Rituals</td></tr>
<tr><td>Fields – Forests</td><td colspan="2" rowspan="2">Hunting/Food-Gathering</td></tr>
<tr><td>Cultivation – Hunting</td></tr>
<tr><td>Humans – Spirits</td><td colspan="2">Bhagat Possession</td></tr>
<tr><td>Male – Female</td><td colspan="2" rowspan="2">Fertility, Fecundity and Sexuality</td></tr>
<tr><td>Bhagats – Bhuts/Bhutalis</td></tr>
<tr><td>We – They</td><td colspan="2">Ancestors, Leaders</td></tr>
<tr><td>Present – Past in the Future</td><td colspan="2">Ancestors, Leaders</td></tr>
<tr><td>Good – Bad (Ethics)</td><td colspan="2">Custom, Tradition</td></tr>
<tr><td>Joy – Sorrow</td><td rowspan="3">Painting
Dance
Music</td><td rowspan="3">Aesthetic Expression</td></tr>
<tr><td>Courage – Fear</td></tr>
<tr><td>Voice – Silence</td></tr>
</table>

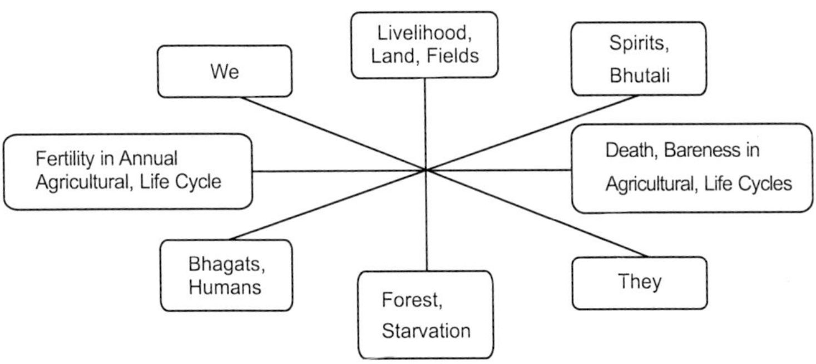

The changing notions of time apparently have not found an adequate resolution within fast changing contexts:

Natural Environment, Agricultural Cycle – Circular Time
Built up Environment, Industrial Cycle – Linear Time
Digital Environment, Virtual Cycle – Momentary Time

The ritualistic incantations, as may be seen above, clearly articulate the material base and the means of production—land, implements, labour, rainfall and ecological conditions, the forests, seeds—the entire production process and very clearly its uncertain outcomes, grains. However, one was intrigued by the fact that the incantations in rituals in contemporary adivasi contexts appear to have no direct reference to or representation of the iniquitous social relations of production, the present political economy and aspirations seeking redressal of the existing injustices; especially given the historical militant political participation of the adivasis in Kulambi village where most of the rituals were observed. Perhaps one's relatively futile attempts at seeking an explanation from the local community and the bhagats were inappropriate in the first place. The incantations in rituals are at best straightforward, empirical expressions of societal symptoms whose basis effectively lie in the ecology and agricultural production relations. As mythical articulations they have an allegorical significance in the sense that J. Clifford describes them, "Allegory (Gr. *allos*, 'other', and *agoreuein*, 'to speak') usually denotes a practice in which a narrative fiction continuously refers to another pattern of ideas or events. It is a representation that 'interprets' itself" (1990: 99). However, they are not analytic in their thrust, uncovering real causes of present conditions in an ideological manner and hence may not refer to social relations of production. Rituals, by their very fossilized nature, help to perpetuate ethnic identity through sustaining tradition. The belief systems expressed in the incantations may often not be understood and be meaningful to the participants in contemporary rituals. Which aspect of ethnic identity becomes a driving force would depend on the character of opportunistic political mobilization. Ethnic rituals are seen by the participants as not being directly related to political rituals as, for instance, electoral participation; because both are considered as practices that have been ritualized in a ritualistic manner. They are in practice viewed as the institutionalization of relatively distinct memories that may not directly influence life and livelihood practices; but are necessary to placate different powers. Another factor might be that the rituals have originated when the material basis of production was more significant; the insecurities of confronting early, institutionalized agriculture under British rule at a time dating back to at least the early nineteenth century or perhaps much earlier given that they might bear the traces of the materialistic Lokayata world view in opposition to the idealistic Vedic Brahmanism going back to over five thousand years, according to D.P. Chattopadhyaya (1978 a/1959; see Chapter 3). Besides, one needs to take into consideration the general adivasi tendency to speak happiness as a form of wish fulfilment and 'imitation magic', as also seen in the content of artistic expression, rather than speak bitterness lest evil befalls one.

One has observed and documented from secondary sources the transformation of some rituals as a para-science with a materialistic basis in agricultural practice to a magical belief system. M.F. Brown (1997) attempts to provide a rational explanation for tribal magical practices that might have a level of adequacy with science and that might find acceptance from a social science perspective. Magic as different from sorcery is seen by him as procedures that result in a perceptible impact on the physical world and as relevant to livelihood. We are in broad agreement with his views. He raises two crucial questions: "Does the persistence of magical thinking imply that there are radically different, even incommensurable, ways of experiencing the world–in other words, autonomous native epistemologies? Finally, is it the job of the anthropologist confronted with magical acts and utterances to explain those practices in terms of local understandings of cause and effect or is it to translate them into categories meaningful to social scientists?" (1997: 121). Our answer to the former question is in the affirmative. Regarding the latter, one is of the view that it is not a question of a choice between sustaining subaltern perspectives on their own terms or explaining them from the perspective of social science. In fact, the challenge is to arrive at adequate and empathetic social science interpretations that uncover the meaning of adivasi ritual practices in the terms of the adivasis. Brown attempts to interpret the case of women Aguaruna Indians of north-eastern Peru in the Amazonian rain forest who tend their chickens by singing to them. Drawing on Tambiah, he sees the possibility of interpreting magical incantations as aesthetic expressions or as a sense of participation and communion that the tribals have with their natural environment: "...magic may 'stimulate' work but is never confused with it. In short, magic is intended to say something, practical work to do something. This analysis rescues magic from the realm of flawed technology or irrational thought and redefines it is a form of self-expression, more aesthetic than operational in its ambitions...". In a later work, Tambiah (1990: 105-110) distances himself from the instrumental/expressive distinction in favour of a different set of complementary principles, which he calls 'causality' and 'participation'. "Causality is typified by the 'language of distancing and neutrality of action and reaction,' whereas participation denotes a sensibility in which a person is immersed in the natural and social worlds, experiencing a primordial oneness of subject and object" (Tambiah 1968: 202 and 1990: 105-110 cited in Brown 1997: 124 and 125). Brown's conclusion, with which one is in agreement, is that "a convincing theory of magic must encompass both the role played by language and magic's strong ties to experimental process" (1997: 126). Tribal societies tend to view practical knowledge as necessary for seeking livelihood, but to be complemented by 'wisdom or visionary insight' as a sufficient condition (1997: 127). It needs to be acknowledged that metaphorical and analogical thinking underlying the process of magical incantations has been an important source of creativity even in science and in cognitive processes. He concludes by suggesting what might be a relevant social scientific approach to magical practices: "Instead of conceptualizing magic as a discrete set of beliefs or practices, we might think of it as a sensibility—an intermediate point on a spectrum ranging from the purely instrumental to the purely expressive, or a state in which cause and effect are mediated by metaphor. Alternatively, we can reserve 'magic' as a provisional label for moments of ethnographic breakdown, when our understanding is challenged by that of our interlocutors, a situation demanding deeper exploration of local ideas about how things come to pass in the world" (1997: 131).

Adivasi magical belief in its original manifestations might be interpreted as a way of progressing towards truth through a process of formulation of tentative hypotheses. This approach has been an important inheritance, though largely unacknowledged, in contemporary times. Frazer makes these points in his exhaustive twelve volume study of legends, myths, taboos, magical and ritual practices throughout the globe: "We are like heirs to a fortune which has been handed down for so many ages that the memory of those who built it up is lost, and its possessors for the time being regard it as having been an original and inalterable possession of their race since the beginning of the world. But reflection and inquiry should satisfy us that to our predecessors we are indebted for much of what we thought most our own, and that their errors were not wilful extravagances or the ravings of insanity, but simply hypotheses, justifiable as such at the time when they were propounded, but which a fuller experience has proved to be inadequate. It is only by the successive testing of hypotheses and rejection of the false that truth is at last elicited. After all, what we call truth is only the hypothesis which is found to work best" (1957: 205-206).

Bogoras analyses the role of incantations during tribal rituals, in a similar manner; a performance which when in-corporated (brought into the body) and imbibed as an existential experience can have more than psychological effects. The whole life of early humans is wound over with all kinds of incantations. The incantation is a symbolic action, something like a child's or an actor's play, a conventional formula with a dramatically active realization. "In a passive state the incantation has no real force whatever. But when enacted, it has a power prevailing over anything" (Bogoras 1925: 209). The adivasi bhagats in Palghar district report that their source of knowledge is primarily the arduous induction process involving abstention from non-vegetarian food and sex that takes place for a period lasting over four months in a remote place within the forest and next to a stream under the guidance of a senior bhagat. However, some also report dreams and trances as the foundation of their insight into recitations that provide meaning to festivals and ritual occasions that serve as markers during the agricultural and life cycles. Especially in a largely non-literate society such as that of the adivasis, rituals and associated incantations from an oral tradition become the bearers of memory and meaning for the collective. Dreams and trances are also based on recollections, but while given a value in adivasi traditions are also admittedly seen to be diffused, erratic and ephemeral as sources of wisdom as compared to the arduous training of the bhagat. Bogoras reports that, "Dreams form the actual material, the basis, the principal source and the practical evidence for the scheme of animism. As to the fact that the visions of dreams (and also of external trances) actually represent the chief source of our religious knowledge, there are a number of important and varied arguments (1925: 241).

Not everything about adivasi rituals, though contextually understandable and relevant to the times, may be considered positively by the standards of contemporary value systems. However, empathetic comprehension requires that one assesses them in terms of their ancient historical origins. For lack of direct evidence this exercise is largely in the sphere of conjecture that is informed by an analysis of the social systemic and logical whole. Examples of practices with a negative valence might be the traces of human sacrifice to placate the female deity, wherever the practice in rare instances continues to exist, and the rituals of attributing evil to the evil eye of the bhutali, the witch, generally a destitute elderly woman who might be harmed to offset her possible claims to land, and in the context of the bhagat's inability to find effective cures for illness in the face of diminishing forest resources and medicinal plants. Some of these practices might be traced to Tantrism which did constitute an expression of ancient, subaltern materialistic beliefs in the tradition of Lokayata philosophy (D. Chattopadhyaya 1978 a/1959). However, these practices might be seen as a result of the perversion of Tantrism where the power of the feminine principle became the object of fixation and the explanatory cause of good as well as evil, in this case the latter. The use of alcohol in rituals holds deep spiritual significance among the adivasis, however, alcoholism might be more definitely attributed to ecological factors, the opening of liquor shops and indebtedness with the intrusion of the 'outsider', and the exploitative character of the social relations of production, as has been discussed earlier.

One of the most insightful analyses of the role of ritualized performances in perpetuating collective memory, and hence of collective identity, solidarity and tradition, that one has come across in the literature is that of Connerton (1989). He writes, "If there is such a thing as social memory, I shall argue, we are likely to find it in commemorative ceremonies, but commemorative ceremonies prove to be commemorative only in so far as they are performative; performativity cannot be thought without a concept of habit; and habit cannot be thought without a notion of bodily automatisms" (1989: 5). Village gossip, in addition, is seen as a means of creating a sustainable communal history (1989: 17). Connerton makes an important differentiation between myths that are recited and the incantations that are part of rituals. "To recite a myth is not necessarily to accept it. What the telling of myth does not do, and what the performance of a ritual essentially does do, is to specify the relationship that obtains between the performers of the ritual and what it is that they are performing. It follows from this that there is an element of invariance encoded into the structure of ritual that is not present in myth" (1989: 54). The following discussion of the different constituent parts of rituals is very relevant to the analysis of the rituals and incantations that mark the life cycle and the annual agricultural cycle on which the livelihood of the adivasis in Palghar district depends. "The performativeness of ritual is partly a matter of utterance: the recurrent utterance of certain characteristic verbs and personal pronouns. Among the verbal utterances most commonly encountered in rites are curses, blessings and oaths; much, if not indeed everything, is thought to depend in each case on the exactitude of the utterance itself... Curses, blessings and oaths, together with other verbs frequently found in ritual language, as for instance 'to ask' or 'to pray' or 'to give thanks', presuppose certain attitudes—of trust and veneration, of submission, contrition and gratitude—which come into effect at the moment when, by virtue of the enunciation of the sentence, the corresponding act takes place. Or better: that act takes place in and through the enunciation. Such verbs do not describe or indicate the existence of attitudes: they effectively bring those attitudes into existence by virtue of illocutionary act...Through the utterance of the 'we' a basic disposition is given definitive form, is constituted, among the members of the liturgical community. The community is initiated when pronouns of solidarity are repeatedly pronounced. In pronouncing the 'we' the participants meet not only in an externally definable space but in a kind of ideal space determined by their speech acts...Performatives are encoded also in set postures, gestures and movements. The resources of this encoding are elementary. In rites the body is given the appropriate pose and moves through the prescribed actions" (Connerton, 1989: 58 and 59).

When deepest aspirations are sublimated into rituals and incantations, they take on the character of a parallel order of reality whose transcendental imaginations of spacio-temporal dimensions have only a symbolic foothold in the real temporal and spatial rhythms of contemporary annual agricultural cycles and individual/generational life cycles. This order of the transcendental rituals might tell us something about real aspirations in given temporal contexts of which they were a more direct expression in the past. However, they persist on their own momentum with only indirect interpretative (allegorical) significance to the present unfulfilled aspirations.

CHAPTER 5

The Mahalaxmi Temple: Cultural, Religious Practices and Belief Systems Within Hegemonic Process

The historical background and the current religious beliefs and practices associated with the Mahalaxmi Temple Complex in Palghar district, Maharashtra provide an illuminating contemporary illustration of the hegemonic process implicit in the adivasi-non-adivasi cultural relations and the inclusive subordination involved in the process. As Kosambi writes: "Fieldwork based upon Poona leads to the conclusion that certain rustic traditions and observances in Maharashtra have their roots in the late stone age. Many nameless village gods have risen from gruesome origins to identification with some respectable Brahmin Deity. A transformation of the cult seems clearly to reflect a change in its human worshippers, from the food-gathering savage, through pastoralist, to agrarian food-producer. The development was not continuous, not always in a direct line. Conflict between the gods generally reflects human group-conflict. Divine marriages, acquisition of a family encourage, and successive incarnations are theological manifestations of social fusion. Such parallel changes in society and religion were repeated in different localities. The apparently senseless myths so illogically put together in our Puranas have a peculiar basis in reality. The villagers continue to live under conditions much nearer to those when the traditions and legends were formed; certainly more so than did the Brahmins who recorded a fraction of the local myth to synthesize it for their own profit" (2016/1962: 75). This historical hegemonic process within the context of the political economy of the region is discussed in some detail in the introductory Chapter 1.

The information that follows has been gathered over several field visits starting from April, 1979 and ending with the present. Apart from observations, across cultures, religious beliefs and economic transactions that mark the phenomenon of this temple, the sources of data have been interviews with non-adivasi Brahmin priests and adivasi bhagats/pujaris (medicine men/priests) associated with the temple and some adivasi and non-adivasi devotees that frequent the temple on special occasions. Limited secondary sources have served to fill in the gaps in information.

The Mahalaxmi temple is situated at the intersection of the Bombay-Ahmedabad and the Dahanu-Jawahar road at Charoti Naka, in Dahanu taluka, Palghar district. This place got its name from the fact that travellers would stop here for chai and roti (tea and bread). Our first field visit to the temple was in April 1979. A non-adivasi doctor attached to the Primary Health Centre (PHC) at Kasa, an important administrative center lying east of Mahalaxmi, reported that the village where the temple is located is Vival Vedhe which has a population of about 700, the vast majority of whom are adivasis living in four hamlets. The village has a primary school and a recently started Ashram (residential) school for adivasis. The majority of adivasi population depends on agriculture, with a minority engaged in manual labour on the then under construction Surya irrigation project under the Employment Guarantee Scheme and with the Timber Board of the Forest Department. To the west of the highway commences the slope that finally leads up to the Mahalaxmi peak. About 500 yards up the slope is the temple, with stalls on either side of the pathway leading up to it during the festivals. In front of the temple and on the right side of it are dharamshalas (guest houses); one financed by a group of Gujaratis from Africa and the other by persons from Surat, in Gujarat. On an open ground there was a fair with a giant wheel, circus, and other forms of entertainment. The Somaya Trust had started a temporary, charitable dispensary while the Kosbad Agricultural Institute had set up an exhibition on adivasi culture. The local Congress MLA had addressed a gathering of school children at a pandal (covered enclosure) next to the temple. About 300 beggars had lined up in front of the temple and were living in its corridors. The Shree Mahalaxmi Mata Renovation Trust had set up an office in front of the temple and was receiving donations that were sought over the loud speakers for the construction of a new temple. Film music was blaring out throughout the day.

1. The Oral Historical Tradition

A Parsi landlord and trader in the region informed us in April 1979 that the location of the temple is the residence of the in-laws of the goddess; her original maternal residence being in Surat in Gujarat. There were two sister goddesses, one has remained and the other has gone. The people of Gujarat have great devotion to the Devi and Mahalaxmi serves as a meeting point of Gujaratis and adivasis from Maharashtra. The image of the goddess used to be closer to the peak of the Mahalaxmi hill and relatively inaccessible to the non-adivasis. A pregnant woman, an adivasi, is reported to have had a dream and the Devi told her that she would appear at the present location near the foothill near the Bombay-Ahmedabad highway at Charoti Naka. Then gradually non-adivasis donated and a temple was built at the present place. There is still a stone image of the goddess higher up the slope and some people do go there. There is a spring emerging from the rock face. A tiger, a totemic symbol of the adivasis, roams the area as protector and people do not go there in the late evening or early morning.

However, a discussion held much later on August 7, 2017 with Rama Kadu, aged 75 years and the police patil of the nearby Dhanavri village suggests the real, oral historical basis of the origins of this temple, though lost in time with indefinite chronology:

> The Sathvis are the priests, but they do not know how to conduct all the religious ceremonies. The Kabulis (the Brahman pujaris/ priests) who are non-adivasis do. They come for a day and then go away. The temple was made of wood earlier. It was situated near the well and then was moved to its present location where it was re-constructed in wood. Only recently has it been reconstructed in stone and marble. The govari (gurakhi, i.e. cow-herd) of the Sathvis found a stone with sindhur (sacred red lead) on it. He showed it to the Sathvis. This was the birth of the Mahalaxmi temple.

Other discussions held much later than the first visit are presented here because they help to clarify the oral, historical traditions among the adivasis. Some factual references might come up later in one's presentation and will serve to enhance further clarity. The chronology of presentation that one has adopted might suggest a free floating narrative of associations; but, that is how a history without scripted documentation might be reconstructed from the nebulous recollections and memory records of the participants, both adivasi and non-adivasi. What is attempted primarily is a general theoretical interpretation from multiple sources. On August 8, 2017, we met Ladkya Ganpath Sathvi, an elderly member of the extended family of Sathvi bhagats now turned pujaris of the temple. His approximate age of 85 provides him a valuable perspective on the past, though overlaid with a fragile memory. He says:

> Mahalaxmi Aai was first up on the hillside. She was propitiated by many persons including two women of the Pagi and Magi families of adivasis. One of these became pregnant and was therefore unable to climb to the shrine. She therefore requested the Devi to come down. Her prayers were heard and the Devi was found in the kasaicha pondha (i.e. in a grassy field with kasai grass) where a spring flowed. The stone had a red tilak (sacred mark) on it. She was then installed as the deity at the site of the wooden temple.
>
> Phad Dev is the Kul Dev (Clan Deities, Hirva and Himai) of the Sathvi clan. But the scrolls which are rolled up also have stories from the Ramayana. At the Pitar Baras (an adivasi festival of ancestor worship held in October), the Phad Dev is taken down in the temple and taken to the house of the Sathvis for five days; then is taken to the hillside and then returned to the temple. For this ceremony three goats, two cocks and three hens are sacrificed. This sacrificial offering takes place not in the temple, but at the home of the Sathvis. One of the Trustees has told the Sathvis that since the Phad Dev is their family Dev, they should take their Phad Dev to their home permanently. But the Satvis refused to do so. Pitar Baras is the day that the pre-engagement ceremony (panchsherya) of the goddess. Mai Baras is the day of the engagement ceremony (badhavni) of the goddess. The wedding ceremony of the goddess takes place at the time of the Jatra (fair in October) and that's why

> people throng the temple. Mahalaxmi's maternal home is in Surat. That's why there are so many devotees from Gujarat.
>
> The Brahmans were asked to come to help out in the temple by the Sathvis as the Sathvis did not know the Vedic verses. The Brahmans come from a village near Palghar and near Saphala and Virar. The Brahmans are slowly taking over the entire shrine. Our children do not know anything about rituals and practices. The stone installed at present as the main deity in the Mahalaxmi temple is not the original stone. The original stone is a much smaller one and is installed at the side. But the smaller deity has the real powers. We were originally from Vivalvedha village. But we were landless. The government gave us land, about four acres, in Dabhon in the name of the Devi. We were also given some land as Patilanchi Pasodi (in view of being village officials). Land has also been given in Surat and Bhilad. The Bhilad land has been given by the government to the Brahmans. The youth who are being initiated into becoming bhagats come before the Devi to get vara (go into a trance) on Pitar Baras.

A legend associated with the temple is that of the Bhim Bandh (dam) as reported by Govind Sathvi, the main adivasi pujari (priest) of the temple in April 1979. This is apparently an attempt to associate the temple originating in adivasi belief systems with the classical Brahmanical mythology in an attempt to seek legitimacy or as a result of a process of hegemonic cooption. Bhim (one of the Pandavas of Mahabharatha fame) had asked goddess Mahalaxmi to marry him and she refused. In anger he said he would direct the waters of the Surya river across the path of the devotees of the goddess by building a dam and thus isolate her from her devotees. He wagered that the dam would be built before the cock crowed. The next day the work on the dam began but before it was completed Devi went there with a cock which crowed and the work had to stop. It is reported that presently there is a rock face with the mark of Bhim's back with the sacred thread. In front of the rock are some formations that resemble traditional bread and vegetables; testimony to the belief that Bhim was supervising the work and eating. Rocks piled on each other may be found across the Surya river about two kilometres from Mahalaxmi, remnants of the reported dam. Another version of this oral tradition we heard from Prakash Sathvi, one of the adivasi pujaris of the temple, during the field visit in October 2015. Goddess Mahalaxmi was travelling to Surat through the forests and on her way she reached a village where Bhim saw her shadow and having followed her, Bhim then came in her way and asked her to marry him. Mahalaxmi laid a condition that if he wanted to marry her, he should create a dam on the Surya River before dawn which would be indicated by the crowing of the cock. Having accepted this condition, Bhim used all his divine strength and started building the dam and even before dawn he almost completed the construction of the dam. Seeing this, Mahalaxmi adopted the role of a cock and crowed which was enough to convince Bhim that he had failed this test and he chose not to complete the rest of the dam. This incomplete condition of the dam can be seen even today in the region. During the Chaitra Pournima (April) jatra (pilgrimage), all the devotees of the goddess visit the site of the Bhim dam. What is common to the two versions of the Bhim dam associated with Mahalaxmi is the resistance of the goddess, a symbol of the adivasi female principle, to the overtures of Bhim, a non-tribal Brahmanical male representation. The legends also suggest a reference to the ancient historical tensions between the patriarchal society of the pastoral migrants and the then tribal, hunter-gatherer matriarchal communities.

The pujaris of the temple in 1979 were from eight adivasi families of the village who were entrusted with the task of looking after the temple. These eight were the descendants of the sons of the Dharma Sathvi, their early ancestor. The chief pujari and the eldest is Govind Laxman Sathvi who is about 60 years old. He has 17 acres in all and his younger brother Ganpat is the Sarpanch (village headman), as also one of the pujaris and an important official in the Jungle Kamgar Society, a cooperative of forest workers. The Sathvi family owes allegiance to the Congress Party (i.e. the then ruling party). Kanha Dharma Sathvi, his nephew of about 35 years of age, is the Police Patil of Mahalaxmi which suggests that the family is politically and administratively well connected. Govind can trace his family tree back to three generations. According to Govind, the family had a lot of land in the past. The entire village belonged to Kanya Sathvi, his grandfather and son of Dharma Sathvi from whom the eight Sathvi families had descended. During the intervening years the non-adivasi landlords 'had eaten up a lot of our lands'. The families are in charge of the temple by rotation for a year and for the rest of the time are engaged in agricultural work. According to Govind, the family that is in charge of the temple for a particular year earns about Rs. 6,000 through donations, however there are many expenses. The head pujari appeared resentful at the destruction of the old temple which stood where the new one was being constructed. It had strong beams, many carvings and several open spaces. The Sathvi family tried its best to see that the old temple was repaired rather than knocked down; but were told by the non-adivasi trustees that a new and beautiful temple would be built along the lines of the one in Somnath.

According to Govind, his forefathers informed the Peshwas who had come to the village on horseback to inquire about the Devi, that this Devi was very helpful to the childless and the poor. The Peshawa asked his forefathers to make an offering and he was granted a child. From that time every year the temple gets an offering of Rs. 125 till today when it is received from the Mamlatdar's (government official) Office. This practice has continued over the British and the post-independence rule. The village had come under the rule of the Jawahar State during the British period. Every year at the time of Chandashi they have been giving a sari for the Devi, Rs. 125 and a salary of Rs. 18 and two flags for Narayan Sathvi, the one who puts the flags; one for the peak and one to be put on the pole in front of the temple. Even though today the power of the Mukne Raja who belongs to the Mahadev Koli adivasis of Jawahar has gone, Yashvant Mukne who is no more and who had once been elected to parliament and his son continue to send these things directly. The significance of the sun and the moon on the flag of the peak which is nine yards and the flag in front of the temple which is five and a half yards indicates that 'Ai' (mother) represented by the moon has come from the direction of the sun floating on the seas. The waters were pulled back and Ai settled on the present peak between four hills which stand today. These four hills are like the soldiers of Ai. The sun and the moon signify that the Ai is as old as them.

It should be noted that the cult of the Mahalaxmi in general goes back to at least the early historical period with its sacred complex being located at the city of Kolhapur. Historical sources indicate that the temple of Mahalaxmi at Kolhapur may have existed from around the seventh century AD onwards. The Mahalaxmi temple at Kolhapur is supposed to be one of the six most sacred sakti pithas where one can obtain salvation. This sakti peetha (seat of power) is of special religious significance as it is believed that one can have all desires fulfilled or attain salvation by praying there. The nature of the sacred complex of Mahalaxmi is of course ambiguous. Is Mahalaxmi the Laxmi, consort of Visnu or Parvati, the consort of Siva, or is she the Adi Sakti the mother of Brahma, Visnu and Siva is a question to which there are many strands of traditions ascribing to one or the other nature of her origin (Dhere 2009). The Devibhagwat Mahapurana gives the prime place in the list of sakti peethas to Kolhapur and the reason it cites is it being the place where Laxmi has always resided. It then lists Mahur and Tuljapur in that order, which are the abodes of Rebuke and Bhavani (Sircar 1973). In the early medieval context the process of state formation went in tandem with the evolution of the local cults and the followers of the same. All the major upcoming dynasties/lineages who attempted to become 'states' made donations to the newly formed sacred complexes in order to harness the followers of the cult to their cause as well as to legitimize their own fledging kingdoms. The offerings made by the adivasi rulers of Jawahar in Palghar district may be seen as part of such a process and is in fact a part of the framework that evolved as the 'tribes' and lineages attempted state formation.

2. The Deity, Adivasis and Non-Adivasis: Socio-Cultural Relations

2.1 April, Ramnavmi, Hanuman Jayanti

To continue the narrative of our field visit in April 1979, it was observed that in one section of the fair there was a collection of traders with onions, potatoes, spices, salt and other daily requirements of the adivasis for barter. The adivasis bring seeds of sag (a vegetable), kherasni (seeds for oil), ringni (a medicinal plant) and other produce gathered from the forests. They get two kilos of onions worth about Rs. 3 as barter for a kilo of seeds worth at least Rs. 10, according to the official of the Primary Health

Centre (PHC). We were informed that rates of unequal exchange for various types of forest produce collected by the adivasis were: For one kilo of gum worth about Rs. 4 they would either get one kilo of pulses, or half a kilo of chillies, or one-fourth kilo of garlic, or one kilo of potatoes, or two kilos of onions, or half kilo of turmeric, according to their need. For one kilo of the following: karandi the adivasis might receive in barter two kilos of onions; for rita (a seed for soap), one and a half kilos of onions; for arandi (used for oil), two and a half kilos of onions. The adivasis camp out in the open, in the spaces around the temple with their rented carts and cooking fires. Some adivasi households of the village rent out their houses to the non-adivasis for the festival period. In front of the temple is a flagpole with a flag on which is a sun and a moon.

It was reported that about two lakh people attend the festival. On Sunday April 15, 1979 the non-adivasis were about 70 per cent of the people. And on the next day, their proportion had dropped to half together with a drop in the absolute number of the devotees. The original Trust, which continued in 1979, was started around the 1940s. The Trust was reconstituted in 2002. The majority of the members were non-adivasis, government officials, landlords and some middle class professionals of the region, together with the adivasi Sarpanch (village head man) of Mahalaxmi and an adivasi pujari of the temple. During the course of our conversation with a non-adivasi trustee, the clerk of the Trust rushed in and complained about an adivasi who in a drunken state accused the Trust 'of putting a foot on the stomach of adivasis'. Our interlocutor replied that the Trust was there to help the adivasis and the temple. According to him the Mahalaxmi tradition goes back to the time of the Peshwas before British rule and has always been with the adivasis.

During our presence at the temple in April 1979, an adivasi offered a cock to the Devi which was not slain but taken away. It was reported that some adivasi women get possessed in front of the image of the Devi. We saw two women getting possessed and making a sound like 'hinska, hinska, hinska!' The non-adivasis generally pick up a tray from the shops close to the temple in which there is sindhur (red lead), ghee (clarified butter), a coconut and sweets. By the side of the temple there is a huge weighing scale attached to the roof. Humans, especially children of formerly childless couples, are weighed against goats, coconuts, fowl, raw sugar, etc which become the property of the Sathvi family. The chief adivasi pujari, Govind Sathvi informed us that whatever is offered in the collection boxes goes to the temple Trust and whatever is offered directly to the pujari at the place of worship becomes the property of the Sathvis. It was reported that 30 per cent of the collections go to the Satvi family and 70 per cent to the Trust.

The fairs and shops start appearing around the temple from Ramnavmi in the month of Chaitra (April). On the first day of the religious festival on the eve of Purnima (the full moon, April 11 of that year), the ornaments and the silver image of the Devi are placed on a rock face. The Purnima Hom (ritual fire worship) is conducted by a Brahmin appointed by adivasi pujaris for the benefit of the Mangelas (a backward caste group) and the Wanis (traders from Gujarat). The rock has the shape of the Mahalaxmi peak and according to one of the non-adivasi Gujarati trustees, the rock has risen spontaneously. On the full moon night, Narayan Sathvi who is the Patil of Wagadi village, gets possessed and climbs the peak to install the flag given to him by Govind Sathvi, the head priest. On the Panchmi (fifth day, April 17) the Devi is bathed, the ornaments consisting of the mask and the crown are removed and entrusted to our non-adivasi, Gujarati informant, the trustee who runs a printing press in Dahanu. The other ornaments are kept with the adivasis. On the Ashtami (eighth day, April 20) there is a Hom (fire worship) where the ears of a goat are cut and it is let loose. The Ashtami Hom is conducted by the adivasi pujari.

The people break their vows through offerings of coconuts, jaggery or goats and cocks. They exhibit the goat in front of the Devi, make it walk around the temple and leave it alive so that the adivasi pujaris can take it. A goat has also to be given to the one who places the flag on the peak together with 500 suparis (areca nuts) and 500 paan (leaf to be chewed) at the time of this festival which appears in April. The adivasi pujari sits as the Yajman at the time of the Ashtami Hom while the Brahmin performs the Hom. When the Yatra (festival period) is over then the Utran Puja has to be done.

> We clean up the temple on Purnima and offer three goats and a cock. The Devi is bathed and a new sari and choli are worn. The meat is eaten by the entire village and our family members have also to cook two bags of rice. The keys of the temple are entrusted to the new adivasi pujari family in rotation.

A goat has also to be given to the one who places the flag on the peak together with 500 suparis and 500 paans at the time of this festival. The expenses related to the temple are reported to be several since about 15 servants of the temple have to be paid and the Brahmin has to be paid the expenses of the Hom (coconuts, bananas, almonds, clarified butter) at the time of the current festival and for the goat which has to be sacrificed on the Ashtami (eight) day. About six or seven Brahmins are needed for different functions. An Aarti (ceremonial offering) is done in the morning and evening every day at the temple.

> Mantras (religious chants) are not said at the time of the adivasi Pujas; that's for the Brahmins who also say some prayers at the time of the Vidhi which runs as follows, 'Keep everyone happy, may the traders get prosperity. Do good for the people and in your goodness whatever you give us is our salary'.

Govind reported that the work of the adivasi pujaris is handed down over generations by the father. On the days of the Ghat Vasvate for nine days they do not eat meat but only rice, dal and milk and only one meal a day. They cannot eat or drink from the hands of a woman. The one who puts the flag on the peak has to abstain from meat from the time of Holi (Shimga) right up to the time of placing the flag and has to eat only vegetarian food cooked with his own hands once a day. He cannot have sexual relations with his wife during this period. The task of placing the flag is given to only one family which has to do it every year. Four or five of his nearest family members accompany him to the peak. He belongs to the Sathvi family from Wagadi village. At 12 midnight, this Sathvi is sent to the hill from the temple once he is possessed by the goddess. He runs to the top, performs the arti, hoists the Peshwa flag and returns to the temple by the highway at around 4 or 5 am. Not a single failure has been reported till today. This Sathvi has complete protection provided by the police who ensure that people do not block his way when he starts running towards the hill. He does not stop for anybody on the way. There are people who jump at his feet to take the blessings from the goddess. Even this does not distract him as he is in a complete trance and has no understanding of whatever is happening around. Govind continued:

> Our forefathers had divided the work among the different families, for example the playing of the musical instruments in the temple. The fakir (Muslim holy man) and the hijras (eunuchs) are also given gifts on this occasion. The hijras are given saris and gifts amounting to Rs. 200. The hijras might be adivasis or non-adivasis. The fakir comes from the Jawahar Sansthan. The Jawahar Sansthan was originally a fakir Gadhi which was given to the Mukne household of the Koli Samaj. The fakir continues to stay there in a Dargha (shrine) in Jawahar. If there is a death in the family the pujari who is entrusted with the temple for a given year cannot perform Puja for 12 days. Then another family of the Sathvis takes over and is paid wages. This is our eighth generation, as far as we can remember, as servants of the Devi. Before that was the time of the Kauravas and the Pandavas. There are bhagats among the adivasis, but we are not bhagats who use rice and put shendur (red lead) on leaves. We are pujaris of Ai and we use suparis (areca nuts). But bhagats are called on Pitru Baras and Maha Baras. They perform certain rituals on these occasions and whip themselves. The Devi who enters the body of the bhagat and this Devi is the same. They take her name and because of that they get possessed.

There appeared to be some difference of opinion on matters of adivasi customs between different representatives of the Sathvi families; as also suggested by attempts to distance the adivasi pujaris of the goddess from the Malhar Koli clan of Sathvis (given their closeness to the Brahmin pujaris) from the adivasi bhagats of the Warlis, as seen in the foregoing narrative. For example, while Govind Sathvi, the adivasi head priest, was insistent that Brahmins are called at the time of their marriages, Kana Sathvi, another pujari family member, stated that Davlaris are called according to adivasi custom. According to Govind, the Warlis require Davlaris and Suvasanis to perform at their weddings; but the Sathvis being Malhar Kolis, Davlaris may be called but it is the Brahmins who perform the weddings. Malhar Koli daughters are not given to the Warlis. Eating is permitted in each other's houses, which was not permitted earlier, but there are no marriage exchanges. Malhar Kolis are higher than Warlis, according to the Sathvi pujaris, and below the Warlis are the Konknas and the Kathkaris who consume the flesh of dead animals. When it was pointed out that the adivasi gods like Vagaya, Hirva and Joting are different from those of the Brahmins and how Mahalaxmi got accepted by the adivasis, Kana Sathvi insisted that,

> The Devi tradition has always been with the adivasis. We did not accept her. Devi was born amongst us. Our forefathers saw her in their dreams and she grew amongst us. The tiger roams in the forest and is the vahan (vehicle) of the Devi. Malhar Kolis recognize the Hindu gods.

We were informed that adivasis, like the non-adivasis, make vows and ask the Devi for children for the childless couples. In addition, the latter would petition the Devi for houses, success in business and for husbands for their women. Do the adivasis ask for more lands, for rains and for adequate grains, we were keen to know. According to Kana, one of the adivasi pujaris, "They ask no! But where does the government give these things?" When one insisted whether they ask the Devi for these things, his response was, "Yes, they ask sometimes."

There are festival periods at the temple that are more specifically that of the adivasis as different from those when non-adivasis also participate. The sharp contrasts in the offerings, the religious practices, in the involvement of the adivasi bhagats as main celebrants and in the cultural practices may be noted. A festival is held at the time of Mahabaras which occurs in the month of Magh (February) when three goats and five hens have to be bought and the whole village has to be fed and given toddy (fermented sap of the palm tree) and daru (country liquor). "Then at the time of Makar, a goat is offered when the doors of the temple are closed and a goat is slaughtered, but not in front of the Ai (mother). Animals are not sacrificed in front of the Ai for she is Laxmi and her food is different." The Mahabaras festival and the Vagh Baras festivals are observed by the adivasis at home in the village as well.

According to Govind, head pujari, festivals at the temple are also held during (August-September) for 12 days when a bhagat (adivasi medicine man) is called and drink and food have to be given to him and his family. For the Magh and Bhadrapad festivals Brahmins are not needed, but rather adivasi bhagats are called. At the time of Bhadrapad, Pitra-Amavasya, the damru (a drum) is played. The bhagat is called and about 30,000 adivasi youth dance throughout the night of the twelfth day of Krishna Paksh, the dark night. The tarfa (a wind instrument made out of a gourd) is played and marriages are arranged between boys and girls. This festival comes before Diwali around August-September. Pitra-baras is celebrated on the twelfth day of the Bhadrapad month. As it is predominantly an adivasi festival, all the adivasis from the neighbouring towns and villages visit the temple. The essential feature of this festival is the tarpha music and dance. The crops that grow during the rain like rice, chawali, pumpkin, cucumber and all the new farm produce is not consumed by the adivasis before this day. On this day, the adivasis hold a fast in the name of Mahalaxmi and they arrive at the temple, show the produce to the goddess and only after that they consume this harvest. This temple is like the kuldev for the adivasis so they come here for the worship. There is a group that performs the bhajan during the worship and they have been traditionally performing this. Other festival occasions are during Dussehra when the pujaris have to do Ghattsthapna which continues for nine days.

We interviewed Sakhya Gobind Baswat, an adivasi farmer from Charoti village nearby. He has four acres of land which normally gives him 10 khandis of grain. But this year owing to the inclement weather, he received only five khandis. The paddy from his land generally lasts his family, consisting of his wife, three daughters and a son, throughout the year. His father had 20 acres which was distributed among his five sons. He says that the adivasis have great faith in the Ai (mother) and ask for favours such as for a child, cure from illness, a house. They do not ask for grains, or rains, or for plentiful crops. He said:

> The rain is higher than the Devi, the Devi has no power over rain. It would have been good if the Devi could control rain. The Devi was benevolent to the adivasis before the old temple was knocked

down around 1975. Today the Trust is building a new temple and the Devi is angry that her temple has been knocked down. There were many beautiful structures of dogs, lion, tigers, etc (totemic symbols of the adivasis) earlier. These have all been dug up and knocked down. The new temple will never be able to capture the beauty of the old.

He has never asked for favours or taken vows (navas) given that he has not had the need to ask for favours. According to this adivasi informant, 15 days before Diwali the adivasis have a festival of their own at Mahalaxmi. There are dances with the tarpha (a wind instrument made of a gourd) and the adivasis make good their vows at that time. He is then employed by the Primary Health Centre to work as a sweeper for the period of the 15 days of the fair. Laxman, an adivasi from Saiwan village, has eight acres of land from which he gets about three khandis (one khandi = ten maunds) of paddy in addition to the coarse grain of vari which lasts the family throughout the year. His family consists of his wife and two children. He brings vari and sells it at the fair to the traders. In exchange he gets potatoes, onions, and turmeric for the rainy season. He arrived in a bullock cart together with three other families and returned the same day by the state transport. He has faith in the Devi and had not made any vows.

There are similar phenomena to the cooption of adivasi religious practices by non-adivasis, caste society in the vicinity; or the adivasis seeking legitimacy under the hegemony of Bramanical Hindu belief. On April 16, 1979 we visited the Santoshi Mata temple at Ashagad village and had an interaction with its non-adivasi trustee. The temple was started in 1961-62 and its pujari, Jethya Rahya Karmoda, is an adivasi. He says that unlike the Mahalaxmi temple which was installed at the given site, the Santoshi temple is a swayambhu, i.e. self-established from an original rock formation. The pujari had a dream in 1961 that the goddess was inviting him to come and worship her at a given place. Till 1971, Jethya used to conduct the temple on his own. A registered Trust was then formed and he was employed by the Trust. His son has completed his elementary education and is a member of the Trust together with several non-adivasis who are major landlords, advocates, traders and persons employed in the service sector in the region.

People had been coming to the temple from 1962; and in 1974, after the formation of the Trust, there was a sharp increase in the number of devotees. At the time of our visit it was popular with both adivasis and non-adivasis. The main day is Chaitra Purnima when about 5,000 people come. A Brahmin performs the Hom and a non-adivasi is the Yajman. The festival lasts till Ashthami (the eighth day). According to the doctor, who was a trustee of the temple:

> Vaghaya means tiger and the tiger is the vahan (vehicle) of the Devi. The adivasis were always Hindus. The pujari used to be very poor before 1961, now he is rich.

Along the Bombay-Ahmedabad highway there is a Vagoba (tiger) temple. In August 1988 we interacted with the priest of the temple who is an upper caste individual from Amravati, Vidharaba region in Maharashtra. At the age of 12, he moved to Bhavnagar in Gujarat. In 1980, he came to the Satevli Ashram in Palghar taluka of the then Thane district. The adivasis told him about the Gav Dev (village deity), a stone formation away from the highway in the valley. During the renovation of the highway in 1980, the adivasis had brought the Gav Dev closer to the highway, applied sindhur (red lead) on it and constructed a temple. Truck and cab drivers now stop and give donations. An adivasi serves as a helper.

On April 22, 2016, we paid another visit to this temple, after a long interval of time, in order to consider the status of our earlier observations. There was a huge crowd near the temple. More than 500 persons—mostly Gujaratis stood in line to take darshan and approximately 70 per cent of the crowd consisted of non-adivasis mainly from the Silvassa area. The local adivasis were expected to throng the area from 8 pm onwards. The pujaris belonging to the Sathvi adivasi clan presided over the proceedings; the various Sathvi families being allotted two hours each to preside and accept earnings. This year was the turn of the Sathvis from Dabhon village, it being said that the festival when the Dabhon pujaris preside is a big jatra. It was also said that a jodi (human sacrifice of a boy and a girl) would be given to the Devi, but this could not be verified. A silver crown was placed on the deity's head in the temple. Some Gujarati devotees offered gold, silver and saris to the

Devi, together with some adivasis offering saris. It was noticed that four goats were also offered by adivasis to the Devi which were not slaughtered in the temple premises, but were taken home by the pujaris. The ceremony regarding the taking of the flag to the Mahalaxmi pinnacle was to begin around 11 pm. We were told that the temple is emptied out. The flag bearer—who is always a Satvi hailing from Waghadi village, will go into a trance. All is quiet. No sound emanates. The flag bearer will come out from the temple, by which door of the temple no one knows. He will be accompanied by a few people. But the last stretch on the Mahalaxmi pinnacle, he does on his own. He returns down around 4 to 6 am. When information that he is returning is received, then all the shops are opened. He applies tilaks on the foreheads of the shopkeepers and they give him cash in return.

A fair is held on this festival occasion with several small stalls on both sides of the way up to the temple, which we had observed close to forty years ago. The main shopkeepers near the temple were the non-adivasis, the shops of the adivasis being in the side lanes. The bhujing (chicken) shops are at a distance from the temple. Visitors to the jatra consume non-vegetarian food, but after going to the temple. Some non-adivasi shopkeepers also said that they eat non-vegetarian food but from the next day after the flag is hoisted on Mahalaxmi hill. Different lanes had shops selling food, bangles, plastic items, footwear and various agricultural implements. The sale/exchange in forest produce had not yet begun and would start the following day. The area had been identified and kept reserved for the traders.

During a revisit to the temple during this festival period on May 4, 2016 we found that more than half the visitors were adivasis. Some of the distinctive features of this festival fair were the bhujing galli where chicken was grilled whole or on skillets on open fires. There was a salt fish lane where stalls were set up mainly by people from the Mithna (Machi) community from the Khatalwad, Sanjan area. Fresh fish was also being sold. Other items of local produce were being sold by the local adivasis, for example, boiled sweet potatoes, targolas in vaatas (counted shares). But the special feature of this fair is the trade in forest and other produce. About 30 shops of non-adivasis involved in the barter/sale of forest produce were situated on both sides of one aisle. The shopkeepers were mainly from nearby areas, e.g. Vadhna, Udhwa and Jawahar. The shops were set up on the day after the first Hom on April 23. The shopkeepers were ready and willing to purchase any type of seeds or forest produce including kaju, kandol (kaag), ringni, karanj, ambadi, takla (tarota), gunj, kaachki (sagargota), vikhra, ambat vela seeds, gum (of any tree including kandol, ain, beheda, shegut, dhamoda). Kaju was the most popular item being traded. The items could be bartered or sold to the shopkeepers, e.g. one could sell the kaju seeds at Rs. 120 a kilo or barter them for 12 kilos of onions. One could also barter the items for a host of other items which were available with the traders, e.g. garlic, daali, haldi, haldi powder and chillies. Ringni and kandol were exchanged for a similar quantity in weight of daali. It was noticed that the adivasis preferred to barter the items, especially for onions, instead of selling them and obtaining cash. Ambat vela seeds fetched a price of Rs. 300 per kilo. The adivasis brought large or small quantities of the seeds and produce. Some brought only about two kilos of kaju seeds, while others brought more than 100 kilos. One adivasi woman informed us that she brought kaju seeds from only one tree and received 60 kilos of onions in exchange.

It was observed that both electronic and manual weighing machines were used by the traders. There were some complaints that the traders were cheating on weight. One woman who received 10 kilos of garlic on barter weighed the garlic on a scale elsewhere and found that she had been cheated of 1.5 kilos. One non-adivasi couple visiting the temple from Baroda observed that as traders themselves they could easily see that the local traders were cheating on weight. There was one stall set up by the Kasa branch of the government-owned Maharashtra State Cooperative Tribal Development Corporation which purchased gum under the Monopoly Procurement Scheme. No other item of forest or other produce was being purchased by the Corporation. The rate of gum was Rs. 95 per kilo. The gum could be exchanged for other items, e.g. nagli, paddy, vari, udid, etc. However, all the items for exchange had been exhausted. The stall was set up late. The person in charge claimed that the stall had purchased about six quintals of gum during the past week. Business was brisk in most of the stalls.

One shopkeeper claimed that he had purchased about two tons of kaju seeds from the start of the jatra. We were informed that traders mainly from Gujarat would purchase the seeds and other forest produce from the traders at Mahalaxmi. Some traders from Vikramgad and Talwada also purchase the produce. If the traders do not come to Mahalaxmi, then the local traders transport the produce to their homes in the nearby area and the large traders then purchase the produce from there. One trader informed us that the large traders would purchase the seeds at the rate that are announced. He said that the rate for kaju seeds had already been announced at Rs. 126 per kilo. We were informed by villagers that while the sale of kaju had increased in recent years, the sale of other forest produce had decreased. Instead of bringing the produce to the Mahalaxmi fair, the villagers now exchanged the produce, e.g. teak seeds, takla seeds, ritha seeds, to traders in the local markets, e.g. Udhwa, Dhundalwadi, Gangangaon, on weekly market days or even every day. The teak seeds were exchanged for an equal volume of potatoes.

2.2 October, Pitra Baras

On October 9, 2015, we carried out a field visit to what might be called the Mahalaxmi Temple Complex consisting of three temples from the peak downwards: The Mahalaxmi Gad, with Dama Bolada as the adivasi pujari, closer to the peak and considered to be the site of the first appearance of the deity in a cave; the shrine presided over by Ishwar Bolada, midway up the slope; and the main Mahalaxmi temple, at the foot of the incline presided over by the Sathvis. We first made a visit to the Mahalaxmi shrine presided over by the adivasi pujari, Ishwar Bolada. It was constructed around 2002 and consists of a small temple and a large shed with a courtyard. Ishwar said that he had a dream that the Devi wanted to descend from the shrine on the top of the hill. A large stone broke away from the Mahalaxmi Gad and was brought down to the present site where he had constructed a shrine. Ishwar refers to the site as being the place where some rakshas (demon) was killed. Many devotees came to the shrine and took vows to appease the Devi if they were granted children or were cured of illnesses. Some of these devotees provided Ishwar with cement sheets for the construction of a shed.

Ishwar faced opposition from the Forest Department when he had constructed the shed as it lies on forest land. But as he had the support of the villagers, the Forest Department backed out.

The climb from Ishwar's shrine to the Mahalaxmi Gad temple was steep. On the way there were two smaller shrines—one dedicated to Hanuman, the other to Mahalaxmi Parekari. While some devotees did pay obeisance at these shrines, neither of the shrines seemed to be of major significance. The temple at Mahalaxmi Gad was in a cave situated on the western side of the Mahalaxmi hill. It is said that the Devi first resided here before she descended to the main Mahalaxmi temple below. The cave is the source of a spring. The cave was low and one could not even sit upright inside. To enter the cave one had to crawl on all fours. Till a few years ago one had to crawl on one's stomach, but the adivasi pujari (i.e. Dama Bolada's father) cut away some of the rock to make the cave more accessible. There were a few sacred spots within the cave. The various shrines to Saunri could be seen in clusters on the roof of the cave and was identifiable by sindhur (red lead) applied to the spots. There was a spot where the original Mahalaxmi deity was supposed to have resided. She has now been brought outside and is placed at the entrance of the cave. A stone with a smearing of vermilion is identified to be Mahakali.

Around 1990, a Trust was formed and under its aegis the entire area outside the cave had been transformed. This Trust appears to be different from the main Mahalaxmi Trust which oversees the main temple at Mahalaxmi. The members of the Trust include both adivasis from the surrounding villages and non-adivasis from Dahanu, Vangaon and Mumbai, with the actual management in the hands of the latter. A three-storeyed structure has been constructed, the ground storey consisting of a hall which houses the deity who has been brought out from the cave. She is accompanied by other goddesses of the Hindu pantheon, including Ambamata. A pujari belonging to the Bolada adivasi family presided and a short distance away two non-adivasis belonging to the Trust also sat officiating over the ritual proceedings. When we visited this temple in the afternoon, about 40 to 50 persons were dancing in a trance to the accompaniment of music played on the dhol (a percussion instrument). Most of those possessed were adivasi women. A few non-adivasis, including some men, were also dancing in a trance which lasted for about 45 minutes. There were three donation boxes, the collection from two of the boxes going to the Trust while that of one of the boxes to the Bolada adivasi pujaris. The monetary offerings made in front of the deity went to the presiding adivasis of the Bolada family. Other offerings in the form of jewels and saris for the deity accrued to the Trust. While the Bolada pujaris had were resentful towards the Trust, they also grudgingly recognized that the number of devotees (and consequently their earnings) had increased after the Trust had undertaken the task of providing facilities to the pilgrims. Part of the ground and first storey constructed by the Trust was within the cave resulting in a total transformation of the cave which is today hardly recognizable as a cave. Rooms had been constructed as kitchens and a long narrow hall for meals for pilgrims in the basement. Some additional constructions were in progress. An additional large construction was in progress about 100 metres to the north of the shrine. Drinking water was pumped up through a pipeline laid from Ranshet village undertaken by the Trust which bore all expenses for water and electricity. In addition all expenses and arrangements for food for the pilgrims were borne by the Trust through donations. Concrete steps from Ranshet village up to the temple had been constructed. Just before one approached the temple, there were a number of small shops selling items required for religious offerings and refreshments owned by the adivasis from Ranshet village.

Most of the visitors to this temple were adivasis from the Davar area of Palghar district, i.e. from the area to the north and north-east of the temple, including many from Dadra and Nagar Haveli and some from Dahanu taluka. The absence of adivasis from the west and south of the temple was significant. Community-wise, one did not notice any adivasis belonging to the Kokna tribe; the adivasis by and large belonged to the Warli tribe. The adivasi pujaris, i.e. the Boladas, belonged to the Malhar Koli tribe. Interestingly, it is said that the Boladas were originally Bhoirs, but due to internal differences some generations ago the Bhoirs of Ranshet changed their name to Bolada. The Bolada pujaris fought within the clan over who would be presiding over the deity. After a dispute which even reached the courts, it was decided that the four major Bolada families would preside one every year. Many of the devotees came every year to the shrine to fulfil vows taken regarding begetting children. Additionally, help is sought from the Devi in illnesses, to get good husbands and wives, to get employment, etc. The Bolada pujaris asserted that the Mahalaxmi at Mahalaxmi Gad was a deity of the Warlis and Malhar Kolis of the local area and was in no way connected with the other Mahalaxmis. They rejected the legend that Mahalaxmi while making her way from Kolhapur to Surat rested on this hillside. They also spoke of how nowadays a story was being constructed that the Pandavas had visited the Mahalaxmi cave. There are cordial relations between the Bolada and the Sathvi adivasi pujaris with participation in rituals by devotees and pujaris in each other's rituals.

On the same day we visited the main Mahalaxmi temple which is located towards the foot of the slope and closer to the highway, to observe the predominantly adivasi festival of Pitru Baras on the night of Amavasya during the month of Bhadrapad, which is also a post-harvest festival for the adivasis. There was a fair with temporary stalls that was set up on the steps leading up to the temple. Alcohol made from the mahua flower was available and in the earlier days there would be adivasi women a little away from the temple who would openly sell this alcohol in pots. However, with increasing cases of drunken violence the police and other government officials have restricted the sale of such liquor during the jatra. The jatra was a fairly small, unlike the one in April. Most of the shops were along the road leading to and from the temple. The shops sold the usual items that one gets at jatras—religious artifacts, prasad, flowers, foodstuffs, toys, household goods, necklaces, etc. Some shops where games of chance were played were observed. A few shops had grilling and selling of chicken pieces on skewers and fresh fish was also sold. The only forest produce noticed was baphli seeds and the bark of some trees to be used for medicinal purposes. No barter of forest or other produce was observed. Some shops sold vegetables and fruit and vegetable produce from the adivasi lands.

In 2012 a massive structure for the new temple was constructed with pillars in granite, replacing the old one made primarily of wood. A flight of steps led one down to an open courtyard.

On the right were facilities for the pilgrims. A small office of the Trust had also been constructed. There were two large towers for lamps in the courtyard. A small shrine to Mahalaxmi Parekari was constructed in the courtyard. Another shrine is also constructed nearby. The main temple was situated a few steps further down from the courtyard. The entrance was flanked by two lions. The temple was double-storeyed with domes. A huge glass chandelier hung from the centre of the temple hall and the deities were at one end of the hall with Mahalaxmi at the centre. Her face was smeared with vermilion. On the left side of the hall, a few scrolls of red cloth were rolled up and hung on the wall. We were told that these were the Phad Dev of the Sathvi clan of adivasi pujaris, which are opened and paid obeisance to from around midnight to early morning and then are rolled up again. When we visited the temple in the evening a small number of devotees, most of whom were non-adivasis, were making their offerings to the Devi. The Sathvi priests were accepting the offerings and there were no Brahman pujaris present. The grandeur of the temple, the composition of the devotees and in fact the entire ambience was very non-adivasi at that time. There was a railing which separated the place where the Aarti was performed from the devotees. The old idol was still there, besides the new one, and was not visible to the devotees as it was blocked by a pillar. The pujaris kept a check on those who were allowed to step towards the old idol for darshan (ritual vision). The ones who were more wealthy, especially the non-adivasis coming from Gujarat, brought sweets and handed them over to the pujaris who kept them close to the idol wherever space was available. Once the Aarti was completed, the sweets were returned to the respective people who took them outside wherever some place was available in the premises and they were distributed. A respondent told us that the Gujaratis celebrated the day of Pitra Baras as Mahalaxmi's birthday, as different from the adivasis for whom it is a day of ancestor veneration. No sacrifice of any animals takes place at Mahalaxmi Gad, at the top of the hill. At the Mahalaxmi main temple no sacrifice of animals takes place within the temple. However, we were told that on the morning after Pitra Baras, chicken and goats are killed in the name of the Devi outside the temple. Regarding human sacrifice, we were told that no human sacrifice takes place at Baras. During the main jatra in April, it is said that once every five years a human sacrifice is made. The Devi takes bhak (Devine bhak ghetle), but this could not be confirmed.

We left the temple premises and returned only after the Arati had begun around seven pm. The Arati was accompanied by drum beating on the Nagara and the occasional blowing of the conch shells. A large number of devotees were present by now, both within the temple and outside in the courtyard. Most of those who were within the temple itself were in a state of trance, prancing up and down or swaying from side to side. Some occasionally shrieked. Many women swayed with their hair flowing, their heads either going up and down or from right to left. One lady stuck out her tongue, kept it hanging out of her mouth for many minutes. We observed that about 15 women had taken out their tongues, some constantly hitting their heads on the ground. Most of those in a trance were non-adivasis, the majority being women. About 10-15 per cent of those present were adivasis. The collective swaying, jumping and shrieking continued for about 20 to 30 minutes. Thereafter, some who were in a trance came out into the courtyard and continued to be in a state of possession for another half hour or so.

The blowing of the tarpha (a wind musical instrument) began sometime later with the first strains from among the crowd in the upper courtyard. Some tribal bhagats were seen in a state of trance and around them adivasis, both young and old, were seen in a state of possession together with a few non-adivasis including some women. Thereafter, the number of tarpha players increased and the playing could be heard from other parts of the courtyard. The focus shifted to one part of the lower courtyard where the possession continued by the adivasis, mostly young men who had completed their training to become a bhagat. Adivasi women were observing the goings-on but were not in a trance. Some young adivasis wished to get into a state of trance but were unable to do so. To assist them some bhagats brought makhvali (jhendu) flowers and agarbattis (incense sticks) near their noses to smell. Some young men got into a trance after such assistance, while others did not despite a continuous effort including physically and rhythmically lifting them up and down.

Suddenly one of the tarpha players changed the tune that he was playing. About four to five of those who were in a state of possession held their arms around each other's waists and began to dance the tarpha dance with a group of another four persons also doing the same. But some were still in a trance and were unable to dance. Soon others who were only by-standers till then joined in the dancing. First only young men and boys began dancing and thereafter women and girls also began dancing. The girls and women danced in a string of five, ten, or twenty, sometimes along with another string of boys and men. The tarpha was danced only by adivasis as the non-adivasis present were only spectators. By this time the crowd had swelled, both within the temple premises and outside in the fair. Thousands of adivasis from the surrounding villages began coming after 9 pm. While girls, women and children were present, more than 80 per cent of the crowd consisted of adivasi boys and men who had come either walking or in vehicles from surrounding villages. As the night proceeded, the entire atmosphere shifted from being non-adivasi to adivasi. We did not observe adivasis from the distant Talasari area as Pitra Baras is now celebrated in a similar fashion in that area. We were told that the number of adivasis who visit the temple had decreased in recent years, as many of them are now followers of different sects such as the Nirankari and Alleluia. One of the respondents mentioned that the tarpha dance and instrument is a symbol of unity between males and females. On the night of Pitra Baras, some people prefer going deep into the forests or on the hills as there are some plants or trees which are reported to have immense medicinal value and it is only on this evening that these plants have an identifiable shine which differentiates them from the others. It is said that collecting some of these herbs and consuming them for the rest of the year helps the adivasis in developing immunity against a number of illnesses. On August 31, 2017, we had an encounter with two relatively young adivasis, Sunil Malvankar aged 28 years of Ambesari village and Naresh Gehla aged 40 of Sakhre village. They threw further light on the phenomenon of medicinal plants collected in the forests at the time of Pitra Baras:

> On Pitra Baras we climb up the hillsides near our villages at night. On that night all the bhagats necessarily go to the forest to collect

> medicinal herbs. At the dead of night, the herbs in some patches in the forest get lit up and shine spectacularly. While bhagats climb up to their hillsides in every village, there are certain hillsides, e.g. Barad and Aaseri near Mendhwan village, where special trips are made. Those who are being initiated to be bhagats are taken to the forest and then they take in the spirit. We do not go to Mahalaxmi to get the spirit. But some youth who may desire to get some special spirit may do so.

Sunil says that he did not believe this, but that he went up to the Barad hillside a few years ago, and indeed he did see the phenomenon.

The playing of the tarpha and dance is related to this joy at the new kharif, monsoon crop. The veneration of the clan deities (Kul Devs), the Khali ritual after harvesting and before threshing, the Gav Dev festival of community solidarity in honour of Vagaya (the tiger), the Mahalaxmi festival at a major cross roads in Dahanu taluka, are all held around this period of the agricultural cycle. We have analysed some of these events separately in Chapter 4. After Diwali and these adivasi festivals, the adivasis, especially the males, migrate in search of work in grass cutting, late harvesting, work in the forests and other agro-industrial labour in brick making, fishing, work on the railway lines, unskilled manual labour in road works, construction and small-scale industries in the coastal towns. So, according to the adivasis, there is no time for song or dance. Presently the tarpha has a deep emotional and spiritual significance to the Warlis, bordering on the magical possession by the Devi. The sound brings joy to the face and dance to the feet of both young and old.

During this time, at around 8.30 pm, one side of the hall of the temple below the Phad Devs that were hanging rolled up on the wall was cleared and an agarbatti stand was placed. A blanket was placed on the floor with some new rice grains (chavlyacha punjlya) and a few coins thereon. In front of that an auj (small drum played with one hand) was placed. Three bhagats belonging to the Sathvi family sat down on the blanket. The central bhagat began singing a song to the accompaniment of the auj while the two on either side responded in song along with the playing of cymbals. The song was the obeisance to the ancestors and is similar to the song sung during the Dis ceremonies. Two or three other persons sat down behind them. Obeisance to the Devi within the same hall continued and outside the hall the focus was on the tarpha playing, possession and the dancing. We were told that when the Phad Dev is opened then the centre of attention shifts to that ritual.

3. Conclusion

Discussing even well intentioned attempts at cultural assimilation, R.H. Brown points out that this process rarely takes place according to principles of equity and without a strong element of hegemonic subordination, especially when it comes to the creation of a national culture based on religion: "More typically, however, the creation of a national culture has been at the expense of crushing or absorbing (after distorting) those cultural components that are economically competitive or politically threatening to the emergent national elites. The destruction of 'parochial' groups may occur even when the central authority is committed to their preservation, because the categories of the dominant discourses warp other cultures in the very act of 'preserving' them or acknowledging their 'contribution'. Thus, in protecting minority cultures, the state typically marginalizes, parochializes and subordinates them. Today as yesterday, difference is reduced to inequality, and equality to sameness...National identity tends to be reified as an integral, absolute value, as an eternal verity that has always existed. Thus nationalism deprives the essentially moral terminology of identity of its relativity, imposing on it a definitional fixity that sometimes is upheld by physical repression" (R.H. Brown in Pfeffer and Behera eds. 1997: 54, 56). The foregoing may be seen as an apt description of attempts at creating a homogeneous national identity based on religion and imposed in an assimilatory manner from above. There is reason to believe that the Warlis resisted several attempts by Brahmins and religious mendicants to draw them into the Hindu fold as a caste during the late nineteenth and early twentieth centuries (Hardiman 1987: 82). In another context, Pati (2016) undertakes a well researched, historical and multifaceted study of dominant religious hegemonic processes in their interaction with subaltern communities in Odisha.

Save's analysis at various instances of his otherwise very useful and detailed ethnographic text on the Warlis is strongly tinged with a patronizing, assimilationist perspective within the Brahmanical, caste structured fold. This in some senses replicates the ancient historical dominance through incorporation and suppression by the external, Vedic Brahmanical influence over the tribal perspective as discussed in Chapter 3 and below; and the continuing exploitative relation with the non-adivasis, especially from the nineteenth century onwards as discussed in Saldanha (2015 a), which Save readily acknowledges. One might also read into his text the influence of Ghurye, his research guide in the 1940s, when he writes: "It has been already said in the chapter on Warli religion, that Warlis are gradually adopting Hindusim. I may go a step further and suggest that even at this stage Warlis can assimilate with the Hindu society, forming a backbone of its lower strata. Warlis' cultural affinities with the Hindus may make assimilation feasible. It is not merely that the Warlis follow some of the customs of the lower caste Hindus, but the latter too in their turn believe like Warlis in witches and evil spirits and sometimes propitiate the gods of Warlis like Waghoba" (Save 1945: 265). Chaudhuri sums up his analysis of the tribe—caste continuum, based on studies of different adivasi groups at different points of time in the contemporary context, and the possible mutual influences in the following manner: "The two major arguments of this paper may now be summed up. (1) Increased Hindu cultural influences on tribals did not invariably necessitate their articulation with the caste-based and hierarchical Hindu social organization. (2) The usual representations of the 'Hinduization' process tend to ignore the will and the subjectivity of the adivasi groups emulating the Hindu cultural and other influences. Integration into the Hindu social organization was conditional on the nature of the countervailing process i.e., the adivasi society's will and efforts to maintain its identity. The integration was easier where the opposite force was weak or non-existent" (Chaudhuri 1997: 78).

Kosambi describes the nature of the hegemonic cooption of tribal cultural practices by the Brahmanical Hinduized, caste mainstream by providing several significant illustrations from the ancient past. Some characteristics of this relatively subtle and non-violent process over a long duration stand out. Assimilation takes place through religious belief in a clearly subordinating manner within the dominant hegemony. The religiosity of the faith-implicit process of assimilation facilitates the relative non-violence; even though the result is a subordination of the incorporated identity. "Like the *avataras* of *Visnu-Narayana*, the various Krsnas gathered mainly different worships into one without doing violence to any, without smashing or antagonizing any. Krsna the mischievous and beloved shepherd lad is not incompatible with Krsna the extraordinarily virile husband of many women. His 'wives' were originally local mother-goddesses, each in her own right. The 'husband' eased the transition from mother-right to patriarchal life, and allowed the original cults to be practised on a subordinate level. This is even better seen in the marriage of Shiva and Parvati which was supplemented by the *Ardha-narisvara* hermaphrodite (half Shiva, half Parvati) just to prevent any separation. Mahisasura (Mhasoba), the demon 'killed' by that once independent goddess, is still occasionally worshipped near her temple (as at the foot of Parvati hill in Poona). The widespread *Naga* cult was absorbed by putting the cobra about Shiva's neck, using him as the canopied (hooded) bed on which *Narayana* floats in perpetual sleep upon the waters, and putting him also in the hand of *Ganesa*. The bull Nandi was worshipped by stone-age people long before Shiva had been invented to ride on his back. The list can be extended by reference to our complex iconography, and study of the divine households. Ganesa's animal head on a human body equates him to the 'sorcerers' and diablotins painted by ice-age men in European caves" (Kosambi, in D. Chattopadhyaya ed. 1978 b: 258-259).

Uncovering the materialist basis of this relatively non-violent synthesis of cultures, Kosambi goes on to add, "To treat all views tolerantly and to merge them into one implies that the crisis in the means of production is not acute. *Fusion and tolerance become impossible when the crisis deepens, when there is not enough of the surplus products to go around, and the synthetic method does not lead to increased production.* Marrying the gods to goddesses had worked earlier (at the time of the Gita, as different from the later polemical Samkara period) because the conjoint society produced much more after the differences between matriarchal and patriarchal forms of property were thus reconciled. The primitive deities adopted into Shiva's or Visnu's household helped enlist food-gathering aboriginals into a much greater food-producing society. The alternative would have been extermination or enslavement, each of which entailed violence with excessive strain on contemporary production" (Kosambi, in D. Chattopadhyaya ed. 1978 b: 261, bracket added; also Kosambi 2009 a: 53). More specifically, as regards the deity Laxmi, Kosambi writes: "... the goddess Laksmi-ai in many villages (in Maharashtra) is a whole set of shapeless red-coated stones, apparently having nothing to do with Laksmi, the beautiful consort of Visnu. This is not a cult degenerated from that of Laksmi, who is called Rakhumai in Marathi, and represented in temples by carved images paired with her husband Vithoba or Panduranga...The food-gatherers worshipped a goddess, while the god first appeared on the scene with pastoral life. The marriage of these Mother-goddesses is a phenomenon of the later conjoint society, as for that matter are those forms of human marriage without which individual maternity or paternity would be meaningless" (Kosambi 2009 d: 834, 835; bracket added).

However, Kosambi's comments may be qualified by the fact that Indian tradition is an amalgamation of various sects, religions and practices that have existed in different contexts at different times. The rise of the local cults and their assimilation in the mainstream, caste society took place mainly in the historical context of state formation processes in the early medieval period when many lineages transited or attempted to become 'states', other than during the Vedic period as a result of the tensions between idealism and Lokayata materialism as contending world views (see Chattopadhyaya, Chapter 3, Section 3). In that process the assimilation to dominant powers, whether stately or religious and in the relation to land, took different forms and shapes. This does not negate the fact that there are innumerable examples of syncretism from below, in this and other adivasi regions, based on respect for difference, mutual sharing of beliefs in a harmonious osmotic manner, and emerging solidarities of a cultural/religious character, based on a political economy that promoted deprivation of vast communities in society; a need that springs from the quest for livelihood and the desire for mutual affiliation, rather than an expression of power of the state or dominant sections of society and the urge to cajole into divisive assimilation. The former syncretism is different from and often opposed to the assimilatory hegemony from above that promotes division and domination under the guise of inclusion and seeks the consent of the subordinate. For a discussion of syncretism see J.J. Roy Burman (1993).

The foregoing discussions should be of special relevance to our interpretation of the historical transitions taking place with respect to the Mahalaxmi Temple Complex in Palghar district; from the adivasi veneration of a mother goddess as a fertility symbol, 'ai' represented by a stone; to the non-adivasi, Brahmanical incorporation of this symbolic image into the Goddess Laxmi; from animal sacrifices being replaced by Brahmanical offerings; with an elaborate temple replacing the old wooden one under the auspices of a Trust dominated by non-adivasis and a gradual predominance of Brahmanical pujaris over the persisting adivasi ones. The final outcome is an amalgamation of adivasi and non-adivasi elements under the hegemony of the latter.

The Pitra Baras adivasi celebrations at Mahalaxmi in October, as narrated above, come around the time of the Gav Dev and the Khali rituals in the villages that commemorate the post-monsoon harvest, Kharif festival. So also the Ram Navami, Hanuman Jayanti celebrations in April fall around the time of the post-winter harvest, Rabi crops. Different communities celebrate their new year around this time of the year. The new year festival of Gudi Padva is celebrated on the first day of the month of Chaitra (April), which also marks the Telugu new year of Ugadi. The nine days to Ram Navami are the Chaitra Navratri dedicated to the mother goddess; the second most important festival days after Sharadiya Navratra which is in the month of October. The foregoing would suggest that the original and typically adivasi part of the festivals at the Mahalaxmi temple had originally in the past and continue in the present to have more to do with the agricultural cycle and the astronomical cycles of the winter and summer equinoxes and the dark and light phases of the moon and the veneration of the mother deity of human and agricultural fertility, rather than the result of Brahmanical influence.

Thus we see that the incorporation of the adivasi fertility deity representing the female principle in the form of a stone image venerated by and presided over by adivasi bhagats, was firstly assimilated as Mahalaxmi with the coming of Brahmanical pujaris yet retaining the status of the bhagats as pujaris as well, though in a subordinate manner; and later with the formation of a temple Trust with a predominance of non-adivasis and the construction of a new temple complex to replace the old wooden structure. Inclusion meant becoming more like us, but at a subordinate level. This process was accompanied by a growing following of non-adivasi devotees from the urbanized areas of Mumbai and Gujarat all of which constitute elements of a social historical, hegemonic process of assimilatory-subordination in a non-violent manner. The gradual cooption by the non-adivasis till they become the majority devotees was facilitated by the fact that the adivasi bhagats, now pujaris, stand to gain economically from the increased incomes from donations and was consolidated by sections of the Warli adivasis, including the pujaris of the Sathvi adivasi clan, acquiring an enhanced tribal social status as a Malhar Koli community as different from the earlier Warli one of lower status (See Chapter 1, Introduction for the historical origins of this transformation). The site of the surroundings of the Mahalaxmi Temple Complex in addition gained predominance as a festival space in the fairs for increased commercial transactions, not always of an equitable character, between the adivasi natural resources and forest produce in exchange for their other consumption needs such as potatoes, onions, spices and salt. If the independent and distinctive cultural identity of the adivasis within a just and pluralistic society that upholds mutual respect of diverse identities be seen as a constitutional value adding richness to the national ethos, then this seemingly harmonious process that assimilates the weak in a subordinating manner, eliding over the social and economic exploitation implicit within the process, is a matter of concern and calls for alternative avenues towards socially just integrative formations.

CHAPTER 6

Adivasi Aesthetic Expressions: Paintings, Songs and Stories

Unlike the rituals related to the life and annual agricultural cycles and the associated incantations that have traditional origins sometimes dating back to early tribal societies and pre-Vedic times, together with their ongoing basis in the contemporary quest for livelihood (Chapter 4); the paintings, songs and stories draw on present-day themes regarding their content while preserving traditional formal elements, reinforcing ethnic solidarities and searching for new meanings for adivasi existence, despite the changing media of expression. One is in accordance with Ghosh's view (1996: 12) that in the context of capitalist globalization, the culture of the subaltern may be considered as a "weapon of the weak", demanding a voice to counter or complement the reduction of culture to that of the powerful and mainstream that is 'distant from the masses and the present'.

1. Warli Paintings

Our interactions with Soma Mashe, a Warli painter, are highly significant in understanding adivasi ethnic identity, especially in the contemporary context, and the relation between art and socio-economic experience. As Dewey writes, "Because experience is the fulfilment of an organism in its struggles and achievements in a world of things, it is art in germ. Even in its rudimentary forms, it contains the promise of that delightful perception which is aesthetic experience." And he goes on to write, "Art is the living and concrete proof that man is capable of restoring consciously, and thus on the plane of meaning, the union of sense, need, impulse and action characteristic of the live creature" (1934/1984: 19, 25). One will be drawing on Dewey's classical work, *Art as Experience* (1934/1984) in order to facilitate an interpretation of adivasi aesthetic expressions.

I first met Jivya Soma Mashe in April 1979 when he was in his mid-forties. He lived in a relatively small hut and his economic condition was precarious. He reported that he started painting on paper with paint and a fine bamboo stick from 1972, as a result of his first contact with a non-adivasi from the city called Kulkarni in 1970. He went to Delhi, won the national award in 1976, 'for keeping alive the ancient traditions of Indian art' from the All India Handicrafts Board. The story of Jivya Soma Mashe is important because his life is closely linked to the early attempts of the Warlis to reach out to contemporary styles and the urban market for paintings, with all its challenges.

He had been drawing from childhood, at first on the ground on the dust, then on mud walls for marriages with savasinis, women who paint the Palghut as described in Chapter 4. All along he had been drawing on wider themes besides the ones that are generally done on the wedding chowk, the ritualistic painting within a square on the mud walls. The award in Delhi was for drawings on the walls. He was a landless agricultural labourer till 1975. He purchased one acre from a Marwari for Rs. 5,000 during the rains of 1978 and three and a half acres from an adivasi for Rs. 3,500 in 1979, from the proceeds of his award. He was planning to construct a well. At present the one acre produces four khandis which would last him throughout the year and he employs labourers to remove the rocks from the three and a half acres. He says:

> Land is what is most important to me and the adivasis. If we have land we have food, money, independence, happiness. I can draw, but I don't even know how to write. The bhuts (evil spirits) are a big sorrow for the adivasis. They give immense trouble. Poverty is also a sorrow. But the biggest sorrow is the Seth Savkar (the landlord, moneylender, trader). The bhuts can be taken out by the bhagat. The bhagat has control over them. But there is no cure for the Savkar. There is no control over him.

Jivya was taking classes for six adivasi boys from the month of Maghshish. In 1978, for six months he was getting Rs. 370 for this work from the government. It was stopped. He continued on his own for two months and had to pay the boys Rs. 80 each for the seventh and eighth months. His paintings of four by four feet sell at Rs. 80, Balu his son's paintings at Rs. 70 and the other boys' at Rs. 40. Contracts are arranged through Vishwas Kulkarni and Kekoo Gandhi, the latter an urban exhibitor and art promoter. According to Jivya, half the amount is kept by the exhibitor for looking after sales. Jivya and Balu's paintings generally sell and Jivya earns on the average Rs. 600 per year.

> *"Why don't you paint sorrowful themes?" I ask him. And he responds, "It is true in the adivasi's life there is a lot of sorrow, but we paint in order to get rid of the sorrow. As I paint and concentrate on it, the sorrow slips away (emphasis added)."*

Mashe continues the narrative of his life story:

> After the death of my mother, father wanted to marry again. So he decided to get rid of his five children. One day he put all of us in a bullock cart and was taking us to Dahanu with the idea of selling us to some Saheb and thus solve his problem. On the way, in a village named Vankas, he met a cowherd who agreed to keep us with him. We could be useful to him to look after his cattle. So father left us with him.
>
> I was the youngest among the five children. I was three and my sister was five and the three brothers were older than us. We all started living with that cowherd. My brothers and sisters used to live with him, but as I was only three years old I was absolutely useless. When the other children used to go to work I would be left alone in the dust. I was so frightened and confused that I could not speak at all till I was eight years old. But mute as I was and entirely left to myself, I started scribbling in the dust. I was happy. After some time the cowherd started harassing us. When it became unbearable my brothers thought of running away. 'We will go back to Vasa, our birthplace,' they said. We younger ones were a burden even for them so they also wanted to get rid of us. We saw them running away. My sister held my hand and we followed them. They kept shouting at us, 'Do not follow us. Go back!' However we kept running after them. We crossed two hills

> and then it was dark. We were afraid. We two couldn't run any more. Other brothers disappeared and my sister and I were left behind. We decided to return.
>
> Next morning we reached a village where one of our relatives was serving in a house. We approached him, but he refused to give us any shelter. Eventually we succeeded in finding another house in the same village, where we were hired for work. Here we worked for years. One day a widow came searching for a son-in-law for her daughter, someone who could also work for her household. She took me to Ganjad. I was married to her daughter. Then I was about 10 years old. In Ganjad, I was also working as a household servant to support this new family. Besides that I started drawing on the walls of huts and tree trunks. This was greatly appreciated by my friends. At the age of 13, I was called to draw pictures in a house for the marriage ceremony. Very soon I became a popular painter of the village. Till today I live in the same village and have been serving in the same house. Now I am about 44 years old. For 24 hours of work, I get Rs. 90 salary for the month. I have three sons and three daughters. The eldest son is married and lives separately. Out of all my children, only the second son is studying in school in the ninth standard.
>
> I have no land. I desire to plough my own farm some day. I am sad my wife has to work far away in the forest for Rs. 3 per day. This she does so that some day we can build a new hut for us. For today, she too, like other workers, has to sleep under the sky without any shelter. Eight years ago, for the first time in my life, I was given papers to paint. I enjoy this work and besides this provides me with some little extra income.

Dewey writes: "I have tried to show in these chapters that the aesthetic is no intruder in experience from without, whether by way of luxury or transcendent ideality, but that it is the clarified and intensified development of traits that belongs to every normally complete experience" (1984: 46). But Jivya's early experience raises the question, what if normal experience is full of contradictions, dead ends and is quite incomplete. In his case the beginnings of aesthetic expression can be a form of sublimation of experience where art completes experience, rather than the other way around. Jivya's most significant experiences were that of poverty, abandonment and exploitation; which in itself is a form of abandonment by unrelated humans. "Impulsions are the beginnings of complete experience because they proceed from need; from a hunger and demand that belongs to the organism as a whole and that can be supplied only by instituting definite relations (active relations, interactions) with the environment" (1984: 58).

I spent the night with Jivya in his hut. The next morning, I continued my dialogue with him with a focus on the thematic content of his paintings on paper which were rolled out on the floor for my benefit. The autobiographical content of his narration differs from the above mentioned in some details, perhaps because we were in a less inebriated state and the likelihood of his being subjected to several such interrogations resulting in boredom. However, the substantive content of pathos continued. The interaction is best represented in the form of a dialogue between Self (S) and Jivya (J):

> S. You were working with Sardar Seth before the Kul Kayda (the 1957, post-independence tenancy legislation that provided land to the tiller), you said.
>
> J. I'll tell you from the beginning. My father left my mother and family to take another woman. I was born at Dhamangaun. My mother died and father took another woman. Father left me, my brother and my sister. My sister and I went to my elder brother. He said: 'Go away, I cannot support you.' We left and as we were walking, we came to a hill that was full of jungles. Night fell and my sister was scared. She began crying. I was quite young. What if the tiger comes. My sister did not know what to do. We set out back for Dhamangaun. We went to our father's sister's place. We reported what happened and asked her what we should do. She told us to get out and sent us away. In Vankas village a Parsi Seth, Khan Bhadur, asked us to stay and told us that he would get us married. We were quite happy. However, we did not stay. I was too young to work. So my sister came and took me to Dhamangaun.
>
> Then my in-laws to be, Pansare, came looking for a husband for their daughter. They brought me to Gujarat. From there I have been working with the Marwari Seth, Sardar Seth. I did not get married to my present wife; I only started living with her. We

could not afford the money for the wedding. We did not even take a loan. Who would give a loan to people like us? I was working with the Sardar Seth till five or six years ago. We were his tenants. Besides that, we had to go to the forest to chop wood and sell it in the market at Dahanu. We used to live on kaneri (a watery gruel made of rice) then. We could afford to buy only two kilograms of kaneri and eat that. My wife was too weak, so she did not go to sell the wood. We thus spent our days. We were working for another Seth before that. The land which I have now bought was originally Sardar's. I bought it from his tenant.

Some years ago, Bhaskar Kulkarni came and asked us, 'Who paints in the village? Five people have to go to Delhi'. Finally four women and I went to Delhi for an exhibition of our paintings. My paintings were accepted. I have six children. The older two sons are married. The eldest is away. I have three daughters and three sons.

S. What are the themes you paint?

J. The rainy season, farming, our houses, wedding chowk, our gods—Naran, Bahram, Kako, Wagho, Joting—all the gods.

S. Don't you paint the themes of sorrow in adivasi life?

J. Yes, we paint that as well. That also has to be painted. I paint the bhuts (evil spirits, he laughs). We paint fewer bhuts nowadays. Nowadays I paint more to get rid of sorrow. As I paint the sorrow slips out of me.

S. Since when have you started painting?

J. Since I was a young child. I used to paint on the ground, with a stick. Gradually I started painting on the walls and then for marriages. They used to give a bottle of daru (country liquor) and a meal; that's all. Women generally paint the wedding chowk. But the women did not paint well, so they used to call me. On the Chowk we have to paint mainly the 'Palgut' God. We also do trees, horses and railways.

S. What are themes for the marriage chowk?

J. Special themes; Hirva Dev, Palgut, Mahadev, Panshire, Narain. God comes first; then comes the sheti (cultivation).

S. What is your Kul Dev? (clan deity; he avoids the question, perhaps because his early nomadic existence deprived him of clear lineage).

J. We do the house there first, and then we draw fields.

S. What are the main needs for adivasis to be happy?

J. If there is money, then you get food, land, grains and vegetables. If you have land, you have everything. Land comes first, then money. If we have land, we will have happiness. That's why I thought I must first acquire land. I bought three and a half acres of land this year for three and a half thousand. The family people work on the land. Children also help, but I have to get outside people to work on the land.

S. What about the movement led by Godutai (G. Parulekar, the leader of the Kisan Sabha from 1944)?

J. Yes, there was a movement in this area. The Lal Bavta (red flag) people came and told us to pay the debt, but not to give up the land to the landlord. There was an adivasi in the area who wanted to sell his land to pay off his debts. I wished to buy that land. I will have to pay off his debts amounting to about Rs. 200. I will have to pay the Collector.

S. Any benefits from the movement?

J. Yes, there have been benefits. Adivasis have got the lands. The oppression of the Seth Savkars (landlords, moneylenders and traders) became less. Before we had to pay the khand (crop share) and also do a lot of veth begar (forced, unpaid labour). We had to buy grains from the government controlled rationing.

S. What is the biggest sorrow now?

J. There are sorrows. Some have happiness, some have sorrows.

S. What party do you vote for?

J. There are two parties here. I do not understand much about it; who must one vote for? I voted for Indira Gandhi. For the cow (symbol of the Congress Party).

S. What do you think about the Lal Bavta?

J. Janata and Lal Bavta have combined now. There has been some improvement recently. For me it is the same to vote for anyone. It doesn't make a difference.

S. Are you going to give up painting now that you have land?

J. I will now paint with a peaceful mind as a hobby. I will do both—land as well as paintings. The paintings will come out better now. When there is insecurity, I cannot paint well. Now that I have land, I will paint with peace. I have done several paintings. They have all been taken away. My son also paints, my third son. Some of the children also paint.

What follows are his comments on his paintings:

The Painting on Gav Dev (the tiger deity of the village) and the Tarfa (musical instrument) dance

S. Do all the villagers, that is, adivasis, non-adivasis, different adivasis come for the Gav Dev festival and the Pada Dev Cheda?

J. This is the Gav Dev festival and the tarfa dance. The tarfa dance is done especially at this time. After that we cannot use the tarfa. Gav Dev is Vagaya (tiger). The Gav Dev is celebrated in the the Kartik month before Diwali. If we do not celebrate the Gav Dev then there is much damage to the village. He is very powerful and is the protector of the village.

S. Where is the Gav Dev of this village?

J. It is out of the village, close by. There are three Gav Devs in Ganjad. It is a big village. These people are playing the tarfa. Men and women are all dancing together. There the villagers are sitting and drinking toddy. Someone is serving toddy. There is the bhagat. The bhagat is brought on this occasion. People are sitting to eat. There are three bhagats. Those are lamps which are put to the gods. This is related to what I said earlier. The lamps are put to the Gav Dev. This is the Gav Dev, the stamp of the tiger. That is a talva; a piece of wood. That is a kul (clan). And the life is the tiger. There is also the sun and the moon. That is a mask. Those are small gods, etc which are kept near Gav Dev. They are to break coconuts. This is the jungle of our village. These are monkeys on the tree. This is the Makar Cheda God. He is the village god, together with Gav Dev. It has the shape of a man, but the face is different; sitting on a horse.

S. Where is it kept?

J. Near the road. A pig has to be sacrificed once in five years to the Makar Dev. This year the sacrifice has to be made. This is the tiger. All these have to be decorated with leaves, monkeys, etc. This is a man and a dog. The dog is following the man. There is an order placed for this painting. I have not been told what to do. I do what I feel like.

S. How do you decide what to paint?

J. It just happens. I do not decide before hand.

S. When do you paint?

J. In the afternoon, in the evenings. I must be interested in painting. I must feel the desire. Then I sit and paint. The mind must pull me to painting. You must be attracted by it. I must feel compelled. That is a man on a tree. These are birds in a formation above the Gav Dev. They are called the Aasra (shelter). That is a peacock.

The Painting of the Marriage Chowk and Related Deities

J. This is a marriage scene. All this is included in the marriage. This is the marriage chowk. This is Palgut, the Devi. This is the main illustration and goddess at the time of the marriage. These are hands. Four hands. Found in all the houses. That is a head.

S. Why are there four hands?

J. That is done from the beginning. Without this out marriages cannot be celebrated. We have to do it. We feel good with the four hands. That outline is the design of the Devi's house. This is the Tangad Dev. Five of them. These are the Govari (shepherds). This is the shape of the god; the shape of a horse (Tangad Dev).

S. What is the function of the Vagaya Dev?

J. He is beneficial to us. He looks after us and protects us, when we go to the Vagaya Dev and make offerings and worship him.

S. Are the functions of the different Devs different?

J. Yes they have different functions. This is Makhar Dev. He is the god of the whole village. This is Palghut Devi, a house goddess at the time of marriage. The Tangad Dev has to be drawn at the time of the marriage. Without him the marriage is not performed. This is the bride, the husband and the wife on horseback. These are the Karavli. They have the coconuts in their hands. The Karavlis are the bride's younger sisters. This woman also does painting.

A Woman: I do, but with a different brush. Jivya has gone ahead. Some stay behind in the second standard or third or fourth. Jivya is now English medium (advanced). He has studied English and has gone ahead.

J. This is the Turai, an instrument played at the time of marriage. This is a Tevrari instrument. This is the Dhol. These are the Bharkari. They are taking toddy for the wedding. These three are the Sahwasinis. They take a coconut in their hands. Their function is to fill the bride's lap (a symbol of fertility). They do the rituals of the gods. This is the Toharkar. He takes a bag and carries a gourd. These are Davlari, three of them. They have lamps in their hands and are like your Brahmins. This is a toddy-walla. These are villagers. This is Kayadakara. They pronounce the marriage. They tell the husband to take the bride. These are the Pancshire, down here on the house. This is the Godya. This is the Ghol Dev. This is the Gangli. These are different gods, Narayan, Himai, Joting, Hirva (peacock feathers). These are the five villagers. These are trees. These are houses. This is the Dev Chowk. We have to do this. All these are trees. First comes this, the Dev Chowk, then are the fields, trees, jungles, birds. First comes Palgut Dev, the house god. This is a five-cornered chowk. The previous is a three-cornered chowk. At the time of marriage we do a four-cornered chowk. Only a four-cornered chowk can be done. The five-cornered chowk I have done to see how it looks. This one of a four-cornered chowk will do at the time of marriage. This is the Basinga, put on the couple's forehead. This is for Sahwasanis to carry in their hands. This is the sun and the moon. That is a ladder.

S. Why do you make a ladder?

J. The ladder is used in the house. It is useful. We first do the Palgut. Then if we get time, we do other things. No special significance of the ladder.

The Painting of the Santoshi Festival

J. This up here is the Santoshi Devi and this is the Palna (cradle). This is the merry-go-round at the fair. This is a new goddess. Not from the beginning. Adivasis are the Pujaris. This was not there many years ago.

Another Adivasi: There was an adivasi who used to work in the fields. One day in his dream the Devi appeared and asked him to do puja. Now he is the Pujari and lives there.

J. This is with her. She cannot stay alone. Six years have passed for the Santoshi devotion. This is a temple. Here is a person falling at her feet. There are people dancing and enjoying themselves. These are people selling tickets. This is a horse.

The Painting of the Fields

J. There are fields. This is rice. This is vari (a coarse grain).

S. You have made many fields?

J. We must have lands. We need lands. It is true that adivasis have little land. It must be seen clearly, the fields. Fields have great importance in the life of adivasis. In the land is our life. Without land, we cannot live.

S. And what about those who do not have land?

J. They have to move around; from place to place seeking work. This is the condition of the adivasis, especially in Dahanu taluka. The Savkars have taken all our lands.

The Other Adivasi : During the rains and before, people are without food and without money. They go to the Savkars and take loans against their coming crops or against grass or rice stalks. The profit is of the Savkars. The adivasis remain in debt. Some take loans against rice. He works and gives the rice to Savkars. People cannot do without these loans. They need money for food during the rains. The Rs. 2 given for mazoori (agricultural labour) is not enough, besides there is not enough work.

J. This is the life of the adivasi.

S. What can be done to get out of this?

J. Adivasis need lands, and if they have lands then they need water and wells.

S. What must they do to get this?

J. Without money we cannot do anything. Who can afford the one, two thousands for land? There is land. It's not that there's no land. But the land is with the Savkar. Those who have land from the beginning, they have land. But the rest have to go looking for work.

S. Whose was the land before?

J. It was the Marwari's lands. He gave lands on tenancy to people without measuring. The Marwaris have come from outside. After the Kul Kayda, some adivasis got land.

S. Before the tenancy whose was the land?

J. Before that, no one perhaps was working on the land. We don't know. This was jungle land. That is a cobweb. The home of the spider. A spider on the trees. There are men moving in the jungle. That's a snake.

S. Is snake a god?

J. Yes, the adivasis perform Nagpanchmi. This is a rat. That a vinchu (scorpion). That is the rain god. When the new rain falls the frogs get married. They are in pairs. Some are punjra (yellow) and some white. They join and mate. That is a worm, that is a crab. That is a well.

S. A well! How many adivasis have a well?

J. That's the question. Very few people have a well. We all rely on the rains. If there is a well then we could have survived in spite of bad rains. Without a well then everything is burnt if there's no rains. We want this. That's why I've drawn. We want this, life must be like this. This is Kamli dance. This is a Padapur Cheda. Jari. This is a dance at the time of the new grains. This is a song, a songhada. These three girls are singing.

The Painting of the Pada Dev (Village/ Hamlet Deity)

J. This is a Dev of the pada. Each pada has a Dev. This is Cheda Dev of the pada. In Ganjad there are 12 padas. Hence there are 12 Devs one for each. If somebody comes to harm, then he is sent away. If an epidemic starts in another village or another pada then the Dev prevents it from coming to their pada. That's why we make offerings to the god. But if the disease spreads in this pada, then we do not make offerings. We get angry with the god. We do the puja of the god every year at the time of the Gav Dev. Only the adivasis worship this god and not the Savkars. The Savkars go to the temples; this god looks after the adivasis. Below the god there is a coconut. There is also a bottle of liquor for the puja (religious ceremony). Here there is a person who covers the toddy with a piece of cloth. Toddy is in a matka (clay vessel). In that corner we see people doing rab (curing and burning of the top soil) in both places. They spread the branches of the trees, the rab is put first, and then leaves and then it is lit. This is done before the rains. Then sowing is done. Then comes the removal of the shoots and the transplanting. They are transplanting here.

S. So this is a complete picture of adivasi life?

J. Yes, but if one went into all the aspects several sheets of papers would be required. The story is very long. This is mainly about the rainy season and the wedding.

S. Which is the wedding season?

J. Weddings are in Maghshish, Maag, Semaga months.

S. In all these aspects you have drawn, which do you think is the most special, most important?

J. First I have to show the land, that's the most important, we need land. Then rains are important. If land is got then one can marry. Then come the festivals. The land, rains, crops, the festivals, and marriage they come in that order.

S. How long did it take you to make this?

J. This painting? About a month. I can't do it fast. It might have taken more than a month.

S. Do you decide beforehand what you will put into your painting? How do you proceed about your work?

J. I decided to do the rainy season. The ideas do not come altogether; as I work, the ideas come to my mind. I think as I work. What should I do now? And now what should I do?

An Old Man : Not everybody can do this.

S. But there are a number of people who do chowk painting.

J. Yes, there are many. They do it fast. In one day.

S. When did you start working on paper?

J. Since 1972, before that I used to paint on the walls. The chowk and other decorative paintings like this together with chowk on the walls.

S. When did you get the award?

J. 1976.

S. Whom did you all vote for at this time of elections?

Old Man: Some say give us the votes, others say give us. We say yes to all. We don't oppose anybody. We won't give you. What we have in mind, to them go our votes. We don't tell the people we won't give you, or give to you. If anyone asks us for votes, we say yes.

S. What do you think, which party has done good for the adivasis?

J. In the beginning, Godavari did a lot of good. The Lal Bavta helped us a lot at the start, freed us from Savkar's market. Vethi went. Savkars used to oppress us when the changes came. Savkars used to say go, get your food from the ration shop. Go away. Today we get no money from them.

S. Today what are the oppressions you suffer from the Savkars?

J. Now it has become less.

Another Adivasi : Now generally, each one manages his own home. When there is a shortage of grains and the rains fail, we have to depend on the Savkars. We are forced to work for the Savkars neglecting our own fields because of economic needs. Now the price of land has gone up. It is Rs. 4,000 per acre. If the land has been levelled and is in working condition producing crops then it is costlier. I had bought waste land.

S. Are you Warlis? Do the Warlis of one village maintain contact with Warlis of other villages?

J. We are all Warlis. We know adivasis in other parts of Dahanu taluka. We maintain contact. People get married to each other, visit friends, relatives in other places; we are all adivasis.

2. Other Cultural Expressions

I was able to observe a range of adivasi cultural expressions at one place during a cultural meet held at Bandghar village, Dahanu taluka, on May 30 and 31, 1993. The cultural festival was a celebration of adivasi identity sponsored by the Indira Gandhi Rashtriya Manav Sangrahalaya, Bhopal and organized by the Tata Institute of Social Sciences, Mumbai and a local people's organization, Kashtakari Sanghatana, as part of the international year of indigenous peoples. While some of the cultural forms had a ritualized character, retaining a link with the past through oral, audio and visual traditions and thus maintaining identity, others had responded to a greater extent to changing ecological and socio-economic contexts thus undergoing what might be called a 'secondary order elaboration' and meeting new needs. Among the latter one might find songs, stories and riddles, and Warli paintings that have undergone modifications to meet the demands of commercial outlets. Story telling is generally done by the Thalawala accompanied by playing on a musical instrument; the palms of the hand being rubbed downwards one after the other on a stick attached to a metal plate with a piece of wax, resulting in a constant drone. A wide range of subjects drawn from the epics, myths and legends, as well as from contemporary events form the content of the stories; with the story teller enjoying great freedom of expression and individual embellishment. The stories are generally told throughout the night between the festivals of Sankranth (January) and Holi (April), after the harvest and before the next sowing season and at the time of the mourning period after a death in the community. Our interactions with the adivasis suggested that the younger generation of adivasis is getting alienated from these cultural practices as a result of films and videos, education and contact with the non-adivasis. Ghorwalla the Thalawalla lamented,

> "The younger generation doesn't know how to paint, how to dance. They don't come for rituals. Entertainment is movies and film songs. They don't like to come for story telling sessions at night. No one is interested in listening and learning these stories from me." And Bhimsen the artist added, "Now the banjo has become a prestige issue. My marriage was without the banjo. But if you ask me about my son's marriage then I have to say that there will be a banjo or the people will look down on me."

One feature was very clear at the cultural meet. While the adivasis of the region belong to various tribal communities and have different ritual and cultural practices, there is a strong bond and realization of collective adivasi status. Economically and in the face of the non-adivasi onslaught and some of the negative effects of state intervention, the adivasis maintain an ethnic solidarity despite tribal distinctions and status differentiation.

Most of the songs suggest a strong non-adivasi and Brahmanical influence. These songs have been learnt by the younger generation generally as a result of contact with non-adivasi cultivating communities and from the modern institutions of schooling. For one, it could possibly be because ritualistic incantations and stories/fables/parables, rather than songs sung individually or on social occasions, have been the traditional forms of oral musical expression. Even paintings have had a ritualistic basis and origin, whereas songs appear to have been the main form of non-ritualistic interactions of an aesthetic character given that they were normally indulged in institutional settings and during informal communication accompanying drinking sessions at the bhonga (the traditional drinking place for toddy) when ghosti karne, engaging in gossip and friendly communication, was the norm. Examples are is as follows, largely recorded at the boarding school, Vangaun village, Dahanu taluka in the 1970s:

Songs with Sticks

What is in the pond, What is in the pond?

There is a lotus in the pond, There is a lotus in the pond,

What is in the lotus, What is in the lotus?

There is Santoshi in lotus, There is Santoshi in lotus,

What is in the Devi, O what is in the Devi?

Songs at Gauri Ganpati Festival

The Gauri Devi is going to Vighna* village to her mother's place Vighna. Let us dance together and then go to the gathering.

The Gauri Devi is going to Vighna, her mother's place. Let's go to the gathering. Let's go to the gathering together with the drummers. The Gauri Devi is going to the gathering. Let's go with the singers to the gathering.

*There is an important temple of Gauri in Vighna village (Jawahar taluka), beyond Kasa.

I Had Gone a Running

I had gone a running to Surat, to Surat,

I brought some manja thread, some manja thread,

Like this I caught a bagla bird*, caught a bagla bird,

And the beak I threw into the sea, the beak I threw into the sea,

I set the trap ready, I set it ready.

*The flesh of this water (sea) bird is used for baiting fish onto the hook line.

Wedding Songs in Gujarati, Women in Bormal Village, Talasari Taluka, December 1, 1979

The bride is being taken away to her in-laws,

Do not cry, what is the use of crying?

You are now the responsibility of your in-laws,

Leave behind the love of your family, brothers, sisters, father and mother,

Take on the love of the house of your in-laws,

Young girl, why are you crying?
The straps of the sandal, the rose flower,
The silken thread should not break,
Wear the sandals and the socks, don't forget them,
The silken thread should not break, Wear the dhoti and the vest,
The silken thread should not break,
Wear the bashing and the garland,
But let not the silken thread break.

Song Sung at Christmas by Warli Christians

The Mokhul flowers (yellow flowers) which used,
To grow so well at my door,
Who has taken them away,
The Vadolin (pandre pesha) of Sanjan has taken it away to sell,
The Vadolin of Palghar ...
The Vadolin of Dahanu ...
The Vadolin of Bombay ...

Davlari Songs Sung at the Wedding, Gurud Pada, Kulambi Village, Talasari Taluka, March 12, 1980

Let the husband and wife stand at the door, the kotwal and the patil stand at the door,
The husband fills the oti of the wife, give her fulfilment,
Savasni, Ishar Dev,
Fill up the baskets, tobacco, the bidi leaves,
Everybody be prepared, put on the topi, put on clothes, shoes,
Let the Porna Godi (name of a god) be ready,
If we are late the wife's people will get angry.

Songs Sung for the Kul Dev, Clan Deities, Generally in February 1980

Tungari winds are blowing,
Put the nagoli shoots into the soil,
The seeds are sown in the fields,
There is a staff tied to the waist,

The Narayan Dev is dancing,

The Hiroba Dev is dancing,

The Himaya Dev is dancing,

The Bharan Dev is dancing.

(These songs of the gods are recited three times a year:

1. Before Holi in February
2. At the time of the new paddy
3. At Diwali, at the time of harvest).

A Wedding Song, 1980

The younger sister of the bride sings:

Brother, don't leave me, take me with my sister,

Even if there's a little rice hanging in the house, we will share it and eat it,

We will share the little 'daru' that there is,

We will share the dal that there is,

We are going to dance for the gods even at night irrespective of the odds.

Wedding Songs, Kulambi Village, Talasari Taluka, May 15, 1979

The way is opened to the relation between the two families, the road is laid, the wires are set, like the telegraph poles,

Your father-in-law, mother-in-law ...

Will be to you as your father, mother ...

Ranga, the bride, your sari is blue,

There is a silver design on the sari,

Your house is also blue,

Wedding Song, Kulambi Village, Talasari Taluka, 1980

Who has taken me?

Malu has taken me,

Taken me to the toddy patta, to the daru patta, to the group of young people, to the young man's place,

Has made a garland of flowers for me.

A Wedding Song

The rains have fallen, the ground is levelled and Nagli grains are sown,
Let the Kokani girl dance with me,
Let the Bahman girl dance with me,
Let the Kathodi girl dance with me,
Let the Mang girl dance with me,
Let the Warli girl dance with me,
Let the Parsi girl dance with me,
Let the Mangela girl dance

Songs of Gauri Ganapati, Vangaun Village, Dahnu Taluka, 1970s

1.

In the lake there is cold water, cold water,
In that there is brother's tiled fort, tiled fort.
On both sides the railway is going, the railway is going,
Ganapati is sitting in the train, in the train,
Where is Ganpati going, Ganapati going?
Ganpati is going to Bhiwandi, Ganpati is going to Bhiwandi,
Whose house is Ganpati going to, whose house?
Ganpati is going to his brother's house, brother's house.

2.

On the banks of the river there is a pumpkin,
Planted pumpkin on banks of river,
Pumpkin grew as creeper,
Then the strings of that Gaurai is trapped,
Run, run O Rawana to release the Gaurai,
Gauri has got up and gone to Bhiwandi,
The Bhiwandi town is big,
The same Rawana has come to beg.

In sharp contrast with the foregoing songs with relatively naïve themes which have been influenced by the hegemony of the dominant culture and belief systems, are the stories that could be more appropriately termed as fables or parables that are closely embedded in the oral traditions of the Warli community. They are communicated by the dhavleris and suhasinis at the time of marriage, the dhakya bhagats during the night watch at the time of deaths and ancestor rituals, thond kahanis told by elders to children and primarily by the earlier mentioned thalawallas who are known as community historians. Prabhu and Balsara of the Kashtakari Sanghatana, a local people's organization, have made a creditable effort to collate and translate some of these oral narratives that serve as a significant historical record of the oral traditions and the diminishing ethnic identity of the adivasis in the face of dominant hegemony (2014). We will attempt to underline some of the salient interpretations that have been provided in so far as they relate to adivasi ethnic identity, urging the readers to refer to the original publication for the stories and the 'painted words' that illustrate them; because constraints of space do not permit reproducing them here. The culture of orality as a firm bond and convivial setting between the sharing narrator and the affirming listener within a community of shared socio, economic and ecological history is the ethos that permeates all the adivasi narratives and the paintings of Koti, Khenvra and Narlya; especially the first fable—Kahankar and Ahankar, The Maker and the Affirmer of the Spoken Word—which is in some senses the centre piece. 'The word is the vehicle of energy' says the wife of the Ahankar, and the elders of the village in the story reiterate a philosophy of life of the adivasis that could well be three centuries old,

> Stories are energy, stories are life, because they hand down our culture and ethos from generations which allows us to live our lives meaningfully. What is the use of living if you don't know who you are and why you think and live life differently? If you really seek your ancestors from whom you can trace your own existence, there is nothing that can stop you, you really can (2014: 6).

Two stories follow that underline the adivasis' symbiotic relation with nature, a relation of interdependence where each contributes to the welfare of the other. The story of the Eagle Mother is reported to be at least four hundred years old dating back to the transition from hunting and food-gathering to early shift cultivation in the forests and the domestication of animals. The principle appears to be that, "other life forms earn their right by virtue of their contribution to the integrity and well-being of the environment and—in turn—to the well-being of humans as one of its members" (2014:17). In a similar vein is the fable of the Pig, the Cat, the Dog, the Rats and the Frogs.

With the story of The Exploits of the Bandicoot begin the narratives of the history of exploitation; from the alienation of the means of production, to the alienation of labour, of livelihoods and the means of survival, and finally to the alienation of the body of the labourer through bondage and sexual exploitation. The fable of Jam the Parsi dates back to the existential reality of alcoholism and indebtedness that began with the introduction of the British Akbari Act of 1874 which gave the collection of excise on toddy and alcohol to the highest bidder; in this case the Parsis who set up their liquor shops and alienated the adivasis from their traditional modes of drinking as part of rituals and everyday pleasures and from the natural resources (date palms, mahua trees) of their own lands. "The Adivasi realized he had lost his soul, so the Parsi came to be equated with Jam, the God of Death" (2014: 37). The story of Kanseri, the female deity of grain, draws attention to the subordination of women with the growing power of the male over homestead, lands, the plough and agriculture resulting in the patriarchal reality of, "The threat of being called a witch remains an ever present threat to all women challenging male domination" (2014: 41). The parable of the Thirty-Six Guiles dwells on the various forms of male oppression and the resistance of women and the ambiguous status of women in adivasi society; respected as representing the female principle of fertility and for their role in the rituals of the life cycle, yet providing a rationalization for evil and feared as such for this attribution. The story of The Barber and the Cat highlights the sexual exploitation by the non-adivasis and the one of The Titu (a bird) and the Fox draws attention to the power of the weak over the strong, of wisdom over guile.

All in all the stories draw on the wisdom of the past to communicate to future generations the truth that underlies their existential realities and thus reinforce their sense of ethnic solidarity. Devi in his extensive anthology of adivasi literature, *Painted Words* (2002), throws further light on the significance of these stories. Discussing the adivasi imagination and their distinctive conceptions of spaces and times and their apparent fusion at multiple levels, he writes, "The tribal imagination, on the other hand (as different from 'secular' creativity), is still to a large extent dreamlike and hallucinatory. It admits fusion between various planes of existence and levels of time in a natural and implicit way. In tribal stories, oceans fly in the sky as birds, mountains swim in the water as fish, animals speak as humans and stars grow as plants. Spatial order and temporal sequence do not restrict the narrative. This is not to say that tribal creations have no conventions or rules, but simply that they admit the principle of association between emotion and the narrative motif. Thus stars, seas, mountains, trees, men and animals can be angry, sad or happy" (2002: x-xi). Realizing that the control over space had been taken away from them, the adivasi mind has an acute and distinctive sense of time. In an observation that has special significance to the publication of Prabhu and Balsara (2014) discussed above, he writes, "In a way, the syntax of language and the grammar of painting are the same, as if literature were painted words and painting were a song of images" (2002: xiii). Adivasi arts draw on past expressions, yet playfully subvert them. "Indeed playfulness is the soul of the tribal arts." While drawing attention to all these insights into adivasi aesthetics, one cannot help lamenting the growing loss of this adivasi world view and ethnic identity in the face of deprivations in the realm of existential realities within the context of dominant hegemony.

3. Conclusions

It might be relevant to interpret adivasi aesthetic expressions, especially the paintings of Jivya Soma Mashe, from the perspective of the epistemological formulation and depiction as presented in Chapter 3, Section 2: An interpenetration of aspects of structured context, agency in process and consciousness expressed through culture. Given that art is an element of the last mentioned dimension, the analysis would in effect entail an elaboration of horizon of subjectivity as experienced culture that reacts back on culture through aesthetic expression. One has tried to transpose the structural elements of more general social phenomena to the sphere of aesthetics in the following manner:

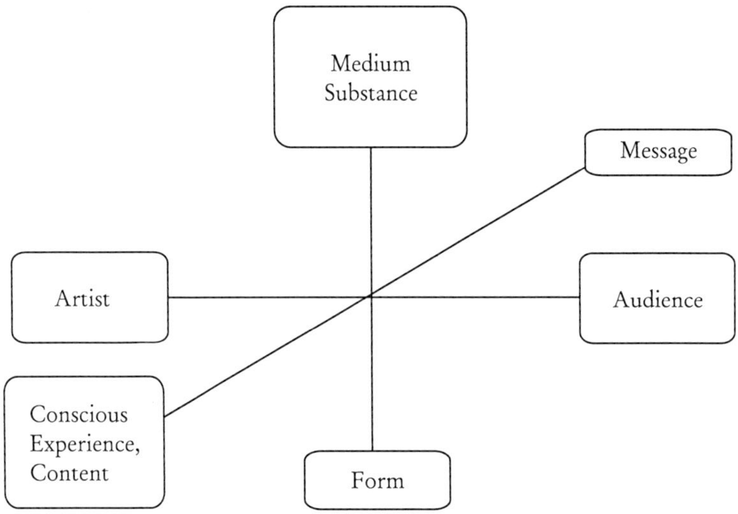

One observes that Mashe's experience emerges from a social context of severe, early economic deprivation and abandonment. This experience results in linguistic silence to begin with and takes the sublimated form of communicative expression through scribbling in the dust, later as ritualistic drawings on the mud walls of the hut through the substantive medium of rice flower paste and a bamboo stick and even later, as a result of 'outsider' influence, drawings using the medium of paint on cloth or paper with a brush. The content of the message also undergoes a transformation from the ritualistic image of the Palghut goddess drawn at the time of marriage on the mud walls of huts together with married adivasi women, Savasinis, to the rhythms of nature and the agricultural operations of everyday life; as well as the audience, from the local adivasi community to the wider national and international market of non-adivasi, commercial buyers and sellers. While the formal elements remain relatively constant, the stylized, sick drawings of primitive tribal expression, there is a tendency as seen in the drawings of other contemporary adivasi artists to indulge in more decorative illustrations. The existential basis that constitutes the well springs of aesthetic expression of the adivasi artists remains rooted in livelihood; the sublimation of the lack of the means for survival or the seeking out of livelihood through exposure to the market with the assistance of non-adivasi intermediaries.

It may be noted that the full gamut of adivasi cultural and aesthetic expressions, as discussed in this publication, continue to contribute to ethnic identity and community solidarity, though to varying degrees. Discussing the artists and the folk forms in West Bengal, Bhattacharya (2014) sees them as acting as mediators between dominant culture and popular consciousness as well as offering passive resistance to that hegemony. While he terms the artists as 'traditional intellectuals' in the Gramscian sense, one sees their potential as playing a role as 'organic' ones. The cultural forms spring from a distinct culture and react back on it reinforcing it. As Dewey writes, "Works of art that are not remote from common life, that are widely enjoyed in a community, are signs of a unified collective life. But they are also marvellous aids in the creation of such a life. The remaking of the material experience in the act of expression is not an isolated event confined to the artist and to a person here and there who happens to enjoy the work. In the degree in which art exercises its office, it is also a remaking of the experience of the community in the direction of greater order and unity" (1984: 81). The rituals and incantations related to the indefinite life cycle and the annual agricultural cycles which are relatively not influenced by contact with the wider non-adivasi community, as compared to paintings, may be seen as a form of aesthetic expression with the most ancient roots and are described in Chapter 4. In this context, Dewey writes, "The sense of communion generated by a work of art may take on a definitely religious quality. The union of men with one another is the source of the rites that from the time of archaic man to the present have commemorated the crises of birth, death, and marriage. Art is the extension of the power of rites and ceremonies to unite men, through a shared celebration, to all incidents and scenes of life. This office is the reward and seal of art. That art weds man and nature is a familiar fact. Art also renders men aware of their union with one another in origin and destiny" (1984: 270-271).

Folk and primitive art are often ascribed several laudatory characteristics that eventually add up to a 'stereotype of positivity' that is in effect a condemnation to mediocrity. These are for example, a lack of complexity that might need explanation, lacking the tensions of the creative process, as timeless in the sense of being highly individualistic or archetypical in nature, and even as lacking in aesthetic qualities. J. and I. Fabian (1980: 290) see a hegemonic and monopolistic character to this apparent depiction of virtue.

Dalmia suggests that Warli painting has great similarities with the neolithic rock paintings of central India of the period between 3000 and 2500 BC and probably indicates its regional origins as well as its rootedness in the discovery of early agriculture. She draws attention to the meaning that present-day art has for the Warlis. Art has a ritualistic, communal and an aspirational character; drawing from the past, providing explanation in the present and direction for the future. "The art of the Warlis then, is part of a ritual tradition and needs to be studied within this context to be fully understood. Ritual art, here as elsewhere, exists for a very specific purpose where it fulfils the aims of the individual and the community....In animating what is recognized as an inner truth, the painting points the way to that which has yet to be achieved. In very real terms, therefore, it provides them with an 'order', a coherency which is needed in their lives" (Dalmia 1988: 10). There is simultaneity of events through images depicted in the paintings which together form a whole. She recognizes that a more comprehensive understanding of Warli art and rituals would need to take into consideration their relation to economic structure and the social relations of production which have not been covered in her book (1988: 11). We have made some attempt to do so in this study of ethnic identity and solidarity by drawing on our earlier studies of the Warlis.

Dalmia raises an important question in the face of increasing demand from the market and from the non-adivasi universe for Warli paintings done by Jivya Soma Mashe and other young adivasis who have followed in his footsteps: "Was Jivya's work likely to be commercialized? At this stage he seemed poised between different tendencies—on the edge of the precipice as it were. His best works revealed a desire to isolate and explore facts of everyday life. He was moving back and forth not only over external reality but over himself. A new, altogether exciting sense of awareness was evident in these works. And he could enhance this with an innate sense of design. But the decorative element could become too formal, losing its vitality and then he appeared to have moved over to the other side. It seemed as if his forms would never unfreeze again.... If Jivya has been able to maintain a balance between his own needs for self-expression and his desire to please the audience and get lucrative offers it is because of an inner sense of integrity as an artist. In other places in the Warli area, however, there has been complete commercialization" (1988: 226, 233). She observes that mounds of stacked paddy and an increase in the size of fields is a running motif in his later paintings. Discussing the paintings of a young adivasi, Balu Dumara, who was trained by Jivya, she writes: "Balu makes no difference between mythical and real events for the two are inextricably fused in his imagination. The sharper his observations of the life around him the more they seem to appear as archetypes. Interestingly enough, important events are arranged by him in a circle which can be considered archetypal, while ordinary day-to-day events are depicted around the circle as a counterpart. The circles in the paintings are perhaps an unconscious formulation of the epic consciousness of the Warlis. The events that take place within these however are concretely real, without any kind of embellishment. But narration demands along with a vivid imagination, an economy of style, an eye for small details and a wide concern for every level of existence" (1988: 239). Our observations suggest that an important symbolic representation for the Warlis is the circle; used during birth, marriage and death rituals. It represents the continuity of time without beginning or end; a series of anti-clockwise, endless and continuously expanding spiral which is also used in a differentiated manner in dance forms, during the music on the tarfa—a repetition of rhythms with varying intonation—and within the flow of the content of ritualistic incantations.

I visited Soma Mashe once again on April 4, 2012, more than 30 years after I first interacted with him and his wife in his relatively small thatched hut on a hillock. He now lived in a set of spacious and 'pucca' (finished with cement and a tiled roof) cottages, closer to the main road in the same village. He had about 11 acres of land and his household dependents had grown to 14 members. He was spending his time working on a limited number of paintings and training three adult and seven young adivasis. He was now in his early eighties, shrunken and more reticent than when I first spent a night with him and was greeted with a warm and enthusiastic response and when he seemed all too keen to explain his life and his art. Age or fatigue as a result of several interactions with representatives of the wider universe of artistic and commercial interests over the years may have resulted in his taciturn behaviour. He perhaps took me for being one of them or a buyer, since I was in fact driven to him by a friend who was a potential investor in art. My valiant attempts to jog his memory of our first encounter were met with failure as I was not carrying the photographs of his large painting on agricultural operations of thirty years ago. His son who had now largely taken over from him dominated the conversation and was keen to display his works which were largely repetitive, stylized and decorative in nature and that would appeal to a wider non-adivasi audience. One could not grudge the relative economic security that Soma Mashe now enjoyed as a result of national exhibitions, awards by way of cash and otherwise and international invitations. However, despite one's limited aesthetic competencies, the impact of the commercialization of adivasi art was self-evident in the works of the next generation, while Soma Mashe appeared to hold on tenuously to his early expression of adivasi rituals, festivals and lived agricultural experience through his limited works.

Writing about the commercialization of folk art from an anthropological perspective and with respect to Central Africa, J. and I. Fabian point to the dangers of the hegemony of the market: "Of course, one might ask, what is wrong with the logic of the market? Some answers come immediately to mind: it leads to grave robbery and cultural thievery on a grand scale, it creates a kind of market where the profits realized by intermediaries are in no relation to the benefits that go to producers, i.e., it creates a kind of exploitation that can be explained but not excused by the mechanics of a free market. In the long run, this sort of art market creates a kind of dependency which is not only political or economic but also intellectual and aesthetic" (1980: 254). The sale of difference based on distinct ethnicity has taken on increasing proportions. Reviewing the international scenario of the market for ethnic products and commenting on this expanding business, John and Jean Comaroff (2009: 142) wonder if this 'ethno-prise' would lead to greater prosperity for the differently disadvantaged or reinforce earlier forms of exploitation through the hegemony of the market.

As this publication was going to press, there appeared the news item of the passing away of Jivya Soma Mashe. I offer this chapter as a small tribute to him for upholding the cultural identity of the adivasis within the labyrinth of dominant hegemony in the manner that he knew and could best.

GLOSSARY AND ABBREVIATIONS

Adivasi: Tribal, literally the earliest inhabitants

Agdi garib: Very poor

AL: Agricultural Labourer

Amhi: We the people, referring to the adivasis

Awar: Mansion of a landlord

Bhakri: A bread made of coarse grains

Bhagat: Tribal medicine man

Bidi: Local tobacco rolled in leaf for smoking

Changle: Well-off, sound economic condition

Daru: Local alcoholic drink now made of fermented jaggery, earlier with mahua flowers

Danda: Business, trading

Dhanya: Grain; struggle for Dhanya is used symbolically for the struggle for economic survival

Fasavnuk: Cheating

Garib: The poor

Garvi land: Good quality land

Ghoni: A sack

Gram Panchayat: Village self-governing body

Guntha: 2.5 per cent of an acre

Hara: A measure of paddy

Khavti: Consumption loan, generally in kind, during lean periods

Kanun: The operational law

Kayda: The law in general or 'the order of things'

Kanneri: A gruel of rice

Karbhari: Senior tribal leader in the village

Khand: A crop share

Khandadia: Husband who lives and works in wife's family in lieu of bride price

Kharif: Monsoon agricultural crop

Khavti: Consumption loan

Langoti: Loin cloth

Lok: People

Lal Bavta: The red flag, i.e. the CPI(M) Party or the Kisan Sabha, a peasant organization

Markut: Beatings

MP: Member of national parliament or Lok Sabha

MP: Middle peasant, according to context

MLA: Member of State Legislative Assembly

Padas: Hamlets of a village

Pandarpesha: Literally, white collar occupation; the landlord-trader-moneylender in this context

Palemode: Crop, labour or land mortgage in return for consumption loan

Paili: The measure of paddy

Pilavnuk: Exploitation

PP: Poor peasant

Rab: Seed bed preparation by burning biomass

Rajkaran: Electoral politics and exercise of power

Rub: Preparation of seed bed by firing biomass

Rabi: Winter agricultural crop

Sadharan: So so, as economic condition

Sarpanch: Elected head of village panchayat

Sarkar: The state or generally government

Savcar: Moneylender/trader

Seth: The landlord, trader, moneylender

Shrimant: The rich

Taluka: Revenue administrative subdivision of district, generally the size of a development block

Taluka Panchayat Samiti: Taluka self-governing body

Tras: Harassment

Vagaya: The tiger deity

Veth: Forced, unpaid labour of tenants

Warkas land: Poor quality rocky dry lands

Zilla Parishad: District self-governing body

REFERENCES

Aminzade, R. (1992): "Historical Sociology and Time," *Sociological Method and Research,* Vol. 20, No. 4.

Bagchi, A.K. and A. Chatterjee (2014): *Marxism: With and Beyond Marx* (New Delhi: Routledge).

Banerjee, P. (2016): "The Work of Theory, Thinking Across Traditions", *Economic and Political Weekly*, Vol. LI, No. 37, September 10.

Barth, F. (ed.) (1969): *Ethnic Groups and Boundaries* (Bergen: Universitetsforlaget).

Bates, C. (1995): "Lost Innocents and the Loss of Innocence, Interpreting Adivasi Movements in South Asia" in R.H. Barnes and others (eds.), *Indigenous Peoples of Asia*, Association of Asian Studies.

Baviskar, A. (2005): "Adivasi Encounters with Hindu Nationalism in Madhya Pradesh", *Economic and Political Weekly*, Vol. 40, No. 48, pp. 5105-13.

Beteille, A. (1992): "The Concept of Tribe with Special Reference to India", Chapter 3 in *Society and Politics in India* (Delhi: Oxford University Press).

___ (1998): "The Idea of Indigenous People", *Current Anthropology,* Vol. 39, No. 2, April.

Bhattacharya M. (2014): "The Folk Artist as Traditional Intellectual and the Culture of Resistance", in Bagchi A.K. and A. Chatterjee (eds).

Bogoras, W. (1925): "Ideas of Space and Time in the Conception of Primitive Religion", *American Anthropologist*, Vol. 27, No. 2, pp. 205-266.

Bonacich, E. (1980): "Class Approaches to Ethnicity and Race", *The Insurgent Sociologist,* Vol. 10, No 2.

Bose, N.K. (1975): *The Structure of Hindu Society*, (trans. with 'Introduction' by A. Beteille) (New York: Orient Longman).

Bourdieu, P. (1990): *"Time Perspectives of the Kabyle"*, in J. Hassard ed. 1990.

Brown, M.F. (1997): "Thinking about Magic" in S.D. Glazier (ed.), *Anthropology of Religion* (Westport: Praeger).

Brown, R.H. (1997): "Representation and Repression: Rhetorics of Ethnicity, Nationalism and Global Community" in G. Pfeffer and K. Behera (eds.), *Contemporary Society: Tribal Studies, Vol. 1, Structure and Process*. (New Delhi: Concept Publishing Company).

Castells, M. (1997): *The Power of Identity*: *The Information Age: Economy, Society and Culture*. Vol. I. (Massachusetts and Oxford: Blackwell).

___ (1998): *End of Millennium, The Information Age: Economy, Society and Culture*, Vol. II, Second Edition (Sussex: Wiley Blackwell).

___ (2010): *The Rise of Network Society, The Information Age: Economy, Society and Culture*, Vol. III, Second Edition. (Sussex: Wiley Blackwell).

Chacko, M.P. (2005): *Tribal Communities and Social Change* (New Delhi: Sage).

Chattopadhyaya, B. (ed.) (2009): *The Oxford India Kosambi, Combined Method in Indology and Other Writings* (New Delhi: Oxford University Press).

Chattopadhyaya, D. (1976 a): *History, Society and Polity, Integral Sociology of Sri Aurobindo* (New Delhi: Macmillan).

___ (1976 b): *What Is Living and What Is Dead in Indian Philosophy* (New Delhi: People's Publishing House).

___ (1977): *Science and Society in Ancient India* (Calcutta: Research India Publication).

___ (1978): "Sources of Indian Idealism", in D. Chattopadhyaya (ed.) (1978): *History and Society: Essays in Honour of Professor Niharranjan Ray* (Calcutta: K.P. Bagchi and Company).

___ (1978 a, first published 1959): *Lokayata—A Study in Ancient Indian Materialism* (New Delhi: People's Publishing House).

___ (ed.) (1978 b): *Studies in The History of Indian Philosophy: An Anthology of Articles by Scholars Eastern and Western*, 2 Vols. (Calcutta: K.P. Bagchi and Company).

___ (1989): *In Defence of Materialism in Ancient India* (New Delhi: People's Publishing House).

Chaturvedi, V. (ed.) (2012): *Mapping Subaltern Studies and the Postcolonial* (London: Verso).

Chauhuri, B.B. (1997): "Tribe-Caste Continuum" in D. Nathan (ed.): *From Tribe to Caste* (Shimla: IIAS).

Clifford, J. (1990): "On Ethnographic Allegory", in Clifford, J and G. E. Marcus (eds.) (1990): *Writing Culture: The Poetics and Politics of Ethnography* (Delhi: Oxford University Press).

Comaroff, J.L. and J. Comaroff (2009): *Ethnicity, Inc* (Chicago: The University of Chicago Press).

Connerton, P. (1989): *How Societies Remember* (Cambridge: Cambridge University Press).

Corbridge, S. (1988): "The Ideology of Tribal Economy and Society: Politics in Jharkhand, 1950-80", *Modern Asian Studies* 22(1).

Dalmia, Y. (1982): *The Painted World of the Warlis* (New Delhi: Lalit Kala Academy).

Dandekar, A. (ed.) (1998): *Mythos and Logos of the Warlis, A Tribal Worldview* (New Delhi: Concept Publishing Company).

Devalle, S. (1992): *Discourses of Ethnicity: Culture and Protest in Jharkhand* (New Delhi: Sage Publications).

Devi, G.N. (ed.) (2002): *Painted Words, An Anthology of Tribal Literature* (New Delhi: Penguin Books).

Dhere, R.C. (2009): *Karveerniwasini Mahalaxmi* (Pune: Padmagandha Prakashan).

Doshi, S.L. (1990): *Tribal Ethnicity, Class and Integration* (Jaipur: Rawat Publications).

Dreze, J. and A. Sen (eds.) (2011): "Putting Growth in its Place", *Outlook*, November 14.

Dube, S.C. (ed.) (1977): "Introduction" in *Tribal Heritage of India. I: Ethnicity, Identity and Interaction* (New Delhi: Vikas).

Eliade, M. (1964): *Shamanism: Archaic Techniques of Ecstasy* (London: Penguin Arkana).

Enthoven, R.E. (1922): The *Tribes and Castes of the Bombay Presidency*, Vol. III (Bombay: Government Press). [First published 1992, Reprinted 1975] (Delhi: Cosmo Publications).

Fabian, J. and Ilona Szombati-Fabian (1980): "Folk Art from an Anthropological Perspective", in Quimby, M.G. and S.T. Swank, eds., *Perspectives on American Folk Art* (New York: Norton).

Flinders, C.L. (2002): *The Values of Belonging* (San Francisco: Harper San Francisco).

Frazer, J.G. (1957): *The Golden Bough: A Study of Magic and Religion*, Vol. I (London).

Gadgil, M. and Guha, R. (1992): *This Fissured Land: An Ecological History of India* (Delhi: Oxford University Press).

Ghosh, A. (1996): "The Problem: A Symposium on Culture and Power", *Seminar*, 446, October.

Ghurye, G.S. (1943/1963): *The Aboriginies "So Called" and Their Future* (Pune: Gokhale Institute of Politics and Economics), republished (1963) as *The Scheduled Tribes* (Bombay: Popular Prakashan).

Godelier, M. (1977): *Perspectives in Marxist Anthropology* (London: Cambridge University Press). (Trans. from Godelier, M. (1973) *Horizons, Trajets Marxistes en Athropologie* (*French*) Paris: Maspero).

Gramsci, A. (1971): *Selection from the Prison Notebooks of Antonio Gramsci*, in Q.R. Hoare and G.N. Smith (eds.), (London: Lawrence and Wishart).

Guha, Sumit (2015): "States, Tribes, Castes: A Historical Re-exploration in Comparative Perspective," *Economic and Political Weekly*, Vol. L, Nos. 46 and 47.

Gurvitch, G. (1990 a): "The Problem of Time" in J. Hassard (ed.) (1990).

___ (1990 b): "Varieties of Social-time" in J. Hassard (ed.) (1990).

Hale, C.R. (1997): "Cultural Politics of Identity in Latin America", *Annual Review of Anthropology*, 26.

Hale, H.E. (2004): "Explaining Ethnicity", *Comparative Political Studies*, Vol. 37, No. 4.

Hall, J.R. (1980): "The Time of History and the History of Times," *History and Theory*, 19, 2.

Hall, S. (1985): "Signification, Representation, Ideology: Althusser and the Post-Structuralist Debates", *Critical Studies in Mass Communication* 2 (2), June: pp. 91-114.

___ (1996): "New Ethnicities", in D. Morley and K.H. Chen (eds.), *Stuart Hall, Critical Dialogues in Cultural Studies* (London and New York: Routledge).

Hardiman, D. (1985): "From Custom to Crime, The Politics of Drinking in Colonial Gujarat", in R. Guha (ed.), *Subaltern Studies*, Vol. 4 (New Delhi: Oxford University Press).

___ (1987): *The Coming of the Devi* (New Delhi: Oxford University Press).

Harvey, D. (1990): *The Condition of Postmodernity* (Cambridge MA and Oxford UK: Blackwell.

Hassard J. (ed.) (1990): *The Sociology of Time* (London: Macmillan).

Ismail, F. and A. Shah (2015): "Class Struggle, the Maoists and the Indigenous Question in Nepal and India", *Economic and Political Weekly*, Vol. L, No. 35.

Jaques, E. (1990): *"The Enigma of Time"*, in J. Hassard (ed.), 1990.

Jenkins, R. (1997): *Rethinking Ethnicity: Arguments and Explorations* (New Delhi: Sage Publications).

Joshi, S. (1991): "Religion and Marxism: Some Theoretical Problems", *Economic and Political Weekly*, November 9.

Kannabiran, K. (2016): "Constitutional Geographies and Cartographies of Impunity, Human Rights and Adivasis/Tribes in Contemporary India", *Economic and Political Weekly*, LI, 44 and 45, November.

Karna, M.N. (1999): "Language, Region and National Identity", *Sociological Bulletin*, 48, 1 and 2, March-September.

___ (2007): "Ethnicity and Democracy: An Uneasy Relationship?", in Bhadra, R.K. and M. Bhadra (eds.): *Ethnicity, Movement and Social Structure: Contested Cultural Identity,* (Jaipur: Rawat Publications).

Khare, G.H. (1958): *Maharashtraci Char Daivate* (Pune).

Kosambi, D.D. (1978): "The Historical Development of the Bhagavad-Gita", in Chattopadhyaya D. (ed. 1978 b).

___ (1985): "Combined Methods in Indology" in A.J. Syed (ed.): *D.D. Kosambi on History and Society: Problems of Interpretation* (Bombay: Department of History), first published in *Indo-Iranian Journal*, Vol. 6, 1962-63.

___ (2008): *Economic and Political Weekly, Special Issue*, Vol. 43, No. 30.

___ (2009 a): "Living Prehistory in India", in B. Chattopadhyaya (ed.) (2009).

___ (2009 b): "Stages of Indian History", in B. Chattopadhyaya (ed.) (2009).

___ (2009 c): "The Vedic 'Five Tribes", in B. Chattopadhyaya (ed.) (2009).

___ (2009 d): "At the Crossroads: A Study of Mother-Goddess Cult Sites", in B. Chattopadhyaya (ed.) (2009).

___ (2016/1956): *An Introduction to the Study of Indian History* (New Delhi: Sage, Mumbai: Popular Prakashan).

___ (2016/1962): *Myth and Reality. Studies in the Formation of Indian Culture* (New Delhi: Sage, Mumbai: Popular Prakashan).

Kulkarni, S. (February 1979): "Class and Caste in a Tribal Movement", *Economic and Political Weekly,* Vol. 14, Nos. 7 and 8.

Malesivic, S. (2004): *The Sociology of Ethnicity (* London: Sage).

___ (2010): "Ethnicity in Time and Space: A Conceptual Analysis," *Critical Sociology*. 37 (1).

Malinowski, B. (1990): "*Time-Reckoning in the Trobriands*", in J. Hassard (ed.) 1990.

Manor, J. (1996): 'Ethnicity and Politics in India,' *International Affairs in Ethnicity and International Relations*, pp. 459-475.

Mehra, J.D. (1977): "The World View of Indian Tribes" in S.C. Dube (ed.): *Tribal Heritage of India. I: Ethnicity, Identity and Interaction* (New Delhi: Vikas).

Mehra, M. and Agarwal, A. (2016): "Witch-hunting' in India? Do We Need Special Laws", *Economic and Political Weekly,* Vol. LI, No. 33.

Misra, V.N and Nagar, M. (1997): "From Tribe to Caste: An Ethnoarchaeological Perspective", in Nathan, D. (ed.) *From Tribe to Caste* (Shimla: IIAS).

Munshi Saldanha, I. (1995): "On Drinking and 'Drunkenness', History of Liquor in Colonial India", *Economic and Political Weekly*, Vol. XXX, No. 37, September 16.

Munshi, I. (2007): *Adivasi Life Stories: Context, Constraints, Choices* (Jaipur: Rawat Publications).

Munshi, I. (ed.) (2013): *The Adivasi Question: Issues of Land, Forest and Livelihood* (New Delhi: Orient BlackSwan).

Nargolkar, K. and V. (1955): *Junglace Raje* (Ghargoti, Kolhapur: Shree Mauni Vidyapeeth).

Nathan, D., Kelkar, G. and Xiaogong, Y. (1998): "Women as Witches and Keepers of Demons: Cross-Cultural Analysis of Struggles to Change Gender Relations", *Economic and Political Weekly*, October 31.

Needham, J. (1956): *Science and Civilisation in China.* Vol II. Cambridge cited in Chattopadhyaya, Debiprasad (1959)

Parulekar, G. (1975): *Adivasis Revolt: A Story of Warli Peasents in Struggle* (Calcutta: National Book Agency).

Pati, B. (2016): "'Hindus Have to Be Born as Hindus', The Magic Wand of Brahmanical Hinduism and Conversions", in M. Radhakrishna (ed.).

Pathy, J. (1984): *Tribal Peasantry: Dynamics of Development* (New Delhi: Inter-India Publication).

___ (1988): *Ethnic Minorities in the Process of Development* (Jaipur: Rawat Publications).

___ (2005): "Tribe, Religion and Nation in the Context of the Indian State", in Chacko, P.M. (ed.).

Pattanaik, D. (2016): "Waiting for Ram", *Sunday, Mumbai Mirror*, August 21.

Prabhu, P. and Balsara, S. translated and collated (2014): *Wisdom from the Wilderness, Painted and Narrated by Warli Adivasis of District Thane* (Vadodara: Sarini and Bhasha).

Prasad, A. (2014): "Class Community and Identity Politics of the Adivasi in Contemporary India", in Bagchi A. and A Chatterjee (eds.).

Przeworski, A. (1985): "Material Bases of Consent", in *Capitalism and Social Democracy* (Cambridge: Cambridge University Press).

Radhakrishna, M. (ed.) (2016): *First Citizens: Studies on Adivasis, Tribals and Indigenous Peoples in India*, Oxford India Studies in Contemporary Society (New Delhi: Oxford University Press).

Roy Burman, J.J. (1993): "Syncretism Ignored", *Mainstream*, May 22.

Sahay K.N. (1977): "Tribal Self-Image and Identity" in Dube, S.C. (ed.), *Tribal Heritage of India. I: Ethnicity, Identity and Interaction* (New Delhi: Vikas).

Saldanha, D. (1984), *A Socio Psychological Study of the Development of Class Consciousness*. Bombay, Department of Sociology, Doctorial Thesis. An edited and updated version was later published as *Structure, Consciousness and Social Transformation: The Adivasis in Thane District, Maharashtra* (Delhi: Aakar Books, 2015).

___ (1988): "Antonio Gramsci and the Analysis of Class Consciousness: Some Methodological Considerations", *Economic and Political Weekly*, Review of Political Economy, Vol. 23, No. 5, January 30.

___ (1989): "Socialization of Critical Thought: Responses to Illiteracy Among the Adivasis in Thane District", *Economic and Political Weekly*, Vol. 24, No. 30, July 29.

___ (1993): "Cultural Communication in Literacy Campaigns: Social Relational Contexts, Processes and Hegemonic Organization", *Economic and Political Weekly*, Vol. 28, No. 20, May 15.

___ (2008 a): "Consciousness and Structure in the Gramscian Perspective: Conceptual Concerns", *Contemporary Education Dialogue*, Vol. 6, No. 1, Monsoon.

___ (2008 b): "Consciousness and Structure in the Gramscian Perspective: Implications for Education". *Contemporary Education Dialogue*, Vol. 6, No.1, Monsoon.

___ (2010): *Civil Society Processes and the State: The BGVS and the Literacy Campaigns* (Jaipur, Rawat Publications).

___ (2015 a): *Structure, Consciousness and Social Transformation: The Adivasis in Thane District, Maharastra* (Delhi: Aakar Books).

___ (2015 b): *The Subaltern Subject in Structured Historical Process: Towards an Epistemological Approach* (Delhi: Aakar Books).

Santoshi, N. (April 10, 2017): "Experts Dig Deep into MP Rock Art History", *Hindustan Times* (Mumbai).

Saul, J. (1979): "The Dialectics of Class and Tribe," *Race and Class*, Vol. XX, No 4.

Save, K.J. (1945): The *Warlis* (Bombay: Padma Publication Ltd).

Shah, A. (2007): "The Dark Side of Indigeneity? Indigenous People, Rights and Development in India," *History Compass*. Vol. 5, No 6.

___ (2010): *In the Shadows of the State: Indigenous Politics, Environmentalism and Insurgency in Jharkhand, India* (Durham and London: Duke University Press).

Sharma, S. (1994): *Tribal Identity and the Modern World*, Tokyo, New Delhi: United Nations University Press, Sage Publications.

Singh, J. (2016): "Communal Violence in Muzaffarnagar, Agrarian Transformation and Politics", *Economic and Political Weekly*, Vol. LI, No. 31, July 30.

Singh, K.S. (1953): *Cultural Anthropology and Other Essays* (Calcutta: Indian Associated Publishing Co.).

___ (1985): *Tribal Society in India: An Anthropo-historical Perspective* (New Delhi: Manohar Publications).

Singh, R.S. (1997): "Tribe into Caste: A Colonial Paradigm", in Nathan, D. (ed.) *From Tribe to Caste* (Shimla: IIAS).

Sircar, D.C. (1973): *The Sakta Pithas* (Benaras: Motilal Banarasidas).

Skaria, A. (1997): "Women, Witchcraft and Gratuitous Violence in Western India", *Past and Present*, No. 155, May.

___ (1999): *Hybrid Histories: Forests, Frontiers, and Wildness in Western India* (New Delhi: Oxford University Press).

Sloan, W.N. (1979): "Ethnicity or Imperialism? A Review Article," *Comparative Studies in Society and History*, Vol. 21, No. 1, January.

Srinivas, M.N. (1952): *Religion and Society Among the Coorgs of South India* (Bombay: Asia Publishing House).

Steur, L. (2011): "Adivasis, Communists and the Rise of Indigenism in Kerala", *Dialectical Anthropology*, Vol. 35, No. 1.

Sundar, N. (2016): "Introduction: Of the Scheduled Tribes, States and Sociology", in N. Sundar (ed.), *The Scheduled Tribes and Their India: Politics, Identities, Policies and Work* (New Delhi: Oxford University Press).

Tambiah, S.J. (1968): "The Magical Power of Words", *Man*. Vol. 3, cited in Brown (1997).

___ (1990): *Magic, Science, Religion, and the Scope of Rationality* (Cambridge: Cambridge University Press), cited in Brown (1997).

Tata Institute of Social Sciences (TISS) (2015 a): *Tribal Sub-Plan in Maharashtra: A Diagnostic Study* (Mumbai: TISS and UNICEF, Maharashtra).

___ (2015 b): *A Tribal Atlas of Maharashtra* (Mumbai: TISS and UNICEF, Maharashtra).

Thapar, R. (2000): "The Theory of Aryan Race and India: History and Politics", and "The Contribution of D.D. Kosambi to Indology" in *Cultural Pasts* (New York: Oxford University Press).

___ (2008): "Early Indian History and the Legacy of D.D. Kosambi", *Economic and Political Weekly,* Special Issue, The Man and His Work, Vol. 43, No. 30, July 26.

___ (2014): *The Past as Present: Forging Contemporary Identities through History* (New Delhi: Aleph Book Company).

The Times of India (2018): "Why Maharashtra's Farmers are Protesting and Why Mumbaikars are Supporting Them: 10 Points", March 12.

Thompson, E.P. (1977): "Folklore, Anthropology and Social History," *Indian Historical Review*, Vol. 3, Issue 2.

Thompson, G. (1941): *Aeschylus and Athens* (London, 2nd ed.) cited in Chattopadhyaya, D. (1959).

Upadhyay, A. (December 1980), 'Peasantization of Adivasis in Thane District", *Economic and Political Weekly, Review of Agriculture*, Vol. 15, No. 52.

Xaxa, V. (1999): "Transformation of Tribes in India: Terms of Discourse", *Economic and Political Weekly*, Vol. 34, No. 12, June.

___ (1999): "Tribes as Indigenous People of India", *Economic and Political Weekly*, Vol. 34, No. 35.

___ (2005): "Politics of Language, Religion and Identity: Tribes in India", *Economic and Political Weekly*, Vol. 40, No. 13.

Xaxa, V. and Others (2014): *Report of the High Level Committee on Socio-Economic, Health and Educational Status of Tribal Communities of India* (New Delhi: Ministry of Tribal Affairs, Government of India).

Index